Spirituality, Philosophy and Education

The idea that education has (or should have) a spiritual dimension is now the subject of increased attention from philosophers as well as educational theorists, policy makers and practitioners. The contributors to *Spirituality, Philosophy and Education* include well-known philosophers as well as educationalists. Between them they bring a depth of scholarly and philosophical rigour to the field and provide wide-ranging explorations and analyses of the meaning and educational significance of spirituality.

The volume explores relations between spirituality and value, spirituality and virtue, scholarship and spirituality, spirituality, science and morality, pedagogy and spirituality, spirituality and aesthetics, spirituality and the curriculum, amongst many other topics. Students of philosophy and philosophy of education, as well as anyone interested in the place of spiritual values in educational policy and practice, should find this collection a major addition to the current literature on the prospects and possibilities of spiritual education, as well as a source of educational inspiration.

David Carr is Professor of Philosophy of Education at the University of Edinburgh, author of *Professionalism and Ethic in Teaching* (2000) and *Making Sense of Education* (2003), and co-editor (with Jan Steutel) of *Virtue Ethics and Moral Education* (1999) all published by Routledge. **John Haldane** is Professor of Philosophy at the University of St Andrews, co-author (with J.J.C. Smart) of *Atheism and Theism* 2nd edition (Blackwell, 2003) and author of *An Intelligent Person's Guide to Religion* (2003). Both have written widely (and sometimes jointly) on questions of religious, spiritual, moral and values education.

Spirituality, Philosophy and Education

Edited by
David Carr and John Haldane

RoutledgeFalmer
Taylor & Francis Group

LONDON AND NEW YORK

First published 2003
by RoutledgeFalmer
11 New Fetter Lane, London EC4P 4EE

Simultaneously published in the USA and Canada
by RoutledgeFalmer
29 West 35th Street, New York, NY 10001

RoutledgeFalmer is an imprint of the Taylor & Francis Group

© 2003 Selection and editorial matter, David Carr and John Haldane;
individual chapters, the contributors

Typeset in Palatino and Gill by BC Typesetting, Bristol
Printed and bound in Great Britain by
Antony Rowe Ltd, Chippenham, Wiltshire

British Library Cataloguing in Publication Data
A catalogue record for this book is available from the British Library

Library of Congress Cataloging in Publication Data
A catalog record has been requested

ISBN 0–415–29669–2

Contents

Author biographies

The Revd Professor **Jeff Astley** is Director of the North of England Institute for Christian Education, and Honorary Professorial Fellow in Practical Theology and Christian Education in the University of Durham. His recent publications include *Choosing Life? Christianity and Moral Problems* (2000) and *Ordinary Theology: Looking, Listening and Learning in Theology* (2003).

David Carr is Professor of Philosophy of Education in the University of Edinburgh School of Education. He is author of *Educating the Virtues* (1991), *Professionalism and Ethics in Teaching* (2000), *Making Sense of Education* (2003) and of numerous philosophical and educational articles. He is also editor of *Education, Knowledge and Truth* (1998) and co-editor (with Jan Steutel) of *Virtue Ethics and Moral Education* (1999).

John Cottingham is Professor of Philosophy at the University of Reading. His books include *Descartes*, *The Rationalists* and *Philosophy and the Good Life*. He is co-translator of the three-volume Cambridge edition of *The Philosophical Writings of Descartes*, and editor of *Ratio*. His most recent book, *On the Meaning of Life* (2002), deals with central themes in the philosophy of religion.

Joseph Dunne teaches philosophy in the Education Department and co-ordinates the programme in Human Development at St Patrick's College, Dublin City University. He is author of *Back to the Rough Ground: Practical Judgment and the Lure of Technique* (1993, 1997) and co-editor (with Frank Litten and Attracta Ingram) of *Questioning Ireland: Debates in Political Philosophy and Public Philosophy* (2000) and (with James Kelly) of *Childhood and its Discontents: The First Seamus Heaney Lectures* (2002).

John Haldane is Professor of Philosophy and Director of the Centre for Ethics, Philosophy and Public Affairs in the University of St Andrews. He has also held visiting positions at the Universities of Edinburgh, Oxford and Pittsburgh and was recently Royden Davis Professor of

Humanities at Georgetown University. His publications include *Atheism and Theism* (with J.J.C. Smart) (2nd edition 2003), and *An Intelligent Person's Guide to Religion* (2003).

J. Mark Halstead is Professor of Moral Education at the University of Plymouth. He has published widely on spiritual, moral, multicultural and Islamic education, and is associate editor of the *International Journal of Children's Spirituality*. He is also co-author (with Monica Taylor) of *The Development of Attitudes, Values and Personal Qualities* (2000), (with Terry McLaughlin) of *In Defence of Faith Schools* (2002) and (with Michael Reiss) of *Values in Sex Education: From Principles to Practice* (2003).

Jonathan Jacobs is Professor of Philosophy and Chair of the Department of Philosophy and Religion at Colgate University, Hamilton, New York state. He works mainly in moral psychology and metaethics. His two most recent books are *Choosing Character: Responsibility for Virtue and Vice* (2001) and *Dimensions of Moral Theory* (2002). He has also published numerous articles on Maimonides and on Aquinas.

John Keast is Principal Manager for Religious Education, Citizenship and Personal Social Health Education (PSHE) at the Qualifications and Curriculum Authority. He was previously County Adviser and Inspector for Religious Education and PSHE in Cornwall Local Education Authority. His teaching experience includes Deputy Head of a Sixth Form Centre, Head of Department and year head in various schools. He has also been an OFSTED inspector and examiner.

Michael McGhee is Lecturer in Philosophy at the University of Liverpool. He is co-editor of *Contemporary Buddhism: An Interdisciplinary Journal*, and author of *Transformations of Mind: Philosophy as Spiritual Practice* (2000).

Terence H. McLaughlin is Professor of Philosophy at the London Institute of Education and Fellow of St Edmund's College, Cambridge. He is co-editor (with J. Mark Halstead) of *Education in Morality* (1999) and (with Joseph O'Keefe and Bernadette O'Keeffe) of *The Contemporary Catholic School: Context, Identity and Diversity* (1996). He has published extensively on issues of education in spirituality and religion in both common and religious schools in liberal democratic societies.

Kevin Mott-Thornton is currently Head of Religious Studies and Philosophy at Sydenham High School (Girls' Day School Trust) in South London. He has contributed papers to recent collections on moral and spiritual education, and his book *Common Faith: Education, Spirituality and the State*, was published in 1998.

Nancy Sherman is University Professor of Philosophy at Georgetown University. She is author of *The Fabric of Character* (1989) and *Making a Necessity of Virtue* (1997) and editor of *Critical Essays on the Classics: Aristotle's Ethics* (1999). She has published over thirty articles in the areas of ethics and moral psychology, and is currently working on a further book, *Stoic Warriors*, for Oxford University Press.

John Sullivan is Professor of Christian Education at Liverpool Hope University College where he teaches (through in-service courses, Master's courses and supervision of doctoral research) in the areas of formation for ministry, and on the connections between theology and education. He is author of *Catholic Schools in Contention* (2000), of *Catholic Education: Distinctive and Inclusive* (2001), and of many essays on religion and education.

Daniel Vokey is a Professor of Philosophy of Education in the Department of Educational Studies in the University of British Columbia Faculty of Education. He is the author of *Moral Discourse in a Pluralistic World* (2001) and of many academic articles on moral and spiritual education and other topics.

Iris M. Yob teaches at Walden University, is Academic Co-ordinator at Collins Living-Learning Center, Indiana University, Bloomington, and a fellow of the Philosophy of Education Society. Her publications as a philosopher of education have appeared primarily in *Religious Studies, Religious Education, Religion and Education, Philosophy of Music Education Review* and *Educational Theory*. She has also published two books for parents: *Keys to Teaching Children About God* (1996) and *Keys to Interfaith Parenting* (1998).

Introduction

David Carr and John Haldane

I

This collection of essays is unusual in its theme. It derives from a long-standing interest of the editors in its concerns, and (to lesser and greater degrees) follows from two previous academic gatherings which they convened in Scotland. The first of these was an international conference on philosophy, education and culture held at the University of Edinburgh in 1997, of which the organiser was David Carr. The second was a smaller meeting on spirituality, philosophy and education arranged by John Haldane at St Andrews University in 2001. (The latter was held under the auspices of the Centre for Philosophy and Public Affairs, which was also one of the sponsors of the earlier Edinburgh meeting.) The 1997 conference included papers on a wide range of issues; but while it amply fulfilled the aim of contributing to philosophy of education generally, it also reinforced the impression that although people in the field were inclined to feel a need for the subject to address the life of the spirit, few made that a direct focus of their enquiries. For this reason alone it seemed appropriate and timely to draw people together for the specific purpose of reflecting upon spiritual formation and its possible relevance to existing educational aims and practices.

Beyond such educational concerns, however, the editors themselves shared the view that in becoming professional and increasingly institutionalised, philosophy has moved too far from an earlier conception of it as being the practice of the love of wisdom, towards a pseudo-scientific idea of itself as specialised research. This is, in part, a consequence of the culture of bureaucracy and oversight that seems the most salient feature of contemporary higher education in Britain, in Continental Europe and even in North America. This culture has led academics to regard the accumulation of a personal research portfolio as of first priority, and it has produced a market environment with an emphasis on novelty, innovation and branding. Those who in the not-so-distant past would have been content to study and to teach the work of greater minds are now encouraged to represent their own thoughts as significant contributions to their chosen fields. Such pretension is unlikely to be the subject of the fraternal correction it deserves, since most are engaged in the same business of talking up their research projects for reasons of appointment, funding and promotion. This state of affairs shows no obvious sign of yielding to a more humane conception of philosophy, or to a more modest estimate of what the average academic could possibly hope to achieve in the course of a career. This makes it all the more important to find ways of and occasions for voicing the older view of philosophy as the practice of wisdom.

So it was that two sets of interests converged: first, that of seeing educationalists address the question of what schooling might aim for in the field of personal formation beyond the acquisition of transferable skills and broad social values; second, that of seeing philosophers engage the issue of the place of wisdom in the practice of their subject. The union of these concerns has shaped something of the recent work of the editors themselves; but more to the point it produced the idea of the St Andrews meeting at which a number of papers were presented under the title 'spirituality, philosophy and education'. The present collection includes these, or descendants of them, plus a number of related pieces by others (several from North America) who share these general interests.

The nature of spirituality and the possibilities of spiritual education are currently of widespread popular and academic interest. That said, much of the recent scholarship on this topic has been rather less than philosophically sophisticated, and it generally inclines to a rather simplistic reduction of spiritual development to moral, aesthetic and other sorts of human formation. It is our belief that the essays presented here offer fresh and more considered approaches to spirituality as a distinctive sphere of human development with distinct educational implications, and that they promise to lead reflection on this topic in interesting new directions.

II

The essays are arranged in three parts. In the first of these John Haldane, Michael McGhee, John Cottingham, Jonathan Jacobs and Nancy Sherman offer philosophical explorations of the concept of the spiritual as this might be understood outside of narrowly religious contexts.

John Haldane begins by noting that 'spirituality' has traditionally been associated with religion but he raises the question of whether it could be understood independently. He considers ways in which it might be brought within moral philosophy, perhaps as an aspect of virtue or character, but argues that it involves a notion of demeanour that has an ineliminably contemplative aspect and which is only indirectly related to other-regarding obligations. Arguing for the autonomy of the spiritual from both the moral and the aesthetic, he concludes by raising the issue of whether, after all, something akin to religious belief is not a precondition for a spiritual demeanour. In a discussion that makes reference to Haldane's and takes issue with aspects of it, Michael McGhee sets out to defend a conception of spiritual life that essentially involves the development of a higher kind of moral understanding and awareness. This is developed with particular reference to the more disinterested and self-effacing aspects of moral engagement, in a way that is not just consistent with, but actually informed by, oriental – principally Buddhist – religious or ethical ideas.

John Cottingham explores a *prima facie* tension between world-views that make spirituality central to life, and the outlook of scientific rationalism which tends to marginalise it. Drawing on both past and more recent philosophy, he argues that this apparent conflict can be resolved: for given that the metaphysical presuppositions of spiritual world-views are beyond the boundaries of science, science itself neither confirms nor refutes them. Since the value of spirituality, moreover, is best understood within a framework of practice, the adoption of the spiritual is rationally justified in terms of the hope of finding a dimension of meaning in life that could not otherwise be secured.

In the next two essays, Jonathan Jacobs and Nancy Sherman establish further thematic and historical links. First, deliberately eschewing any religiously grounded perspective, Jacobs explores the possibility of developing a conception of spirituality drawing on the resources of virtue ethics. Specifically, he aims to show that a largely Aristotelian conception of virtuous conduct makes possible a spiritual appreciation of the world and human life, even when virtue is understood in broadly naturalistic terms, and he concludes that just as pleasure completes or perfects activity in general, so spirituality completes and perfects virtue. Meanwhile, Sherman provides an introduction to Stoic practical philosophy arising out of her experience of teaching at the US Naval Academy in Annapolis, Maryland. She addresses several questions including the general one of whether, and if so how, philosophy may be relevant to life, and the particular one of how Stoicism may speak to contemporary military lives. Her conclusion is that the Stoic tradition, and philosophy more generally, have things to teach about the importance of character, education, and mutual dependence and responsibility.

The second part of the collection consists of essays by Mark Halstead, Joseph Dunne, Iris Yob, John Sullivan and Jeff Astley, in which these authors examine various dimensions of spirituality. In bringing together religious, ethical and aesthetic aspects of spiritual experience Halstead's paper serves as something of a bridge between the first and second parts of this volume. His main purpose is to explore the analogical and metaphorical uses of spiritual discourse which he regards as well exemplified in poetry and other imaginative literature. Halstead examines spiritual metaphor by reference to the work of John Donne and other seventeenth-century metaphysical poets, paying particular attention to their employment of images of sexual love as worldly analogues of divine love.

Joseph Dunne's paper asks about the fate of spirituality when it is severed from its traditional moorings in philosophy and religion. He suggests that the prominence in contemporary culture of MacIntyre's aesthete, therapist and manager, while undermining of ethics, creates a hospitable environment for ersatz versions of 'spirituality'. He further argues that some recent work in philosophy, by Weil, Murdoch and Gaita – though not by MacIntyre himself – helps us to recover an adequate conception of the spiritual by reference to the Platonic notion of truth and goodness as 'needs of the soul'. In her contribution, Iris Yob questions the deeply dualistic character of much received spiritual discourse by giving critical attention to the work of various modern and contemporary Christian thinkers. She argues that in distinguishing too sharply between soul and body, traditional religious discourses of spiritual experience and development have often failed to do justice to other dimensions of spiritual experience. Thus, without denying the importance of both reason and tradition, she argues for a more inclusive conception of spirituality which allows scope for the physical, affective and 'feminine' aspects of spirituality.

In a paper which in many respects plays a key role in bridging the theoretical and practical concerns of the collection, John Sullivan sets out to show that it is hardly possible to understand the enterprise of scholarship and learning without reference to qualities and attitudes which may aptly be regarded as 'spiritual' – and which are, at all events, not at all well captured by contemporary discourses of educational policy-making. From this viewpoint, the essay provides a significant basis for criticism of present day 'target-oriented' trends.

In the last essay of this section, after developing an analysis of the human 'horizontal' and 'vertical' dimensions of spirituality, Jeff Astley asks whether spirituality is constitutive of human flourishing as such, or if there is a distinctively spiritual sort of flourishing, of rather more limited scope or appeal. This leads him to a consideration of the conceptual and educational difficulties for naturalistic accounts of human well-being raised by both ideas of moral and spiritual disinterestedness and by deep spiritual assurances of the worth of human life.

The third part contains essays by John Keast, Daniel Vokey, Terence McLaughlin, Kevin Mott-Thornton and David Carr that engage issues of educational practice and policy-making. As a useful prelude to this, John Keast's paper constitutes a critical survey of the political, educational and other interests and concerns behind the recent spate of official UK policy documents and initiatives directed towards spiritual, religious, moral and values education. In particular, he provides a useful sorting of the different kinds of more and less instrumental considerations which have fuelled such initiatives.

Next, acknowledging the difference between religious and spiritual education, Daniel Vokey begins by considering the case for the latter grounded in a concern for a more meaningful school education and the development of 'whole' persons. He then proceeds, however, to review a range of major socio-cultural, political and institutional impediments to the realisation of any such aims. In the last section of his paper, however, he more optimistically sketches a number of possible projects which might conduce to more spiritual goals in public schooling.

Also looking at the context of recent schooling debates, Terry McLaughlin explores the possibility of 'education in spirituality' in common schools. The elusive notion of 'spirituality' is brought into clearer focus by drawing a distinction between 'religiously tethered' and 'religiously untethered' conceptions of spirituality, and the implications and problems of basing spiritual education in the common school on one or the other of these conceptions are then explored. Still, McLaughlin concludes that certain forms of 'education in spirituality' in the common school are defensible, although a number of dangers need to be identified and avoided.

In re-emphasising the practical importance of distinguishing between an educationally suitable notion of spirituality as such, and the various forms of spiritual development that might be based upon it, Kevin Mott-Thornton's paper reconnects with some of the themes explored by McLaughlin. Again considering the context of moral and social diversity, he argues that there is a serious tension between the delivery of adequate spiritual development and the ideal of common schooling, favoured by social democratic liberals; and he proceeds to propose a strategy for the development of local community and school cultures of spiritual and moral formation that might go some way towards easing such tension.

In bringing the collection to a close, Carr takes a broader look at past and present popular, theoretical and other perspectives on spirituality with a view to providing some basic mapping of the various available spiritual educational options. Distinguishing between three general conceptions of spirituality for spiritual education – the *traditional*, the *modern* (or constructivist) and the *postmodern* – Carr concludes that the traditional conception, despite its often religiously grounded nature, still promises to provide the most philosophically coherent and educationally viable account of spiritual experience and development.

III

It should be clear from the foregoing that there is much in these essays that will be of interest to those working in the fields of philosophy, philosophy of education, and educational theory and policy-making. Consonant with the subject matter, however, we hope (and expect) that readers will find themselves reflecting on their own condition as far as the life of the spirit is concerned. Certainly the editors feel themselves challenged on this score, but also inspired by some of the ideas presented here. It is often said that we live in an age of spiritual hunger: amidst the affluence and the bustle there can be heard the cry for simplicity and stillness. We are not altogether sure to what extent this is true. Many people seem perfectly happy with consumer culture and city-sizzle; and not all who prefer quieter ways would identify their desires as spiritual ones. Admittedly, there is a tendency to apply the terminology of spirit and spirituality to any inclinations towards reflection or gentility; but this is a merely lazy and stipulative definition. There is, therefore, a case to be made for the diagnosis of spiritual malaise, and much work would need to be done to persuade the patient of the correctness of this or that analysis. We can no longer assume that people are familiar with traditional philosophical and religious ideas, let alone that they are acquainted with specific associated accounts of 'spirit' or 'soul'. Much of what passes as contemporary spirituality seems an encouragement to indulgence and self-satisfaction: 'stop being self-critical; find time for yourself; attend to your own personal needs; celebrate being you; don't let yourself feel guilty; don't let others determine your values; share the pain.' Often this would-be wise counsel is couched in prose that lurches between psycho-babble and management-speak, and generally it treats the reader as witless or infantile. The irony of this state of affairs hardly needs commentary.

The issues raised in this collection are evidently ones of wide academic interest and personal and social concern. In conceiving the idea of the St Andrews meeting on the subject, and then in preparing this volume, the editors have worked with the aim of stimulating and helping to shape a serious discussion of the place of spirituality in both philosophy and education. Their hope is to see such discussion reflect some of the ideas canvassed in the following chapters, but whether and how that may happen they and the authors fervently appeal to others to ensure that such issues are discussed: a culture that neglects the life of the spirit is one that has not long to live. If this last thought seems rhetorically excessive, it is worth considering whether that may be because the light cast upon the condition of life by the presence of spirituality is now already dimmer than it once was. One can never 'go back', but in going forward one may benefit from comparison with, and lessons drawn from, the past.

Part I
Philosophy and spirituality

Chapter I

On the very idea of spiritual values[1]

John Haldane

'Vain is the word of that philosopher which does not heal any suffering of man.'

Epicurean saying

I

It is rare for an academic philosopher in the Anglo-American tradition to discuss the subject of spirituality. This might once have been attributed to a view of philosophy as confined to conceptual analysis and the theory of logic. Now, however, when almost every aspect of human life has been made the subject of some department of 'applied philosophy', it could hardly be said that the subject of spirituality lies outside the sphere of reasonable philosophical enquiry. Yet it is almost entirely neglected.

There is another reason why academic philosophers might not think to explore the subject. For 'spirituality' smacks of religion, and not of the interesting metaphysical aspects that form the subject-matter of natural theology, but of those devotional and pietistic preoccupations that are felt to belong to the affective domain, if not to the sphere of irrationality. Occasionally a passing philosopher will, so to speak, stop at the church door and approach the credulous man in the pew in order to point out what nonsense talk of spirituality really is. In an essay entitled 'What is "spirituality"?' (Flew 1997), Antony Flew performs such an exercise by looking at several terms with which the word is linked: these are '*spirited, spirit, spiritist, spiritual* and *spiritualist*'. He distributes these into various categories: psychological disposition (*spirited*), incorporeal substance (*spirit*), those believing in the latter (*spiritists* and *spiritualists*), and then that pertaining to higher human characteristics, or to non-earthly matters (*spiritual*). As an atheist who regards immaterialism as absurd, Flew barely lingers over the incorporeal, but he dwells awhile to denounce modern educationalists who favour policies of spiritual development in the (state) 'maintained school system'. Readers familiar with Flew's spirited writings may feel that by this point he had been joined in the aisle by a couple of restless hobby horses.

Certainly, when educational theorists talk about 'spiritual development' they are usually either struggling to take a last dip in the shallows of the ebbing tide of faith, or engaged in the practice of aggrandising the ordinary, or else doing both at once. The appreciation of art and music and the cultivation of a concern for the feelings of others are worthwhile educational activities, but their point and value is made less and not more clear by describing them as parts of 'spiritual development'. Yet increasing numbers of educationalists are adopting this way of speaking, and requiring teachers to act upon it, specifying the need, for example, to induce in children 'experiences of awe and wonder' (National Curriculum Council 1993, and Office for Standards in Education 1994). One may well ask at what? Are attitudes grouped under the heading of the 'spiritual' intelligible, save as focused upon transcendent phenomena? Even putting the point in terms of intentional objects and appearances, the question is whether the spiritual can be anything other than the religious. That indeed is one way of introducing the subject of this essay: can there be non-religious spirituality? And if so, what might be its forms?

Within religious domains the 'spiritual' certainly has definite meanings. Theologically its uncontested home is Christianity in which it refers to matters concerning the indwelling of the Holy Spirit whose gifts are courage, knowledge, reverence, right-judgement, understanding, wisdom, wonder and awe, and whose fruits are listed by St Paul in his Epistle to the Galatians. Widening out from this, one may say that the spiritual life is that given to the search after an inner awareness of God, a condition pursued through prayer and meditation and attained through grace. My concern here, however, is not with the theology of grace. Rather I am interested in the possibility of non-religious spirituality, and in the thought that this may not just be philosophically credible but that it is a central aspect of philosophy itself.

II

English-language philosophy consists very largely of logic, metaphysics, epistemology and ethics. Since there is so much of the last of these, an increasing amount of which is practically oriented, this might seem the place to look in expectation of finding something relevant to my interest. In fact, however, contemporary ethics is remote from what I have in mind in thinking about non-religious spirituality. It was not always so: the ancients, especially, engaged in styles of reflection about conduct that bear the mark of spiritual meditations. Before coming to that, however, let me say more about the contemporary scene.

One may conceive moral philosophy in terms of three levels of thought and discourse. At the base lies ordinary pre-philosophical moral thinking involving judgements about what is good and bad, right and wrong, and virtuous and vicious. At the next level there are more or less systematic structures of justification of these first-level judgements (such moral theories as utilitarianism, Kantian deontology, and so on). At the third, top-most level there are philosophical accounts of the status of first-order claims and of second-level justifications (metaethical theories). The last of these levels draws on general arguments and theses in logic, metaphysics and epistemology and is not distinctly ethical in content whereas the second is. Interestingly, however, the main growth in recent moral philosophy has been in 'applied ethics' which consists in deploying particular moral theories in relation to the problems encountered in first-order moral thinking. It is a downward movement from theory to practice (Haldane 1996).

As such, applied ethics is often of little autonomous intellectual value, which is not to say that it may not be well done and useful. More problematically, however, it can sometimes be corrupting of the spirit of true enquiry into value and requirement. So far as the first limitation is concerned, this style of thought often contributes little to the identification of moral dilemmas and problems than that already accomplished by those whom they affect, and it rarely questions the adequacy of the moral theories it applies. The tendency to intellectual corruption, meanwhile, arises from the applied nature of the exercise. There is a real sense in which the philosophical work has already been done, and this means that the applied ethicist is just working out the conclusion of a series of syllogisms whose major premises express the favoured moral theory and whose minor premises are provided by the facts of the case. This leaves out of account the possibility that looking hard at the situation and at related ones may itself disclose moral features not previously conceptualised within the theory. In this sense applied ethics prejudges moral issues and thereby disposes the practitioner to exclude the possibility that he or she might learn something new and of general *moral* interest from attending to cases.

In this respect it differs from traditional casuistry, for the casuists were generally alive to the possibility that particular departments of human activity might have area-specific moral features whose adequate characterisation requires the formation of concepts that are not specifications of broader ones defined within a general moral theory. Certainly there are philosophers who think hard and well about moral, political and cultural issues and who make imaginative and helpful contributions to thinking about them, but this activity is not essentially philosophical and similar styles are often adopted by high-grade journalists and social commentators.

What we have within contemporary academic philosophy is a good deal of necessarily technical epistemology and metaphysics, some of it deployed in metaethics; a fair amount of subtle moral theory; and considerably more applied ethics. In almost none of these areas taken individually or collectively is there scope for, let alone evidence of, anything that begins to look like spirituality. In order for that to seem surprising, however, I need to show why one should expect philosophy to have anything to say about this aspect of human experience.

III

Let me offer two pathways towards this expectation: one *phenomenological*, the other *historical*. In the middle of the nineteenth century Thoreau wrote that the mass of men lead lives of quiet desperation. Evidence of this is provided in literature, in the press, in doctors' surgeries, through personal acquaintance, and by knowledge of one's own circumstances, all of which suggest that many people are ill at ease with the human condition as they experience it. Many of us are desperate and many of us are sad; and the sources of our distress are not easily removed.

While many privations may not befall one, their very possibility casts a shadow across human lives. Those who are betrayed or bereaved, those who long for recognition or for love, those who experience rejection, those who fear their own impulses, those who are ill or dying, those who are clinically depressed, or who fear creeping insanity, those who labour with mental or physical handicaps, or who struggle with sufferers, those who are victims of injustice, all are in a position to discern the frailty of the human condition, and to see beyond the possibility of immediate and temporary relief to the facts of unredeemed suffering, weakness, solitariness and death. Given all of this, human beings often ask whether there is any spiritual truth that might counter, alleviate or help to deal with these facts, and they often suppose that it might be the task of non-religious philosophy to say whether there is any such truth. Clearly this supposition reflects the still popular belief that philosophy has something to do with the meaning of life. Such, however, is the growing ignorance within the profession of the broad history of the subject, and such has been the extent of specialisation with accompanying technicality, that many philosophers are genuinely puzzled when they encounter these expectations. The fact that 'philosophy' means love of wisdom (*philosophia*) will be set aside as being of purely antiquarian interest.

Not all academic philosophers are as unwelcoming to questions about the possibility of finding meaning in life (or even of finding *the* meaning of it). One who has taken them seriously is David Wiggins, who explored the first of these themes in an important lecture given to the British

Academy. Entitled 'Truth, invention and the meaning of life' (Wiggins 1976) this has been the subject of some discussion but mostly for the bearing of parts of it upon certain metaethical issues. As interesting, however, are Wiggins' attempt to structure the quest for meaning and his suggestion that progress towards discerning it calls for a phenomenology of value. He writes:

> Working within an intuitionism or moral phenomenology as tolerant of low-grade non-behavioural evidence as is literature (but more obsessively elaborative of the commonplace, and more theoretical, in the interpretative sense, than literature), [the theorist] has to appreciate and describe the quotidian complexity of what is experientially involved in a man's seeing a point in living. It is no use to take some existing moral theory – Utilitarianism or whatever it is – and to paste on to it such *postscripta* as the Millian insight 'It really is of importance not only what men do but what manner of men they are that do it' . . . If life's having a point is at all central to moral theory [as Wiggins had suggested it is] then room must be made for these things right from the very beginning.
>
> (Wiggins 1976: 136–7)

Wiggins has not, to my knowledge, pursued this aspect of his essay further. One reason is perhaps the thought that it is not for the theorist *qua* theorist to say what meaning consists in but only to say what finding meaning is. As a corrective to preaching this may be apt, but it also suggests a residual attachment to the view that philosophy can only be conceptual analysis, and it assumes a distinction between describing an activity and engaging in it which is in some tension with the recommendation to the *theorist* (not the non-philosopher) to adopt the method of moral phenomenology. It also puts strain on the idea associated with Wiggins' metaethical epistemology, that certain concepts are only available to one who shares the evaluative interest they express. In other words, describing what it is to find meaning may require evaluative concepts fashioned in the effort to describe the constituents of meaning itself.

More to the present point, however, is Wiggins' assumption that the issue of the meaning of life is among the central questions of *moral* philosophy. Whether that is true depends upon the scope of the expression 'moral philosophy'. Among definitions of the term 'spiritual' identified by Flew is 'of or pertaining to the higher moral qualities'. Noting that this is offered in explanation of one of the earliest uses of the term, Flew speculates that the word '*moral*' should be interpreted as it was in the old contrast between moral and physical sciences; in other words as pertaining to higher human faculties. In this very wide sense the meaning of life may be a subject for moral philosophy, but it is clear from what he writes that Wiggins is thinking more narrowly and locating it within *moral theory*.

This is inappropriate and one consequence of placing the topic there is that it is unlikely to receive the attention it needs. This indeed may be part of the reason why this aspect of Wiggins' lecture has not been pursued by moral theorists. The relevant point is best developed by returning to the attempt to identify non-religious spirituality as a subject for philosophical attention. Hearing that someone was interested in this a philosopher might well direct them to ethics, or perhaps to aesthetics having in mind experiences of the sublime. But if I am right spirituality is not to be located entirely within either of these domains or even in their union, and, if we confine ourselves to these fields, we shall not make much progress in answering the question of whether there is anything philosophy can offer to cure, alleviate or confirm the quiet desperation felt by many as they experience what life brings before them, or to validate the sense that some have that all can be well.

IV

I have already indicated why one might not hope for much from applied ethics or from metaethics. For while the latter is substantial it is not itself normative but analytical and ontological, and while the former is normative it does not provide a theory of value but presumes one or another such account. Moral theory itself may seem more promising, but while it is certainly concerned with value and requirement its domain is essentially that of right conduct in relation to moral subjects, and this is only a part of spirituality and perhaps then only *per accidens*.

I might have said that morality concerns norms of conduct regulating *interpersonal* relations. That would have passed muster at one time, but now it would be judged question-begging so far as concerns the rights of animals and duties to oneself. Neither of these examples is uncontentious, yet they can probably be accommodated by speaking of intersubjective relations. If we now believe that non-human animals have rights that is because we have come to view them as members of an enlarged community of moral subjects. One might attempt the same analysis with regard to non-sentient nature; but that is less plausible, which I take to be reason for thinking that the extension of rights to trees and valleys is untenable. This is not to say, of course, that there are no environmental values. The idea of duties to oneself is more problematic. Some sense might be made of it by regarding people as temporally and aspectually structured objects. Thus one might contend that the claim that Oliver has a duty to himself to stay sober, say, is to be analysed as holding that Oliver at t 1 has a duty in respect of Oliver at t 2; or again that Oliver *qua* party guest has a duty to Oliver *qua* driver. (Intoxication rarely being instantaneous, this latter analysis will also involve temporal slices or indexes.) But this dubious ontology is a high price to pay for saving a notion that may have little to recommend it.

The idea that morality is definable in terms of interpersonal conduct, intersubjective relations or, in my preferred account, right conduct in relation to moral subjects, is given support by the form and content of familiar moral theories. Although consequentialism and deontology differ in their account of the primary objects of assessment, favouring effected states of affairs, and actions, respectively, they share a list of the candidates for evaluation, namely intention, action and outcome. In short they agree that a moral theory is a theory of *conduct,* and they offer as guiding principles the well-being (happiness) or standing (autonomy) of those included within the scope of action.

Someone might agree that neither of these dominant styles of moral theorising is suited to make sense of the fears and anxieties that constitute the quiet desperation of mankind, let alone to alleviate or to confirm them, or again to make sense of the hopes men have that the cultivation of spiritual values may bring peace of heart and mind. Yet they may suggest that I have omitted an important range of moral theories designed to embrace this sort of thing, namely virtue ethics. The appeal to virtue as it was first made in analytical philosophy by Elizabeth Anscombe (Anscombe 1958) and related neo-Aristotelians suggested a way of acknowledging that not everything is down to the maximisation of happiness, while also allowing that what one should feel and do are not duties of pure reason or cosmic prescriptions, but may be grounded in naturally discernible facts about what is of benefit to rational animals. A further aspect of its merit and the one most emphasised in recent years is the suggestion that an ethic of virtue is not committed to codifiable and abstract rules of conduct but can locate the ethical in the broader constitution of human agency, taking account of character, emotion, social context, and even of fortune and misfortune.

All of this is to the good but it does not alter the fact that contemporary virtue theory is presented by its advocates as an account of *morality,* which is to say it is offered as an alternative to consequentialism and deontology as providing an account of right conduct. In emphasising the importance of emotion and of character generally, and in allowing reasoning about action to give equal place to the interests of the agent, it is certainly a much richer theory, but it remains a normative account of practical reasoning primarily in the sphere of intersubjective relations. Whether others are involved in one's actual deliberations is a contingent matter but a moral theory has, of its nature, to be able to give account of rightness and wrongness under such social headings as charity, justice and honesty.

That is what virtue theory claims to do and that is why it remains first and foremost a theory of *morality*.

My suggestion, however, has been that there is a further area of human existence, the spiritual, which is not essentially concerned with action in relation to the rights and interests of others and which has something to do with how one experiences the world and with what one makes of that experience. It is, I suggest, primarily a matter of what *personal demeanour* or mode of being one develops in the face of reality as one understands it in some more or less philosophical way. Earlier I mentioned that in antiquity the existence of such matters was recognised and catered for within philosophy and I shall touch on this shortly, but first let me anticipate and set aside another attempt to reduce the spiritual to a more familiar category of value.

V

A focus on experience and on the contemplation of it, instead of on conduct, may prompt the thought that what I am looking for is already a subject of extensive study within philosophical aesthetics. No doubt part of what is liable to be included within spirituality, such as a cultivation of the sense of the glory of nature, overlaps with the proper business of aesthetics. As with the attempt to locate spirituality in moral theory, however, much will be left behind if one hives off what can plausibly be dealt with under the heading of the theory of beauty and related categories. Meanwhile an expansion of the idea of the aesthetic to include the philosophy of adversity, despair, reconciliation and hope, etc. will undermine its claim to have a well-defined subject-matter. To one side lies the error of inappropriate aestheticisation, and to the other lies the danger of a loss of identity for aesthetics itself.

Of course, these remarks presuppose some account of the aesthetic. It is that which has occupied the central ground since the subject was born in the eighteenth century. Abstracting from detail, the aesthetic involves pleasure or disgust taken in the contemplation of things regarded as objects of experience not essentially connected with practical interests. (Although this type of account is associated with Kant and other Enlightenment and post-Enlightenment authors it is anticipated in the Middle Ages. Aquinas, for example, writes that 'good means that which simply pleases the appetite, while the beautiful is something pleasant to apprehend' (Aquinas 1914 [1271] Ia, IIae, q.17, a1 ad 3).) One may view events in one's life and recurrent aspects of the human condition in that way, but since life is something to be lived, or for some poor souls something to be abandoned, to view it in that way is to be disengaged from it. Spirituality as I am concerned with it, however, and the meaning of life as that which exercised Wiggins, are not to be identified with disengagement. Stepping back may be in order, but the point will typically be to step forward again so as to make some readjustment in one's demeanour and in the pattern of one's living.

To summarise: there seems little difficulty in understanding the idea of spirituality and of the spiritual life within the context of religious thought. In Christianity especially these are given definite content by reference to the indwelling of the Holy Spirit and to practices of prayer, meditation and devotion by which the soul progressively partakes in the life of God – not substantially but relationally as an adopted child might increasingly partake in the life of a family. (I use the analogy of participation in the life of a family rather than that of a parent given that in Christian mystical theology partaking in the life of God involves entering into the mutual Divine life of three persons.) When we turn to (non-religious) philosophy, however, a question arises whether any form of spirituality can find a home there. Yet even the most cursory reflection upon human experience, and on the efforts of great writers and others to give expression to it, suggests that there is a domain of thought, feeling and action that is concerned with discerning the ultimate truth about the human condition and with cultivating an appropriate mode of being or demeanour in response to that truth. The phenomenology is compelling, the concerns are intelligible, and for some reason intelligent people persist in supposing that it must be a central part of philosophy to deal with these matters and therefore look to it to do so.

Philosophers themselves, at least in the dominant Anglo-American tradition, either ignore such appeals; suggest that they are confused in ways similar to those in which some metaphysicians suggest that people are mixed up when they ask about first or ultimate causes; or else, if they are inclined to grant that questions of non-religious meaning and spirit do arise and call for attention, they point to moral theory or possibly to aesthetics as being the relevant departments to visit.

While this last option has the merit of recognising that there is something to be catered for, it errs in consigning it to moral philosophy as this is now understood, for that is concerned essentially with rightness of conduct, and first and foremost with conduct bearing upon other moral subjects. Contemporary virtue ethics remains a version of moral theory concerned principally with action. Likewise, aesthetics is concerned principally with disinterested contemplation of objects of experience. Spirituality involves intellect, will and emotion and is essentially contemplative, but the process of discovering the nature of reality, evaluating its implications for the human condition and cultivating an appropriate demeanour in the face of these, is not reducible to ethics, nor to aesthetics. Yet unless philosophers can show this enterprise to be confused or exclusively religious, they are open to the charge of neglecting something of fundamental, and perhaps of ultimate, human importance.

VI

Earlier I commended Wiggins for engaging the question of life's meaning. Let me next draw upon an interesting essay (by Anthony Quinton entitled 'Character and will' (Quinton 1998). In his perceptive and witty discussion Quinton practises what he allows may have the appearance of 'lexicographical needlework', sorting out the differences between the closely related concepts of *personality*, *temperament* and *character*. Then he turns to consider the 'distinctly marginal, even furtive, role [of character and will] in organised [i.e. philosophical] thinking about morality' (p. 39). What Quinton says about character is very useful for my purposes and it suggests that while he locates the formation and re-formation of the self within the domain of moral philosophy he might be persuaded, as might Wiggins, that it is better to mark out a new field of study bearing the title the philosophy of spirituality.

Quinton relates *personality*, *temperament* and *character* in point of their depth, stability and malleability within the structure of the human psyche. *Personality* lies on the surface, being a matter of manner or style, though linked to something deeper. *Temperament* is the most stable element within personality and consists in broad orientations towards optimism and pessimism, sociability and solitariness, and so on. *Character* is more deeply rooted than personality and may be viewed as an enduring (though not unchangeable) structure of acquired habits of feeling and choice. I would add that it includes, at least in its deepened form, tendencies towards and away from significant recurrent features of human life. Indeed, strength of character is central to what I have called 'demeanour'.

Quinton's discussion harks back to the psychology of Plato and Aristotle, and in keeping with that tradition he considers the relation between character and virtue, concluding that while character takes in habits of affection and will, it is not as such virtuous or vicious in the sense that one does not know simply on account of knowing that someone has a character whether it is a good or bad one. Good character is one whose habituated dispositions are towards things of positive value; bad character one whose habits are oriented towards the negative. For my own purposes I have chosen to speak of positive and negative *values* rather than of good and bad *ends*, for the latter are too readily interpreted in moral terms. More to the point, although Quinton refers these issues to moral philosophy he notes that his favoured notion of character comprises *three* of the four main Platonic virtues – prudence, courage and moderation – but expresses some doubt about the inclusion of justice conceived of as 'the self-denying suppression of one's own interests for the sake of people other than oneself' (Quinton 1998: 42). The point, of course, is not to deny the value of justice but to question whether it is central to the subject of study, namely *character*. I am in a position to suggest why this doubt is apt: justice is centrally a matter for moral philosophy, i.e. for moral theory, while the study of character is part of the philosophy of spirituality.

VII

Historical support for the claim that quiet desperation and other non-eccentric conditions of the soul or psyche are proper subjects for philosophy comes from the period of classical antiquity. Plato and Aristotle have been mentioned, but of greater relevance are the Stoics. Ancient Stoicism came in three phases: (i) the *Old Stoicism* of Zeno, Cleanthes and Chrysippus, the last of whom provided its most systematic formulation; (ii) the *Middle Stoicism* of Posidonius, and (iii) the *Late Stoicism* of Seneca, Epictetus and Marcus Aurelius. Like the Epicureans the Stoics were concerned with *ataraxia* (untroubledness), though their diagnoses of its causes, their remedies, and their understanding of good psychic health, all differ. Also there are significant differences between Stoics of the three periods. In general, whereas the early practitioners were materialistic monists of atheist or pantheist orientation, late Stoicism seems to accommodate the suggestion of a transcendent deity and to be dualistic. What unites the various strands, however, is a view about the tasks of philosophy and the need to cultivate inner peace.

The French scholar Pierre Hadot has made a series of interesting studies of the aims and methods of the six ancient schools of philosophy, namely *Stoicism, Epicureanism, Platonism, Aristotelianism, Cynicism* and *Pyrrhonism,* arguing that each reflects and in turn seeks to develop a permanent possibility of the human spirit (Hadot 1995). I shall not even attempt to summarise his many conclusions but I do want to extract one or two points so as to advance my own discussion. First, Hadot discerns in the ancient traditions, especially in the Stoics, a distinction between '*philosophy*' conceived of as the formation of the soul, and *discourse about philosophy* understood as the investigation of the nature of things, and to a lesser extent our knowledge of them. This is related to the more familiar distinction between practical and speculative philosophy. But whereas modern, recent and contemporary thought has invested greatest effort and talent in the pursuit of speculation in the form of epistemology and metaphysics, the ancients give priority to practice, and within that to the cultivation of wisdom and the development of the spiritual life. Epictetus observes that 'the lecture room of the philosopher is a hospital' (Epictetus

1995 [c. AD 100] 3, 23, 30) which is to say that his work is the cure of souls. Later he writes: 'How shall I free myself? Have you not heard it taught that you ought to eliminate desire entirely? . . . give up every-thing . . . for if you once deviate from your course, you are a slave, you are a subject (Epictetus, 4, 4, 33)'.

Hadot's reading of such texts is both informed and imaginative. It encourages him to make three claims of great interest. First, that much more of the writing of antiquity belongs to philosophy in the sense of the practice of wisdom than has been commonly supposed (more strikingly, that these texts concern and in some cases *are* spiritual exercises). Second, and in opposition to the assumption that the notion of spirituality is in origin a religious one, that Christianity appropriated this area of reflective practice from pre-existing philosophical traditions, and even took over 'as its own certain techniques of spiritual exercises as they had already been practised in antiquity' (Hadot 1995: 206). Third, that the historical interest of all of this is perhaps its least significant aspect. Responding to Foucault's use of his work Hadot writes:

> I think modern man can practise the spiritual exercises of antiquity, at the same time separating them from the philosophical [metaphysical] or mythic discourse which came along with them. The same spiritual exercises can, in fact, be justified by extremely diverse philosophical discourses. These latter are nothing but clumsy attempts, coming after the fact, to describe and justify inner experiences whose existential security is not, in the last analysis, susceptible of any attempts at theorisation or systematisation . . . It is therefore not necessary to believe in the Stoic's nature or universal reason.
>
> (Hadot 1995: 212)

The exercises Hadot refers to, what Foucault called '*pratiques de soi*' (practices of the self) (Foucault 1984), are designed to free one from (inappropriate) attachment to exterior objects and the pleasures deriving from them. By regular self-examination one checks the tendency to exteriority, and by contemplating the impermanence of things one masters oneself, attaining happiness in interior formation. Writing up this exami-nation, or better, perhaps, examining through writing is one form of spiritual exercise. Where Hadot takes issue with Foucault is in claiming with the ancients that the movement toward interiorisation is 'inseparably linked to another movement, whereby one rises to a higher psychic level, at which one encounters another kind of exteriorisation, another relation-ship with the "exterior"' – or what one might term the 'real' (Hadot 1995: 211). One may reasonably seek further specification of this movement. A major direction of development is likely to lead to the inexpressibility of a mystical encounter, but other possibilities include moderate versions of Platonism and even naturalistic Aristotelianism.

I wish, though, to challenge the claim that spiritual formation may proceed independently of the truth of the accompanying metaphysical discourse. Presumably Hadot recognises limits to how wrong one can be at the speculative level while keeping on track in the practice of wisdom. Also, there is reason to link the two as constituent components of a single enterprise, such that the content of spiritual formation depends upon its metaphysical complement. I spoke of spirituality involving an appropriate demeanour. It may be asked 'appropriate to what?' Suppose, by analogy, someone were persuaded that the Christian God exists, but then seemed wholly unmoved by this acceptance. One would say that religiously speaking conversion had not yet begun. For *that* belief requires the formation of a demeanour appropriate to its content.

Likewise, a reductive materialist convinced that his philosophy gives the ultimate truth about reality should ask how in the face of this he should compose himself. It seems unintelligible to suppose that *nothing* follows for the enquirer from arriving at a fundamental view of reality be it physicalist or theist. Not only is there the issue of how to compose one's spirit, but the content of the metaphysical belief must condition the character of the resulting demeanour. The Christian will move towards familiar religious practices, and the reductive physicalist whose metaphysics is not so different from that of the Old Stoics may wish to explore their spirituality. Hadot is wrong to loosen the link between philosophy and philosophical discourse; spirituality and metaphysics go together.

VIII

Finally, I turn to the themes of consolation or abandonment as these are suggested by Boethius's *Consolation of Philosophy*, a work of the early sixth century inspired by Stoicism and Neo-Platonism, and the *Abandonment to Divine Providence* of Jeanne Pierre de Caussade,[2] a French Jesuit of the seventeenth and eighteenth centuries (de Caussade 1975 [c. 1730–40]). I have written about Boethius elsewhere (Haldane 1992) and here only extract the idea familiar from Platonism that whatever the contingencies that affect us, however bogged down we are in material things, we have the power to engage intellectually with transcendent realities outside of space and time. Whether these be forms, essences or universal natures they lie beyond fortune and misfortune, and in engaging them we too are raised up, if not wholly or permanently at least for as long as intellectual contemplation endures. That is one kind of spirituality. Whether we can avail ourselves of it depends on the truth of its metaphysics; but even if we can, happiness through intellection is surely redemption for the few.

De Caussade, by contrast, is concerned to emphasise the universal accessibility of Christian spirituality:

> In reality, holiness consists in one thing only: complete loyalty to God's will. Everyone can practise this loyalty, whether actively or passively.
>
> To be actively loyal means obeying the Laws of God and the Church and fulfilling all the duties imposed on us by our way of life. Passive loyalty means that we loyally accept everything God sends us at each moment of the day . . . [this] is even easier since it implies only that we accept what often we cannot avoid, and endure with love and resignation things which could cause us weariness and disgust . . . But what is the secret of finding this treasure? There isn't one. The treasure is everywhere. It is offered to us all the time and wherever we are. All creatures, friends or foes, pour it out in abundance, and it flows through every fibre of our body and soul until it reaches the very core of our being . . . This is the true spirituality which is valid for all times and for everybody . . . It is the ready acceptance of all that comes to us at each moment of our lives.
>
> (de Caussade 1975: 24–6)

Whether it is universally valid depends on the truth of certain doctrines and this is not the place to assess those. If, however, the form of this spirituality seems attractive even to the non-religious, can some version of it be refashioned on a non-theological world-view? There is some reason for thinking that this may be possible. Suppose, however, that it is not. This raises another question. If it should seem after all that the necessary condition for the possibility of spirituality is some religious truth, and if the need and possibility of spirituality should seem compelling, then might we have the beginnings of an argument for religion? I leave the task of answering that question to another ocasion (Haldane 2003).

NOTES

1 This is a revised version of an essay of the same title that appears in O'Hear (ed.) 2000.
2 The *Abandonment* was composed posthumously from a series of works and letters addressed to members of a community of Visitation Nuns in Nancy for which de Caussade acted as a spiritual director.

REFERENCES

Anscombe, G.E.M. (1958) 'Modern moral philosophy', *Philosophy* 33; reprinted in G.E.M. Anscombe, *Ethics, Religion and Politics: Collected Philosophical Papers, Volume III*, Oxford: Blackwell, 1981.

Aquinas, St Thomas (1914) [1271] *Summa Theologiae*, London: Washbourne.

de Caussade, J.P. (1975) [c. 1730–40] *Abandonment to Divine Providence*, trans. J. Beevers, New York: Image, Doubleday.

Epictetus, *The Discourses* (1995) [c. AD 100] *The Discourses of Epictetus*, trans. R. Hard; ed. C. Gill, London: Everyman.

Flew, A. (1997) 'What is "spirituality"?', in L. Brown, B.C. Farr and R.J. Hoffmann (eds), *Modern Spiritualities: An Inquiry*, New York: Prometheus.

Foucault, M. (1984) *History of Sexuality*, Volume 3, *Care of the Self*, trans. R. Hurley, New York: Pantheon.

Hadot, P. (1995) *Philosophy as a Way of Life: Spiritual Exercises from Socrates to Foucault*, A.I. Davidson ed. Oxford: Blackwell.

Haldane, J. (1992) 'De consolatione philosophiae', in M. McGhee (ed.), *Philosophy, Religion and the Spiritual Life*, Cambridge: Cambridge University Press.

Haldane, J. (1996) 'Applied ethics', in N. Bunnin and E. Tsui-James (eds), *The Blackwell Companion to Philosophy*, Oxford: Blackwell, 2nd edn 2002.

Haldane, J. (2003) *An Intelligent Person's Guide to Religion*, London: Duckworth.

National Curriculum Council (1993) *Spiritual and Moral Development – Discussion Paper*, London: National Curriculum Council.

Office of Standards in Teacher Education (1994) *Social and Cultural Development*, London: OFSTED.

O'Hear, A. (ed.) (2000) *Philosophy, the Good, the True and the Beautiful*, Cambridge: Cambridge University Press.

Quinton, A. (1998) 'Character and will', in A. Quinton, *From Woodhouse to Wittgenstein*, Manchester: Carcanet.

Wiggins, D. (1976) 'Truth, invention and the meaning of life', *Proceedings of the British Academy* LXII; reprinted in D. Wiggins, *Needs, Values, Truth*, Oxford: Blackwell, 1987.

Chapter 2

Making spirits attentive
Moral-and-spiritual development

Michael McGhee

I

If schools are required to provide for the 'spiritual and moral development' of pupils and officials are required to inspect their provision, what *conception* of this development should prevail? Is there a common conception, equally acceptable to religious and non-religious teachers? How, for instance, can secular humanists, without hypocrisy, and knowing that hypocrisy always shows, help to provide for the *spiritual* development of their pupils, if they believe that the idea is tied up with religion? Need it be so tied up? And, if not, why should it command the consent of religiously committed colleagues?

This is an area of conflict and political compromise, and what I shall attempt here, all too inchoately, and on the margins of the debate, is to indicate a notion of 'moral-and-spiritual development' that depends upon a significant distinction to be made within the interior conditions of *conduct* that I think can be sustained independently of the Judaeo-Christian context that has traditionally been invoked in the West to make sense of it.

i

In the introduction to the 1995 SCAA Discussion Paper, *Spiritual and Moral Development,* we are told that the 1988 Education Reform Act 'sets education within the context of the spiritual, moral, cultural, mental and physical development of pupils and of society' (p. 3). This is a mouthful of context to set education within, and it is not clear that we need separate accounts of the development of this and the development of that. Nevertheless, and ominously, the paper looks first at 'spiritual' and then later at 'moral' development. Admittedly it sometimes *refers* to them together (using the phrase 'spiritual and moral development'), but it *treats* them separately in a way that suggests that they have been *conceived* separately too.

Now this phrase, 'spiritual and moral development', does not to my ear sound quite right, and I feel more at home with the then Sir Ron Dearing's perhaps unconscious correction of the phrase in his Foreword, where he refers approvingly to 'moral and spiritual development' and to 'moral and spiritual growth'. I am not suggesting that someone who puts the words in this latter order is less likely to *conceive* them as separate, and nor do I think that we cannot *treat* them separately at all. But if we do so we should be clear that we are thereby abstracting out different aspects of a totality, and it is better to be clear about the nature of the totality first. So I prefer to keep the two adjectives 'moral' and 'spiritual' together and in that order as a kind of portmanteau expression that indicates a necessary connection or indivisibility. In my subtitle I have placed hyphens between them, to indicate a kind of rising curve in which the condition of morality ascends towards and transforms itself into the 'spiritual' in a single line of development, and so to lock them in together, to show that their connection is an essential rather than accidental one. In other words, my suggestion is that whether or not we are comfortable with the word 'spiritual', the reference of the term includes the interior conditions under which a certain kind of *ethical* development takes place. I might as well indicate now what kind of development I have in mind.

ii

Some of our descriptions of conduct are cautiously adverbial and this *can* be a means of refusing to commit ourselves to an opinion about its spirit, or motivation, or real source. Thus we might agree that someone acted generously, without agreeing that they acted out of generosity (or because they were generous), that they acted justly, but not necessarily out of a sense of justice (or because they were just), that they acted honestly, but not in a spirit of honesty (or because they were honest), acted charitably, but not out of charity (or because they were charitable).

The point of course lies in the motivation, and the nature of the attention one extends to others. There can be venal or self-serving reasons for acting justly, or generously, or honestly. Indeed, one aspect of a person's moral-and-spiritual development is some *discernment* of the spirit in which an action is performed. It seems that when we refer to *the spirit of an action* we name the character or nature that it expresses. There are negative counterparts: in a mean spirit, for instance. We name interior dispositions, say what kind of spirit a person is. But the spirit of an action is something that can be distilled and concentrated or strengthened.

Thus it may well be objected that though I have invoked the word 'spirit' what we have here are moral rather than 'spiritual' distinctions. I shall come back to this, in order to try to show that I am drawing on one of the founders of Christianity, St Paul, whose writing is so crucial for our understanding of the origins of the term 'spiritual'. For the moment, though, allow me at least to suggest that some of the qualities we might originally think of as being 'moral' may attain the status of 'spiritual' to the extent that compassion, say, or generosity, or the sense of justice, seems to refer not to a single moral possibility of action, but to a coiled set of possibilities, each one transcending the last in scope and concentration. The compassion of Christ, or of the Bodhisattva Tara, reaches beyond my own, I take it, not only in its stability, its force and intensity, but also in its scope and conception. What is significant here is the idea of a kind of spiral transcendence, an indefinite possibility of development. We rely on the latter stages of the spiral to provide us with the vantage-point from which we can think of the earlier ones as at least steps towards 'the spiritual', if indeed we are inclined to invoke that language.

iii

But now, it is hard not to notice that the framers of the Education Act managed to avoid referring to the *religious* development of pupils as among the dimensions that underpin the curriculum and the ethos of the school. The SCAA Discussion Paper attempts to solve the pluralist, cultural problem by locating the religious within the category of 'the spiritual'. It also implies that one can talk about 'spirituality' without reference to religious belief, *and* engage in 'collective worship'. There is no reason why secular schools shouldn't teach Religious Education, but I have my doubts about 'collective worship'. This could be replaced by 'inspirational assemblies', which probably already go on under the name of 'collective worship'. My sense of the SCAA document, though, is that it attempts to present religion as a *form* of spirituality, so that it can also present 'spiritual development' in alternative, non-religious forms. The trouble is that it also wants to offer an account of 'the spiritual' independently of 'the moral'. But it is not a straightforward matter to break the connection between religion and 'spirituality'.

I suggest that any notion of 'spirituality' that is conceived independently both of religion *and* of moral life is enfeebled and attenuated. There is evidence of such attenuation in the SCAA document. But we can, I think, have a sufficiently robust notion of the spiritual that is *non-religious* as long as we stay in touch with moral life. However, the connection with moral life is essential even if we retain the connection between spirituality and religion. If, though, we retain that connection *without* reference to morality, we end up with a one-sided and partial notion of spirituality rather than a feeble and attenuated one. So can we avoid these two errors?

II

In his seminal paper, 'On the very idea of spiritual values' (Haldane 2000; see also this volume, Chapter 1), John Haldane suggests that 'the spiritual' is an area of human existence 'which has something to do with how one experiences the world and with what one makes of that experience. It is, I suggest, primarily a matter of what *personal demeanour* or mode of being one develops in the face of reality as one understands it in some more or less philosophical way' (p. 62; this volume, p. 18).

I appreciate this notion of a 'personal demeanour', and it seems proper to qualify it with that 'in the face of reality', or with 'how one experiences the world'. However, I am not so sure about the 'primarily'. Although a significant aspect of 'spirituality' is captured by the idea of a certain demeanour 'in the face of reality', it is only *one* aspect: one that needs to be set alongside a person's demeanour towards others, for instance. I also have a reservation about qualifying 'in the face of reality' by the further phrase 'as one understands it in some more or less philosophical way'. I do not wish to exclude it altogether, but I suspect an intellectualist bias here, and a particular movement of thought I shall try to diagnose.

i

At the beginning of his paper Haldane reminds us what an expression like 'spiritual life' would traditionally have been used to refer to. 'the spiritual life is that given to the search after an inner awareness of God, a condition pursued through prayer and meditation and attained through grace'(p. 54; this volume p. 12). I do not have a problem with this as an account of part of 'the spiritual life', as theologically conceived and developed. A crucial point for our purposes, though, is whether we think of this enterprise as undertaken in the first person singular or in the plural. It seems to me that theologically it is the latter that is properly dominant, providing the context for and a perspective on the 'spiritual life' of the individual. If, however, we think primarily in terms of the singular, it is hard to see how our ethical relations can have any centrality for our spiritual lives. And indeed Haldane denies any such centrality.

But if we think in terms of a community whose members are struggling with their own unregeneracy and mutual destructiveness, things start to look different. The 'inner awareness of God' becomes a matter of sensitivity to the still small voice, to promptings of the Spirit that are precisely focused on conduct and its consequences. A person's 'spirituality' is established in an inner awareness of the action of that breath of the Spirit that speaks to us of what we do and fail to do. Here is an inner state that stands in need of outward criteria.

ii

The immediate issue is whether there is anything left to refer to if we remove the religious, specifically theological, context that gave us precisely this language of 'spirituality'. If we omit the religious dimension, and break the connection with conduct, staying in the first person singular, it looks as though all that is left of our inner awareness of God, and our personal demeanour in the face of God's will, is a personal demeanour in the face of reality 'as one understands it in some more or less philosophical way'.

What is the motivation for the addition of this qualifying phrase? It seems to me that spirituality has been defined here as an attitude to the ultimate nature of reality, so that if one does not believe in God, and does not therefore take up an appropriate attitude to His existence, all that is left for one's attitude to the ultimate nature of reality to attach itself to is mediated by some alternative metaphysical position – well, the *only* alternative metaphysical position that Haldane allows: materialism. The question of whether there can be a non-religious spirituality thus becomes the question of what kind of demeanour there can be in the face of reality conceived atheistically.

iii

But there are other candidates than the metaphysical for the position of a 'reality' towards which one can take up a personal demeanour that has some claim to being 'spiritual'. One thinks about a person's tranquillity or otherwise in the face of success or failure, say, their demeanour in the face of injustice, false accusation, adversity or loss, as measures of what we might reasonably call their 'spiritual state', the state of their 'spirit'. We see it in the fortitude with which someone bears an illness or looks after a sick wife or husband or parent. Or, to make the connection with the other issue I want to question, namely the relation of spirituality to conduct, we may measure a person's spiritual state by their capacity for forgiveness, by their refusal to boast or condescend to others, by their passion for peace-making. We may measure a person's spirituality by the vitality of their sympathetic awareness of others, and their discernment of the nature of their needs. This is not simply another direction for a personal demeanour, however, but is the traditional *criterion* by which, in a religious context, it is possible to judge someone's awareness of the presence of God. By their fruits ye shall know them. Those who do not love do not know God. Whether a person is genuinely possessed of an inner awareness of God is revealed by the nature of their inner awareness of others, because, to put it crudely, it is of this that God speaks. Thus the theology, where the criterion of spirituality is precisely demeanour and conduct.

But John Haldane's account seems at best ambivalent about the connection with conduct. For instance, he says that right conduct 'is only a part of spirituality and perhaps then only *per accidens*' (p. 60; this volume, p. 16). That 'perhaps' has been removed, though, and the *per accidens* underlined when he comes to the notion of a personal demeanour: 'My suggestion . . . has been that there is a further area of human existence, the spiritual, which is not essentially concerned with action in relation to the rights and interests of others' (p. 62; this volume, p. 18). I think I would say by contrast that it *is* essentially so concerned, though perhaps 'rights and interests' is not the phrase to capture the idea of a passion for the welfare of others. The same contrast is made a little later, when he makes it clear that in talking about the spiritual his focus is 'on experience and on the contemplation of it, instead of on conduct'. My reason for drawing attention to this is that it seems to me that conduct is a criterion of the presence of any kind of demeanour that we want to call 'spiritual', and that this provides us with a way into our subject, which concerns education and moral and spiritual development. Maybe the point is that the reference to 'the spiritual' is to what comes from a person's inmost being or *spirit* as it encounters what it perceives as a higher, holy spirit: and that its expression is always more or less impeded by the *flesh*.

To take the discussion further, though, we need to attend to one of the Christian sources that has given us the word 'spiritual' in the first place, so that we can see what we can learn from the theological context from which I have claimed we can disconnect it.

III

St Paul's Epistle to the Galatians is not addressed to a single individual, but to the *Galatians*, that is, to an assembly of early Christians, a Church or congregation, and the nature of Paul's rebuke – 'You stupid Galatians' – is instructive. It might be said that the letter is also addressed to individuals, but if it is, it is addressed to them as individual *members* of a congregation whose behaviour towards one another is not as it should be. If we keep this in mind we may be able to find our way between the Scylla of individualism and the Charybdis of communalism. However, the course we chart between them involves different conceptions of the moral life, and we have to negotiate between the Pauline contrast between the Law and a freedom from the Law that is not merely licence, between the flesh, or our lower nature, and the guidance of the Holy Spirit, and between the presence and absence of faith in Christ Jesus. I really cannot give a proper or competent account of this theological complex, and all I want to do is to discover a recognisable analogue that will give us grounds for thinking that there is something distinctive that constitutes the moral and spiritual development that teachers are supposed to provide for. In this connection it is worth noting that it is in Galatians that Paul refers to the Law as a schoolmaster (Tyndale) or a tutor (New English Bible), which might provide us with an ironic comment on this discussion, but also the means towards a solution to a problem.

i

The gifts of the flesh and the gifts of the Holy Spirit, as Paul presents them, are primarily exemplified in contrasting forms of human relationship. A 'spiritual' life is thus a life lived by a community of persons, specifically of the faithful, under the guidance of the Spirit. Paul contrasts it with a life of mutual destruction. The extremities are between giving licence to our 'lower' nature, and becoming 'servants to one another in love'. The spirituality of the latter is constituted by its being an expression of a nature transformed by the breath or action of the Holy Spirit. But in between there is the Law. Paul offers us a vision of fundamental conflict, between the guidance of the Spirit and the desires of the flesh. And here is the crucial contrast:

> *Anyone can see the kind of behaviour that belongs to the lower nature: forni-cation, impurity, and indecency; idolatry and sorcery; quarrels, a contentious temper, envy, fits of rage, selfish ambitions, dissensions, party intrigues, and jealousies; drinking bouts, orgies and the like . . . But the harvest of the Spirit is love, joy, peace, patience, kindness, goodness, fidelity, gentleness, and self-control. There is no law dealing with such things as these.*
> (Galatians 5:19–23)

ii

I am tempted to interpret this last sentence in the following way. There is a sense in which the Law, and obedience to the Law, mitigate the worst effects of the natural dispositions and expressive states of the flesh or our lower nature. The Law puts a curb on them or contains them. The specifically Pauline and Christianising move is then to say that 'The law was a kind of tutor in charge of us until Christ should come, when we should be justified through faith; and now that faith has come, the tutor's charge is at an end.'

But the point is that the Law already reveals or articulates some discernment or awareness of obstructed promptings theologised as the promptings of the Holy Spirit. The crucial human experience is that we cannot give expression to that spirit in our actions because of the opposing strength of contrary inclinations and the darkening of our vision by the flesh. To the extent that I live my life in accordance with the law I put a curb on my natural but destructive inclinations and succeed thereby in acting 'morally'.

However, the harvest of the Spirit also includes a contrasting set of expressive states and natural dispositions: 'the life I now live is not my life, but the life which Christ lives in me.' The conduct that flows from the working of the Spirit is the natural expression of the Mind of Christ, and it is not conduct that is determined by the law, but conduct whose interior condition now supersedes it. We feel the breath of something higher acting within us that gives us the freedom to act with a new kind of spontaneity, not admissible before, since what was spontaneous then was more likely to be the flesh than the spirit.

But what are we to do with all this? St Paul provides us with the kind of context within which the notion of 'spirit' and its derivatives have a particular sense and refer to determinate phenomena within the terms of a particular theology. It could all have been expressed differently and the same crucial distinction sustained. The immediate point, however, is that the spiritual refers us paradigmatically to a particular kind of abundant life that is the free life of our spirit, of our inmost being unfettered by the demands of the flesh. It is not so much that *I* as an adopted child of God participate in the divine life, but that *we* as adopted *children* of God participate in that life, and we do so to the extent that we live a life of 'faith active in love': 'let us work for the good of all, especially members of the household of faith.'

iii

The upward curve that I indicated earlier with my hyphens takes us from a conception of morality as determined by law towards a form of freedom guided by the Holy Spirit that guides us to what lies innermost. It seems to me that there is a clear sense in which we can focus the notion of moral and spiritual development around this particular development in conduct, and the expressive spirit in which we act, whether we accept the theology or not.

The way we conduct ourselves is an expression of our inner or our spiritual state. We do not need to think in terms of the working of the Holy Spirit in order to secure the distinction that the notion of the Spirit is invoked to explain. However, the phenomenology may well be a phenomenology of grace, the sense that it is not I but Christ who lives in me, so that just as I start to identify a new principle or source of action within me, I identify myself over against it. That sense of things is no doubt reinforced by the reflection that whereas I can at least sometimes follow the requirements of the law by strength of will, can at least sometimes conform my behaviour to the law despite the sway of contrary inclinations, I *cannot* so produce those actions that are the harvest of the

Spirit, and this because they are not to be understood as the product of will, but as the expression of an inner state or condition.

iv

But what about the faith in Christ Jesus that is supposed to free us from the law, and is the *condition* of the guidance of the Spirit? It seems to me that minimally it is constituted by a leap, but this leap of faith is a leap of the imagination, towards the figure, the representation, the exemplar, of a higher kind of life, a life manifestly desirable because it is free of the felt oppression of the flesh and the 'mutual destruction' that comes in its wake. Clearly there are many representations of this kind in world literatures and religions, and it would be seriously inappropriate to restrict ourselves to one particular tradition, or to one figure, or to one gender. But here I am merely offering an account of one main source of the *language* of 'spirituality'.

Only under the condition that a person has a lively and abiding sense of the presence of this exemplar, who already embodies for us what that higher life consists in, *and which we are already drawn to and admire*, are we likely to hear the promptings of the Spirit, rather than the promptings of the flesh. To the extent that the mind conforms itself actively and imaginatively to the mind of Christ, our lower nature to some extent recedes from the centre of consciousness, because we have planted there at least the seed of another possibility of consciousness. So there is a meditative aspect to this, a calming of the passions, which allows other forms of motivation to crystallise and come into focus, forms of motivation already imperfectly present and adumbrated by the Law. Under such a condition we start to become alert and attentive to the presence and situation of others in a way not previously available. In thus becoming aware of the promptings of new impulses we might well start to think in terms of the promptings of the Spirit rather than of the spirit. 'If we live in the spirit let us walk in the spirit.'

On the other hand, I think we need to be wary of the Pauline impulse to use the image of crucifixion in *this* context, an impulse that recalls the brutal treatment of the black horse in the *Phaedrus*: 'And those who belong to Christ Jesus have crucified the lower nature with its passions and desires.' One of the things we have learnt from Nietzsche and others is that this can be a disastrous remedy. The energies that the flesh locks in stand in need of transformation, not crucifixion. But for this to happen the flesh needs to become quiet; so let us turn to Shakespeare and my main title, 'Making spirits attentive', for a quasi-secular account in a different idiom of the silencing of the flesh and the emergence of the spirit that is thus released.

IV

The SCAA Discussion Paper, as we saw, 'is intended to guide schools in their understanding of spiritual and moral development' but also 'to demonstrate that these dimensions apply not only to Religious Education and collective worship but to every area of the curriculum and to all aspects of school life'. This *could* have radical implications. But the irony is that the radical thing would be to make more pervasive than seems possible under present conditions what has always been done in schools: music and drama. I mention these particularly only by way of emphasis, because they constitute *events and occasions* in the life of the school that have a particular impact.

i

The first part of my title alludes to a famous passage in a scene between Shylock's daughter Jessica and her lover Lorenzo in the last act of *The Merchant of Venice*. The lovers are at Belmont, in a grove before Portia's house. They are moved by the stillness of the beautiful moonlit night, and Lorenzo calls for music: 'soft stillness and the night/ Become the touches of sweet harmony'. I think this says more than that such nights are a suitable time for the playing of music. There is an inner unity between the one and the other, in that both can have a similar effect on us: 'soft stillness and the night' may touch us in the same way that music does, bringing us into a mood whose quality we may indicate by reference back to its cause, that we register by that very talk of soft stillness and the night. The mood is harmonious, and, as the speech develops, it is seen to be one in harmony with the music of the spheres, except that though this latter harmony 'is in immortal souls' . . . 'whilst this muddy vesture of decay/ Doth grossly close it in, *we cannot hear it*' (my italics). Or at least not usually. The harmony of the spheres, though, is not the main issue. Soft stillness and the night provide an image of a revealed depth of the mind (the night) and the condition upon which that depth depends (soft stillness). This muddy vesture of decay is the flesh and what it grossly closes in is our sense of, our own attunement to, the harmony of the spheres.

The musicians enter and start to play. The lovers listen, and Jessica says, 'I am never merry when I hear sweet music.' Lorenzo replies: 'The reason is your spirits are attentive' – spirits, as in animal spirits, become quiet and attentive in the sudden awareness through harmony of higher, celestial but also fellow spirits. Lorenzo now describes a typical classroom scene:

> 'For do but note a wild and wanton herd,
> Or race of youthful and unhandled colts,
> Fetching mad bounds, bellowing and neighing loud,
> Which is the hot condition of their blood –
> If they but hear perchance a trumpet sound,
> Or any air of music touch their ears,
> You shall perceive them make a mutual stand,
> Their savage eyes turn'd to a modest gaze
> By the sweet power of music. Therefore the poet
> Did feign that Orpheus drew trees, stones, and floods;
> Since nought so stockish, hard, and full of rage,
> But music for the time doth change his nature.
>
> (V.i)

This is a thought we find developed in Schiller, and it is one we find also in Plato. And if we ask, change his nature from what? we find that the answer already given, 'stockish, hard, and full of rage', is further delineated in the famous closing lines of the speech:

> The man that hath no music in himself,
> Nor is not mov'd with concord of sweet sounds,
> Is fit for treasons, stratagems and spoils; . . .
> Let no such man be trusted.
>
> (V.i)

It might seem from this that Shakespeare is here clearer about what our nature might be changed *from* than about what it might be changed *to*. He offers us a description of the first, but not apparently of the second: little more is *said* to spell out the latter. But then he manages one of his unsettling dramatic fusions, in which the interior logic of the poetic discourse, and the action of the play, are advanced at the same time. Lorenzo ends his speech, and bids Jessica 'mark the music', and as it plays Portia enters, with her waiting-woman, Nerissa. Portia is the shining embodiment or exemplar of that change of nature that, as Lorenzo has just told us, music can effect 'for the time', so she is genuinely a vision brought forth by the music, as well as the instrument in the play of justice and mercy. She *instantiates* what Shakespeare means, her entrance secures the point of the speech.

ii

As she approaches Belmont, Portia observes the candle shining in her hall:

> How far that little candle throws his beams!
> So shines a good deed in a naughty world.
>
> (V.i)

The Arden editor, John Russell Brown, refers us to Matthew 6:16, 'Let your light so shine before men.' Indeed the passage that follows it registers the theological or spiritual ambience set up by Lorenzo's speech, which invoked Diana, and which might also be thought of as a preparation for her entrance in the form of Portia. 'When the moon shone, we did not see the candle' . . . 'So doth the greater glory dim the less.' When she hears the music, Portia remarks that 'it sounds much sweeter than by day', again indicating the heightened perception that comes with the stilling of the mind, and her waiting-woman sagely notes that 'Silence bestows that virtue on it.' Again we are given the sense of the silence of the night as a contrast with the bustle of the day, with the implication that the self-revelation of the soul requires silence, and is imaged by the night, our fleshly clamouring and the press of affairs imaged by the day. We could not properly attend and appreciate the music of the nightingale by day, 'when every goose is cackling'.

What is important for my theme is the *common human experience* of the power of beauty and of art, of 'the sweet power of music', to change 'for the time' our nature. What this 'for the time' suggests is the idea of an *interlude* in which what Eliot referred to as 'the usual preoccupations of the conscious mind' briefly recede to the periphery in favour of an intense listening or concentration, which provides a portal to a transformation or re-ordering or re-direction of the energies of the psyche whose intimations then become more manifest and more audible.

iii

I hope you will forgive my failure to resist at this point a Buddhist connection, and yet another idiom. The purpose of *samatha* meditation in the Buddhist traditions is precisely to calm down our quotidian thoughts and desires, including the *kleshas*, sometimes translated as 'the defiling passions', but maybe better rendered 'mental afflictions'. And the point of the exercise is to make available what emerges under the condition of that calming or stilling of thought and desire, namely, the releasing and strengthening of what are called skilful mental states (*kusaladharmas*), such as loving-kindness (*metta*) and generosity (*dana*). Like other Asian and East-Asian traditions Buddhism does not have a word to translate that very theological word 'spiritual', but it is apparent that similar distinctions are being invoked here with the same degree of importance attached to some notion of transformation. The silencing of the *kleshas* is the condition for the emergence of skilful states, but that emergence comes about through a concentration that is supposed to increase alertness and bring a person to insight into 'the way things really are'. Now this is a phrase that stands in need of interpretation – we do not need to go into upper case, for instance. But though I cite a Buddhist context, there is space here to locate the contemplative aspect that is strongly underlined in Haldane's paper.

iv

I hope that these reflections can be seen to tend towards a certain conclusion about providing for the moral-and-spiritual development of children. *It is the role of teachers to make spirits attentive in ways that open up the possibility of a certain kind of ethical transformation.* The Law was once the tutor: it is now for teachers to allow children to see how the Law mediates between the flesh and the spirit. Perhaps it is overwhelmingly important to say that this needs to be done by *acts of showing,* and that *saying* too much is a pedagogical error especially here. Music and drama become important, then. In his paper Haldane remarked that

> The appreciation of art and music and the cultivation of a concern for the feelings of others are worthwhile educational activities, but their point and value is made less and not more clear by describing them as parts of 'spiritual development'.
>
> (Haldane 2000: 54; this volume, p. 12)

This is a comment on the SCAA document, and it seems to me that his assessment of what it actually says is accurate. However, Shakespeare's reflections seem to imply, not that music is a *part* of spiritual development, but that 'the sweet power of music' can *conduce* to such development, can lead us to the threshold of possibilities that might not otherwise come to our minds. Art and music, drama and poetry can be liminal or threshold activities. In that case it does not seem unreasonable that those who are charged with 'the spiritual and moral development' of our children should seek to provide an artistic and musical and such other environment as makes their spirits at least intermittently attentive. This is the provision to be 'inspected'.

v

But the reference to *activities* should prompt us to acknowledge that in the Shakespearean scene we are focused only on the experience of being a member of an audience. That can be a shared experience of the silencing of egocentric and communal impulses. What seems to me at least as important, perhaps far more important, is the experience of *participation*.

This does give children 'a sense of community' as the SCAA document requires. But that does not quite capture it. What is needed is the sense of that community which unexpectedly emerges when we put aside 'the gifts of the flesh' and engage in collaborative activities that transcend them.

If we took this notion of participation seriously, I can imagine a scenario in which there is a real (i.e. funded) shift of emphasis in education, one in which 'moral-and-spiritual development' becomes a genuinely leading idea. It would not be much talked about, but acted out, a multiplicity of small-scale activities. There is another thing to be said here. Good teachers bring an energetic joy and enthusiasm to their teaching. Whatever else they teach, they teach their demeanour. This is what determines the ethos of the school, and we register it by means of the atmosphere.

But the SCAA document makes a dismal move at this point. It quite rightly asserts that teachers transmit values to pupils consciously or unconsciously, but a dreary instinct then needs to tie down or capture the ethos with some kind of documentary evidence, a Statement of Values, with which these consciously or unconsciously transmitted values have to be consistent. We are told that the ethos of a school 'may be apparent through a statement that sets out . . .'. Here is the pervasive, nervous, bureaucratic impulse, comfortable only with *saying*, uncomprehending of acts of *showing*. The ethos of a school is not apparent through a statement, it is *palpable* 'mark the music' is what I say.

REFERENCES

Haldane, J. (2000) 'On the very idea of spiritual values', in A. O'Hear (ed.), *Philosophy, the True, the Good and the Beautiful*, Cambridge: Cambridge University Press, pp. 53–71. This paper also appears in a revised version in this volume; see Chapter 1.

School Curriculum and Assessment Authority (1995) *Spiritual and Moral Development*, Discussion Paper No. 3, London: SSCAA.

Chapter 3

Spirituality, science and morality

John Cottingham

It is probably pointless to offer a precise definition of the idea of spirituality, nor, in this paper, shall I attempt it. But I shall indicate some of the
strands that make up the idea. My purpose in doing so will be to explore
a certain tension (which I think most people implicitly recognise) between
what might be called the outlook of scientific rationalism, on the one
hand – an outlook which has little time for the idea of spirituality – and,
on the other, an approach which takes the idea of the spiritual dimension
in life very seriously. The eventual aim of the paper will be to show that
these two differing approaches can coexist. To take the spiritual dimension
seriously need not involve quarrelling with any of the values and achievements of scientific rationalism (though it will tend to see science as
presenting an account of human existence that is in a certain sense incomplete); and, conversely, scientific rationalism need not dismiss the spiritual
domain, since the insights offered in the latter realm are not in competition
with the theories and explanations of the scientist. Though the main
themes of the paper are those of spirituality and of science, it will be
clear from the outset that questions about spirituality inevitably intertwine
with central *moral* questions about how life should be lived; and it will
emerge towards the end that the moral credentials of the spiritual life
play an important role in defending its value.

SPIRITUALITY VERSUS SCIENCE

Michel Foucault, in a 1982 seminar held at the Collège de France,[1]
explored the concept of spirituality in terms of an ancient notion with its
roots in pre-Christian philosophy – what the Greeks called *epimeleia
heautou*, very roughly and crudely, looking after yourself. Socrates (in the
Apology) reproaches his Athenian accusers for being very concerned with
things like wealth and reputation, but not having the faintest concern for
the improvement of their souls.[2] Not just 'know yourself' (the Delphic
motto to which, as we know, Socrates was strongly drawn), but, as part

and parcel of that self-knowledge, take care of yourself, look after yourself, pay attention to what is the most precious and important part of yourself.

The idea of care of the self, though it clearly does not exhaust the domain of the spiritual, does seem to capture an important part of what most people understand by it. It is an idea which modern academics do not tend to associate with Socrates: most of us prefer to see him as a wholly rationalistic figure, and construe the *exetastos bios*, the 'examined life' which he recommended, as principally a matter of analytical logical enquiry. But in fact it is difficult to read what Socrates says about his inner voice, about the search for purity of conscience and integrity, without seeing the 'examination' he advocates as indeed possessing the 'spiritual' dimension identified by Foucault. Foucault goes on to show how this notion of self-examination and care for the self resonates throughout subsequent Hellenistic thought, in the Epicurean 'therapeutic' conception of philosophy, and the Stoic notion of the care of the soul.[3] Later, of course, the notion becomes the cornerstone of much Christian asceticism.[4]

The notion of 'care of self' no doubt has cognitive implications: the famous Augustinian 'inward turn', for example, is partly a search for a more adequate grasp of one's own nature, and like the Delphic injunction that preceded it, and the Cartesian programme that succeeded it, it is recognisably part of the philosophical enterprise of extending our knowledge and understanding. But in many of its manifestations it is also, importantly, a matter of *practice* – techniques of meditation, techniques for the examination of conscience, and so on.[5] And rather like the physical routines embraced by the devotee of the gym and the workout, such exercises are aimed at producing a significant change in the subject.

These strands in the notion of spirituality – the stress on disciplines and exercises, the goal of internal transformation – seem to take us light years away from the modern enterprise of philosophy, at least as typically conceived by the majority of its academic practitioners in the Anglophone world. The title of a recent book by Michael McGhee, *Transformations of Mind: Philosophy as Spiritual Practice,*[6] strikes a surprising chord precisely because most of us do not think of philosophy as a way of changing our lives, except in the purely academic or professional sense – enabling us to earn a living, progress in a career, and so on. Or perhaps that is a little unfair: perhaps we do expect to be changed by our subject in the sense that it may give us a better understanding of the conceptual landscape, the nature of knowledge, the kinds of justification that can be offered for our actions, the relationship between the mental and the physical domains, and so on. Such improved understanding can be very extensive, and, like any improvement it will of course involve an alteration. But the kind of alteration involved is, if I may put it this way, of an essentially scientific nature: we *enlarge the terrain of our knowledge*. What is not, or only very rarely, envisaged as part of the fruits of philosophy is that more radical interior change – *metanoia* is the Greek term – a change of heart, a change of the kind that leads to a fundamental shift in the flow and direction of one's life.[7]

Yet it was transformation of this more radical kind that was the goal of the earlier philosophical systems that put a premium on the 'care of the soul'. Foucault, in the seminar just referred to, defines 'spirituality' as 'the set of inquiries, practices and exercises (including self-purification, ascetic techniques, self-denial, etc.) which constitute, not in terms of knowledge, but *of the very being of the subject,* the price to pay for gaining access to the truth.'[8] This implies that the truth is never simply given to the subject as he or she is, but requires some inner modification of our receptivity (a conversion, a subjective transformation). And by the same token, particularly in the religious developments of this notion, there is the idea of a reciprocal 'response', as it were from the other side: the truth imparts blessedness, bestows tranquillity on the soul: 'there is, in the truth and in the access to it, something which fulfils the subject and completes, or transfigures, the very being of the subject.'[9]

If such a model can seem alien to us now, this is very probably connected with the rise of modernity. When Descartes announced his 'method' in 1637, the 'method for rightly conducting reason and reaching the truth in the sciences',[10] he inaugurated a new phase in man's relationship to the world – one in which an aggressive self-confidence was increasingly to displace the submissive contemplation of an earlier age. The advent of the 'Cartesian moment', as Foucault calls it, proclaims that the subject is capable, in himself, and simply by exercising the appropriate cognitive skills, of discerning the truth and gaining access to it. This need not mean that the truth is always simple and straightforward (Descartes did actually believe as much, but modern scientists know better);[11] but it does mean that the pursuit of truth becomes a matter of applying certain objective procedures (what we now call the scientific method), rather than depending on any programme of internal transformation. As Foucault puts it:

> If we define *spirituality* as the form of those practices which presuppose that the subject, as he is, is incapable of attaining the truth, but that the truth, as it is, is capable of transfiguring and saving the subject, then we must say that the *modern age,* the age that connects the subject to the truth, begins as soon as we postulate instead that the subject, as he is, is indeed capable of attaining the truth, but that the truth, as it is, is not capable of saving the subject.[12]

There are details of Foucault's analysis one could quarrel with, but in broad outline his account of the dawn of modernity seems to me persuasive. And if he is right about the shift from spirituality to science, a plausible diagnosis of that shift presents itself. As long as mankind was confronted by a universe whose potentially devastating operations he could not hope to understand or control, the best he could aim for was to transform a natural response of helpless anxiety into one of tranquillity and acceptance; and the path of spiritual practice offered the hope of 'salvation' through interior disciplines of contemplation and calmness. But with the advent of modern science the possibility opens out of making ourselves 'masters and possessors of nature' (*maîtres et possesseurs de la nature*), in Descartes' famous phrase: rather than having no recourse but to modify our subjective responses to the world we can now start to understand its objective workings, and in understanding them, set about harnessing or changing them to our advantage. Science makes obsolete the earlier goal of spiritual salvation, as it begins to place real and practical solutions to the problems of humanity within our own hands. The shift is captured perfectly in the passage just alluded to from Descartes' intellectual autobiography, a text aptly viewed as the manifesto of modernity:

> [My discoveries in physics] opened my eyes to the possibility of gaining knowledge which would be very useful in life . . . Through this we could know the power and action of fire, water, air, the stars, the heavens and all the other bodies in our environment as distinctly as we know the various crafts of our artisans; and we could use this knowledge for all the purposes for which it is appropriate and thus make ourselves as it were masters and possessors of nature . . . [W]e might free ourselves from innumerable diseases, both of the body and of the mind, and perhaps even from the infirmity of old age, if we had sufficient knowledge of their causes and of all the remedies which nature has provided.[13]

SPIRITUALITY AS A RESPONSE TO FINITUDE

The picture that emerges from our analysis so far has the virtue of simplicity: the traditional concerns and practices grouped under the heading of 'spirituality' turn out to have been superseded, made redundant if you wish, by the goals and methods of modern science. But unfortunately, or perhaps fortunately, the truth turns out to be far more complicated than that. Within a decade of articulating his proclamation of science as the new saviour, Descartes became acutely aware of how limited a salvation it could provide. 'Instead of finding ways to preserve life', he wrote to a correspondent in 1646, 'I have found another, much easier and surer way, which is not to fear death.'[14]

Why the disillusionment with the promise of science? The question might seem otiose to the modern reader, having seen all the problems (pollution, overcrowding, climate change) that the scientific revolution has generated. But these recent worries, pressing though they are, are in one sense relatively superficial; and it is perfectly possible that science itself, given a century or two, may manage to solve them. The deeper worry, hinted at by Descartes in his more mature writings, is that however far the march of scientific rationality may take us, it cannot remove that most fundamental aspect of the human condition – our dependency, our finitude, our mortality. It is curious how little this basic feature of human existence is acknowledged and reflected upon in the voluminous writings of moral philosophers. This is a point nicely brought out in Alasdair MacIntyre's most recent book, aptly named *Dependent Rational Animals*:

> [Facts] . . . concerning our vulnerabilities and afflictions and those concerning the extent of our dependence on particular others are so evidently of singular importance that it might seem that no account of the human condition whose authors hoped to achieve credibility could avoid giving them a central place. Yet the history of Western moral philosophy suggests otherwise . . . [M]oral agents . . . are . . . presented as though they were continuously rational, healthy and untroubled . . . Aristotle . . . anticipated . . . a great many . . . in importing into moral philosophy the standpoint of those who have taken themselves to be self-sufficiently superior.[15]

The point can be pushed further than MacIntyre himself takes it. The self-deluding 'superiority' he speaks of is not just a bumptious failure to acknowledge our inherent human dependency, but is also a kind of arrogance about the powers of human reason: we, the philosophers, take ourselves to have the wisdom to lay down a recipe for the good life, and we, the scientists, claim to have the theoretical knowledge and technical know-how to achieve the desired result. This is the 'proto-Californian' vision that inspired the young Descartes, when he envisaged extending our lifespan and eliminating the physical inconveniences of the ageing process.[16] And indeed the dream is by no means intrinsically absurd: perhaps another century or so may see much of the Cartesian-Californian programme realised. Yet the Psalmist's words 'Lord let me know my end . . . that I may be certified how long I have to live'[17] are a chilling reminder that there is one fact of life, its inevitable eventual end, that can never be 'sorted', as the current jargon has it – one limit that science will never be able to eliminate.

This is not merely an objective condition, concerning the flux of change and decay within which inhabitants of this physical universe must operate; it also has a subjective aspect, having to do with our inner human response to the external facts. Our finitude we may share with countless fellow-creatures; but it is the unique privilege, or curse, of humans to be able to *perceive* that finitude in all its starkness. And it is this that gives humans their characteristic restlessness, that perpetual undercurrent of *Angst* which Heidegger somewhat ponderously termed the 'existential mode of the not-at-home [*das Nicht-zu-Hause*]'.[18]

Even more sombrely, Heidegger also spoke of human life as 'Being-towards-Death'.[19] But the sombreness should not be interpreted as a piece of personal snivelling or whining, of the kind familiar, for example, from the poems of Philip Larkin.[20] More reminiscent, rather, of the Socratic insistence that life is a preparation for dying,[21] it should be seen instead as stemming from an acknowledgement of the yawning gap between what we are, and what we aspire to be, between our fundamental limitedness as mortal creatures, and our ability to see beyond that limit. And this thought in turn links up with the notion we began by exploring – that of spirituality as internal change. If the gap between what we are and what we aspire to be is beyond the power of scientific rationality to close, the Californian-Cartesian route, for all the short-term benefits it may bring, sooner or later comes up against a brick wall: it reaches the limit of its power to allay the *Angst* that is inseparable from our human nature. So recourse must be had elsewhere, not to further scientific advance, but instead to interior modification, the kind of modification which aims not at changing, but at coming to terms with, the way things are.

Further light is thrown on the origins of this idea in a remarkable study by Pierre Hadot of the spiritual dimension in ancient philosophy:

> All spiritual exercises are, fundamentally, a return to the self, in which the self is liberated from the state of alienation into which it has been plunged by [anxiety]. The 'self' liberated in this way is no longer merely our egoistic, passionate individuality: it is our *moral* person, open to universality and objectivity, and participating in universal nature or thought . . . The practice of spiritual exercises implied a complete reversal of received ideas: one is to renounce the false values of wealth, honors, and pleasures, and turn towards the true values of virtue, contemplation, a simple life-style, and the simple happiness of existing.[22]

Hadot is here summarising a number of elements which he sees as common to the Socratic and Hellenistic traditions of philosophy as spiritual practice. Some of the elements mentioned seem to invoke ideals of personal flourishing, on the one hand, and universal morality, on the other, which are familiar from the discourse of virtue ethics and of moral theory respectively; and this in turn invites the question of how far the pursuit of spirituality is supposed to be either necessary or sufficient for the attainment of *eudaimonia*, or of moral goodness, or both. These are fascinating questions, which I do not have space to pursue here. But whatever the answers may be, Hadot himself is clear that he wants to resist the kind of reductionism which would give spiritual practice a merely instrumental role, or try to subsume it entirely within the domain of ethics. There may, for example, be a temptation to see the ancient spiritual agenda summarised by Hadot as merely a rather solemn and austere kind of virtue theory, one where inner asceticism takes the place of outward flourishing as the key to *eudaimonia*. Hadot goes on to make it clear, however, that to construe the philosophical exercises of antiquity as simple 'moral exercises' is to underrate their significance:

> These exercises have as their goal the transformation of our vision of the world and the metamorphosis of our being. They therefore have not merely a moral but also an existential value. We are not just dealing here with a code of good moral conduct, but with *a way of being*.[23]

If we connect this with our earlier discussion of Foucault, it turns out that Hadot's use of existentialist language in describing ancient spirituality has a particular aptness. For what Foucault sees as the traditional impulse of spirituality, the interest in care for the self, is on his view reincarnated in the existentialist movement in modern philosophy, the movement which runs from Schopenhauer and Nietzsche through to Heidegger, and the psychoanalytically inspired postmodernists such as Jacques Lacan. Foucault finds in the writers mentioned a focus on two questions which are absolutely characteristic of the spirituality tradition in philosophy: the problem of what the subject must be like, what he must become, in order to gain access to the truth, and the reciprocal question of how the access to the truth so gained has power to transform elements of the subject.[24]

It may be worth digressing, just briefly, to make a point here about the 'analytic–continental' divide in philosophy which so much preoccupies us at the start of the twenty-first century. It is, I think, by now generally agreed that the division cannot satisfactorily be characterised simply in terms of stylistic criteria – notwithstanding the complacent judgements about the 'clarity' and 'rigour' of their way of doing philosophy that some practitioners on one side of the divide are still prone to indulge in. Foucault's remarks suggest to me a more fruitful way of making the distinction, in terms of scientific versus spiritual models of philosophising: the one based on paradigms of enquiry which aim to conduct an objective investigation entirely in abstraction from the state and status of the investigator (except where the investigator's sensations or observations may happen themselves to be part of the data), while the other takes the *being* of the subject, in something like Heidegger's sense, as central to the enquiry. Kierkegaard's somewhat unhappily phrased and often misunderstood slogan, 'Truth is subjectivity', points to certain aspects of the so-called 'continental' mode of philosophising which connect with this: philosophy is conceived as an activity which is hermeneutic rather than analytic, transformatory rather than descriptive, aimed not so much at dissecting reality as at disclosing and deepening the significance of my encounters with it. Seen this latter way, the philosophical enterprise is quite closely continuous with religious and psychoanalytic modes of thinking – modes which (hardly accidentally) tend to be given short shrift by adherents of the science-inspired analytic model of philosophy.

To resume the thread of my argument and to conclude this section, what I have been suggesting is that the cluster of human responses we commonly label 'spiritual' – which may include meditation, prayer, fasting, self-examination and the like, and which are aimed at the transformation and purification of the self – can plausibly be construed as attempts to come to terms with the *finitude* of the human condition. But they need not be interpreted as betokening a contra-scientific or pre-scientific outlook, nor by the same token are they necessarily liable to be pushed aside by the rise of science, for the simple reason that the core human predicament on which they focus is not within the domain of problems that science can aspire to solve.

SPIRITUALITY AND FAITH

There is, however, a key element in the concept of spirituality which has not so far been addressed, namely that it is generally supposed to be connected with certain presuppositions about a supernatural or transcendent realm. The description of a set of techniques for changing one's life could be no more than a self-help manual, or a book of advice on mental and physical health; for it to have a spiritual dimension, at least as most people understand that term, something further is required, namely a claim or claims of some sort about the (ultimate) nature of reality, about the true character of the cosmos and man's place within it. In short, spirituality is what may be called a *metaphysically freighted* notion. This aspect now needs to be looked at, since it may seem to put at risk the reconciliation between science and spirituality which has just been proposed.

The metaphysical aspect is, in fact, already recognised in Foucault's characterisation of the spiritual, when he talks about the transformation of the subject through contact with 'the truth'. And it is clearly evident in the ancient philosophical systems aiming at the 'care of the soul': the Stoics, for example, strove for a life lived 'in agreement with nature', an ideal that presupposed that the cosmos is a rationally governed order, and that mankind, in virtue of the exercise of reason, could be a harmonious part of that cosmos, attuned to the nature of the whole.[25] Christian systems of spirituality make an even more direct and striking metaphysical claim, that the practice of prayer, fasting and so on will fit the soul for communion with its creator and sustainer. The Buddhist system, aptly described by Michael McGhee as a 'non-theistic form of spiritual practice', might seem to be an exception; but in fact it turns out to carry a considerable metaphysical freight, albeit of a somewhat austere kind. Change and impermanence are the ultimate features of reality, human individuality an illusion, and the possibility of enlightenment is open only to those who can cease from striving and attachment and allow the false sense of selfhood to dissolve away into the shifting flux that is all there really is.

Given that the domain of the spiritual, in its various manifestations, is always metaphysically underpinned, it might be thought that the tension between spirituality and scientific rationalism reappears with a vengeance. For the default position of modern scientific rationalism is laid down unambiguously enough in what has been pretty much standard orthodoxy since Hume and Kant: science deals with testable descriptions of the phenomenal world, philosophy investigates the conceptual presuppositions of those descriptions, and any further claims about the nature of the supposed ultimate reality that may ground or support the phenomenal world must lie beyond the limits of rational knowledge, for ever 'shut up from human curiosity', as Hume so graphically put it.[26] That being so, the advocate of spirituality as a response to the human predicament seems to be faced with an impasse. It may be clear enough, as suggested earlier, that science cannot heal the anguish generated by the fragility and dependency of the human condition; but this may be a tragic part of our lot that we just have to put up with, if it turns out that the escape routes grouped under the domain of the spiritual are available only at the cost of stepping outside the bounds of sense.[27]

One possible way out of the impasse is suggested by some remarks of the Oxford philosopher Adrian Moore, at the conclusion of his recent book *Points of View*. Moore evidently has a great deal of sympathy with the idea of the spiritual impulse as a response to human finitude. Yet he is sufficiently in tune with Kantian post-critical orthodoxy to want to dissociate his religious inclinations from the need to make metaphysical claims about a transcendent supernatural realm. Spiritual aspirations that talk the language of theism take us beyond the bounds of the sayable. So what Moore advocates instead is a compromise which might be called 'quasi-theism':

> I would urge us, in the same way that Kant urged us, to adopt a regulative principle to proceed *as if* God exists. This principle answers . . . in

a way that nothing else answers to something deep within our finitude. It is a device which we would be free to abandon if ever we knew how to be finite. While we are still learning, however, it is our only way of sustaining *hope* . . . To proceed as if God exists is to proceed as if . . . what ultimately matters enjoys a kind of infinite resilience.[28]

Moore concludes his argument with a 'chilling paradox', namely that believing in God may help us to come to terms with the fact that there is no God. 'Not only is there reason to believe in God even if God does not exist. There may be reason to believe in God *because* God does not exist' (ibid.). The paradox does indeed have an icy chill to it, but it is far from evident that it is compelling, at least in the form in which it is presented. If the Kantian constraints (which Moore has been accepting throughout the rest of his book) mean that talk of a transcendent deity is beyond the limits of rational knowledge, it is not clear how the non-existence of God can be a 'fact' that we need to come to terms with. Kant himself was perhaps clearer on this point, insisting that his exposure of the limits of philosophical reasoning did not at all give support to atheism, since his position was that claims not just about the existence but also about the non-existence of God were equally off limits to reason.[29]

However that may be, the proposal to proceed 'as if' God exists does strike me as suggestive of a promising way forward for the defender of the spiritual domain, though not quite in the manner Moore suggests. The traditional notion of religious *faith*, which has often been seen as crucial for those embarking on the path of spirituality, turns out to be very close to proceeding 'as if' God exists, since it involves, in effect, committing oneself in the absence of proper cognitive credentials (compare Kant's famous assertion that he 'abandoned [or went beyond] knowledge in order to make room for faith').[30] Or, as Thomas Aquinas put it, faith 'makes good the deficiencies' of the other senses.[31] How can this kind of transformation operate in the absence of properly certified belief? The answer seems to me to lead us back to the key element of spirituality which was underlined at the outset of this paper, namely the importance which spiritual programmes have traditionally given to *praxis* – to prescribed techniques and disciplines of prayer, meditation, self-purification and the like. It is after all common human experience – in relationships, in jobs, in undertakings such as marriage and the raising of children – that praxis can do its work, can involve us, stimulate us, re-orient us, carry us along on a tide of faith or commitment, without any need for prior theoretical certification.

The primacy of praxis over theory turns out to be central in the religious thought of Blaise Pascal, a thinker who famously observed that the God he revered was a God of 'love and consolation', the God of a living tradition of worship, not the God whom the philosophers purported to establish by 'useless and sterile' abstract argument.[32] From a purely cognitive point of view, Pascal argues (in somewhat proto-Kantian mode), God's existence cannot be established by the human intellect: having no parts or limits he is 'infinitely beyond our comprehension', and 'we cannot know either what he is, or if he is.' But in the remarkable passage that follows, he proceeds to urge his listeners to set about acquiring a belief in God by following the path of praxis, by acting as if they believed:

> [Y]ou must at least realise that your inability to believe comes from your passions . . . Your desired destination is faith, but you do not know the road. You want to cure yourself of unbelief, and you ask for remedies: learn from those who were hampered like you and who now wager all they possess. These are people who know the road you would like to follow; they are cured of the malady for which you seek a cure; so follow them and begin as they did – by acting as if they believed, by taking holy water, by having masses said, and so on. In the natural course of events this in itself will make you believe, this will tame you.[33]

The passage comes in the context of Pascal's famous 'wager' argument – that the sacrifices involved in living a religious life are well worth the chance, however remote, of an infinite reward in the next life.[34] Such a bet has not found many supporters either among atheists (who tend to find the self-interested calculation both absurd and squalid), or among theists (who think it misunderstands the nature of salvation); but fortunately we do not have go into that issue here, since the spiritual tradition we have been discussing in the present paper proposes clear benefits of a far less ethically and theologically problematic kind – the care of the soul, tranquillity of mind, release from the false pursuits of egoism and material gain, a closer awareness of the mystery of life, the 'simple happiness of existing', and the other rewards of spirituality noted by Hadot and others. If there are such benefits accruing to those who take the spiritual path (and this is in part an empirical issue), the 'Pascalian' challenge comes down to this: why not take the plunge and start the journey, rather than agonising over the epistemological credentials of the associated religious doctrines – doctrines which it is in any case beyond the scope of theoretical reason to establish or refute?

The sceptic will answer here that if the proposed benefits of the spiritual outlook (tranquillity of mind, for example) rest on false or unsupported metaphysical claims, they are bought at too great a price. Even if we acknowledge all the *Angst* generated by the raw dependency and finitude of human life, nevertheless to purchase assurance at the cost of a leap of faith is rather like buying tranquillity by ingesting a calming pill or undergoing a course of hypnotism: it may do the job, in a crude pragmatic sense, but only at the cost of another and more degrading dependency – dependency on a drug, or an illusion.

This is a serious challenge, and to respond to it fully would require a great deal more space than is available here. But the first step towards answering it will be for the defender of spiritual praxis to be more specific about the precise form of spirituality that is in prospect. There are, of course, many kinds of 'spirituality' on offer, and some do indeed seem nothing more than ways of exploiting human weakness, little better than techniques of mass hypnosis or cynical manipulation. But there are other forms which even their most detached critics would find it hard not to see as vehicles for genuine moral and aesthetic value: consider the purity and resonance of a Gregorian chant when properly done by a religious community whose whole being seems intent on the submerging of self to the demands of worship; or the stillness and humility that seems apparent on the faces of those who have immersed themselves in long years of training in meditation. Such observations are of course no conclusive proof of the integrity and value of such lives, but they surely count as some evidence in their favour.

In essence then, this kind of defence of spiritual praxis involves appeal to the maxim 'By their fruits shall ye know them.' The advocate of spirituality is not simply proposing any old expedient. Rather, he or she is advocating a particular path, grounded in a tradition which can provide some evidence of its moral credentials – some evidence that its adherents have gone some way towards a deepening of their own self-awareness and their compassion for others. The desired peace of mind and other 'benefits' of the spiritual life are not quick fix palliatives, but organically related to the deepening process at which the spiritual disciplines aim. It is against this sort of background that it is possible to make such celebrated claims as these: 'The fruits of the spirit are love, joy, peace, longsuffering, gentleness, goodness, faith, meekness, temperance.'[35]

This stress on the moral credentials of the (right kind of) spiritual path may now seem to incur a rather different objection: if the advocacy of spirituality depends on the supposed link with the attainment of moral goals, or morally good states, why not pursue those moral goals directly, as it were, in an ordinary secular context, without the need to proceed via a religious package with all its associated rituals and metaphysically problematic doctrines? It is certainly no part of this paper's aims to criticise any secular system of ethics, or to argue that the pursuit of moral goals necessarily requires some kind of spiritual underpinning. Several important aspects of the relation between the spiritual life and the moral life – in particular whether the first is either a necessary or a sufficient condition of the second – are (at least for the purposes of this paper) left entirely open. Nor is the argument of the paper that the adoption of the spiritual path is the *only* appropriate or conceivable response to the kind of existential impasse generated by our human vulnerability.

Our argument, in its bare bones, has been this: first, the spiritual path is, and has long been, a characteristic human way of coping with the aspects of the human predicament just described. Second, the *way* in which that coping is achieved is important: forms of spirituality are to be assessed, in part, by their moral credentials. Third, the spiritual life characteristically carries a metaphysical freight: it involves claims which are not within the domain of rational knowledge. But, fourth, that is not as serious an obstacle as it may seem, since (as the 'Pascalian' argument shows), immersing oneself in the relevant practices can generate commitment without the need for prior epistemic certification.[36]

The upshot is that science and spirituality are not, after all, in competition. Science indeed provides an increasingly full description of the phenomenal world – perhaps one day it will even be complete. But even if completeness were achieved, it would still not rule out (any more than it would rule in) the possibility of a transcendent realm beyond the phenomenal world – a realm whose objects, as Kant put it, may be objects not of knowledge, but of faith.[37] There will of course be those who shun the very idea of 'faith' as a cognitively irresponsible leap in the absence of any proper grounds for belief. And from the outside, that is perhaps how it will always seem. Yet from the inside, from within the structure of regular and systematic praxis, things will, as Pascal reminds us, be very different. The spiritual path beckons; and in view of the signal benefits it offers to provide, the old Pascalian question resounds with renewed force: *Qu'avez-vous à perdre?* What have you got to lose?[38]

NOTES

1 Foucault 2000: 143ff.
2 Foucault 2000: 149. See Plato, *Apology* [395 BC], 29d5–e3; cf. 30a6–b1; 31b; 36c.
3 For Epicurus' notion of philosophy as 'therapeutic' cf. Long and Sedley (1987), 25C. For the Stoics, see e.g. Seneca, *Epistulae morales* [AD 64], x. See also Hadot 1995: 83–6.
4 Texts cited in Foucault 2000: 154 include Gregory of Nyssa, *De Virginitate* [c. 390], Chs. XII and XIII.
5 Cf. Foucault 2000: 155–6.
6 McGhee 2000.
7 In its New Testament usage, the term *metanoia* may be translated 'repentance' or 'conversion'. Cf. Acts of the Apostles: 'God hath granted repentance unto life (*metanoian eis zoen*)' (11:18).
8 Foucault 2000: 159; emphasis added.
9 Foucault 2000: 161.
10 *Discours de la méthode* [1637], title (AT VI 1: CSM I 111). (For these references, see Adam and Tannery (1964–76), and Cottingham *et al.* (1985–91).

11 Letter to Huygens of 10 October 1642 (AT III 797: CSMK 215).
12 Foucault 2000: 163; emphasis added.
13 *Discourse*, part vi (AT VI 62: CSM 142–3).
14 Letter to Chanut of 15 June 1646 (AT IV 442: CSMK 289).
15 MacIntyre 1999: 1–2 and 7.
16 Cf. Descartes, *Conversation with Burman* [1648], AT V 178: CSMK 353.
17 Psalm 39:5 (Book of Common Prayer version [1662]).
18 Heidegger 1957: 189 and 1962: 233.
19 *Sein-zum-Tode*, op. cit. (1957) 234 (German), (1962) 277 (English).
20 Cf. Philip Larkin, 'Aubade', originally published in *The Times Literary Supplement*, 23 December 1977.
21 'The true philosophers, Simmias, are always occupied in the practice of dying', *Phaedo* [c. 380 BC], 64.
22 Hadot 1995: 103–4.
23 Hadot 1995: 127; emphasis added.
24 Foucault 2000: 166–8.
25 See Long and Sedley (1987), no. 63A and B.
26 David Hume (1975) [1748], sectn. IV, part 1, p. 30.
27 'Postmodernist' thinkers sometimes reject this standard view of the boundaries of human knowledge; see Caputo and Scanlon 1999: 2–3; see further Cottingham 2002: 5–19.
28 Moore 1997: 278. For Kant's 'quasi-theism', cf. *Critique of Practical Reason* [*Kritik der Praktischen Vernunft*, 1788], Part I, Bk. ii, Ch. 2, §v. First emphasis in original; second emphasis added.
29 See the Introduction by Robert Merrihew Adams, in Kant (1998), vii ff.
30 Kant (1965) [1781/1787] p. 29. Cf. Kaygill (1995), s.v. 'faith'.
31 From the hymn *Pange lingua* [1260]. Compare Aquinas (1975) [1260] p. 39.
32 Cf. Blaise Pascal, *Pensées* ('Thoughts') (1962) [1670], no. 449.
33 Pascal, *Pensées*, no. 418. trans. J. Cottingham.
34 For an excellent discussion of the wager and its relation to faith, see Jones (1998).
35 Galatians 5:22–3.
36 Further aspects of the 'Pascalian' argument are developed in Cottingham 2003: ch. 3.
37 Kant cites the existence of God as one of the 'objects of faith' (*credibilia*) in the *Critique of Judgement* [*Kritik der Urteilskraft*, 1790], §91, sectn. 3, contrasting such matters with matters of opinion (*opinabilia*) and matters of fact/knowledge (*scibilia*).
38 Pascal, *Pensées*, loc. cit. (towards end of no. 418). I am most grateful for helpful comments received when I gave earlier versions of this paper at the Conference on Spirituality, Philosophy and Education held at the University of St Andrews in March 2001, at Rhodes University, Grahamstown in February 2002, and at Trinity College Dublin in June 2002.

REFERENCES

Adam, C. and Tannery, P. (eds) (1964–76) *Œuvres de Descartes*, 12 vols, revised edn, Paris: Vrin/CNRS. [Originally published 1897 and 1913]. Referred to as 'AT'.

Aquinas, Thomas (1975) [1260] *Summa contra Gentiles*, trans. A.C. Pegis, Notre Dame, Ill.: Notre Dame University Press.

Caputo, J.D. and Scanlon, M.J. (eds) (1999) *God, the Gift, and Postmodernism*, Bloomington: Indiana University Press.

Cottingham, J. (2002). 'Profondità e postmodernismo' ('Profundity and Post-modernism'), *La Società degli Individui* 14.

Cottingham, J. (2003) *On the Meaning of Life*, London: Routledge.

Cottingham, J. *et al.* (1985–91) *The Philosophical Writings of Descartes*, Vols I and II, translated by J. Cottingham, R. Stoothoff and D. Murdoch, Cambridge: Cambridge University Press. Referred to as 'CSM'. Vol. III, The Correspondence, by the same translators plus A. Kenny, Cambridge: Cambridge University Press. Referred to as 'CSMK'.

Descartes, René (1637 etc.), see Adam and Tannery (1964–76) and Cottingham *et al.* (1985–91).

Foucault, M. (2000) [1982] Seminar at the Collège de France of 6 January 1982. Published as 'Subjectivité et vérité' in *Cités*, ed. Y.C. Zarka, Vendôme: Presses Universitaires de France, vol. 2.

Hadot, Pierre (1995) [1987] *Philosophy as a Way of Life*, Oxford, UK and Cambridge, USA: Blackwell. Originally published as *Exercises spirituels et philosophie antique*, Paris: Etudes Augustiniennes.

Heidegger, Martin (1957) [1927] *Sein und Zeit*, Eighth edn, Tubigen: Niemeyer.

Heidegger, Martin (1962) [1927] *Being and Time*, trans. J. Macquarrie and E. Robinson, New York: Harper & Row.

Hume, David 1975 [1748] *Enquiry concerning Human Understanding*, ed. L.A. Selby-Bigge, rev. Nidditch, Oxford: Clarendon Press.

Jones, Ward E. (1998) 'Religious conversion, self-deception and Pascal's wager', *Journal of the History of Philosophy* 36: 2.

Kant, Immanuel (1952) [1790] *Critique of Judgement [Kritik der Urteilskraft]*, trans. J.C. Meredith, Oxford: Clarendon Press.

Kant, Immanuel (1965) [1781/1787] *Critique of Pure Reason [Kritik der Reinen Vernunft]*, trans. N. Kemp Smith, New York: St Martin's Press.

Kant, Immanuel (1998) [1793] *Religion within the Boundaries of Mere Reason [Die Religion innerhalb der Grenzen der bloßen Vernunft]*, Cambridge: Cambridge University Press.

Kaygill, H. (1995) *A Kant Dictionary*, Oxford: Blackwell.

Long, A.A. and Sedley, D.N. (eds) (1987) *The Hellenistic Philosophers*, Cambridge: Cambridge University Press.

MacIntyre, Alasdair (1999) *Dependent Rational Animals*, London: Duckworth.

McGhee, M. (2000) *Transformations of Mind: Philosophy as Spiritual Practice*, Cambridge: Cambridge University Press.

Moore, A.W. (1997) *Points of View*, Oxford: Clarendon Press, p. 278.

Pascal, Blaise (1962) [1670] *Pensées*. ed. L. Lafuma, Paris: Seuil. An English version is available by A.J. Krailsheimer (Harmondsworth: Penguin, 1966).

Chapter 4

Spirituality and virtue

Jonathan Jacobs

There is, I believe, a plausible and philosophically interesting conception of non-religious spirituality. It is plausible and philosophically interesting because of how it is connected with virtue and a number of issues in moral psychology. I wish to show that virtuous activity makes possible a spiritual appreciation of the world and human life, even when virtue is understood in broadly naturalistic terms.

The discussion will make reference to a number of Aristotelian insights and arguments. While this is not a presentation of Aristotelian doctrine, there are resources in Aristotle's philosophy that are especially relevant. In fact, many of the ways in which contemporary understandings of value, happiness, and the meaning of life are stunted, jejune, and inadequate supply powerful motivations for a reconsideration of those resources. Their importance does not depend on specific Aristotelian claims that there is a single best kind of life for human beings or that all of the capacities that are constitutive of human nature can be exercised in an integrated, harmonious manner. The resources in question have considerable merit even when detached from those theses.

The central element of the view to be presented is that spirituality completes and perfects virtue. The more fully an agent exercises and enjoys exercising virtue, the more the agent is able to recognize and appreciate spiritual value. I am speaking of virtue very broadly, in regard to a wide spectrum of human excellences and activities, and not confining it to moral matters. That breadth is important to the view in ways I will indicate.

I

The relation between virtuous activity and pleasure is an apt starting point. Aristotle argues that virtuous activity is naturally pleasing and he says of virtuous agents that 'the life of these active people is also pleasant in itself' (Aristotle 1999: 1099a 7). 'Actions in accord with virtue are pleasant by nature, so that they both please lovers of the fine and are pleasant in their own right. Hence these people's life does not need pleasure to be added [to virtuous activity] as some sort of extra decoration; rather, it has its pleasure within itself' (Aristotle 1999: 1099a 16–17). Later on, in Bk X, he writes:

> But in all such cases it seems that what is really so is what appears so to the excellent person. If this is right, as it seems to be, and virtue, i.e., the good person insofar as he is good, is the measure of each thing, then what appear pleasures to him will also really be pleasures, and what is pleasant will be what he enjoys.
>
> (Aristotle 1999: 1176a 16–19)

Moreover, pleasure completes an activity and the pleasure proper to an activity supplies the agent with a reason to continue to engage in that activity. Pleasure is not what makes activities valuable – it is not what *constitutes* them or their ends to be good. The good of activities depends upon their natures and their objects, and good activities are accompanied and motivationally reinforced by pleasure (which, because of the character of the activities, are good pleasures).

An important part of this overall moral psychology is that agents' pleasures depend in significant ways upon their characters. The dispositions of judgment, desire, and affect that are second nature to the agent shape what the person finds pleasing, and also shape one's reasons to continue engaging in certain activities. Virtuous agents enjoy good pleasures. They have a *correct* view of what is valuable and worthwhile. Aristotle notes, 'For the same things delight some people, and cause pain to others; and while some find them painful and hateful, others find them pleasant and lovable' (Aristotle 1999: 1176a 10–11). He goes on to add:

> And if what he [the virtuous agent] finds objectionable appears pleasant to someone, that is not at all surprising; for human beings suffer many sorts of corruption and damage. It is not pleasant, however, except to these people in these conditions.
>
> (Aristotle 1999: 1176a 20–24)

It is evident that there are bad or shameful pleasures, enjoyed only by those with bad character. If, for example, some agents find the degradation or the suffering of others to be humorous or pleasing, that raises no serious question for us whether there might be real good in those things, or whether good is altogether person-relative and subjective. Rather, the enjoyment of what is base or shameful is evidence of the corruption of those who take pleasure in such things. Perhaps we could, to at least some extent, *argue* someone into seeing some activity as good, but that person will only genuinely and fully appreciate it as such through having a character such as to enjoy it. And, if the person has poor character to begin with, it is doubtful that the presentation of reasons will bring him to see things differently, simply because of the ways in which considerations weigh with him. The possession of reason does not ensure that the agent will have the developed ability and willingness to accept and enact good reasons.

This is because making valuative judgments and deliberative decisions that can withstand critical scrutiny depends upon capacities and modes of awareness and appreciation acquired and cultivated through habituation. The sorts of attention, consideration, and making of discriminations necessary for sound judgments of worth have to be *learned*. The notion that agents can do well at fashioning conceptions of good on their own, without the education of habituation is, frankly, wildly implausible. Self-determination depends upon developed deliberative and reflective abilities, not an alighting of volitional or appetitive interest here or there, followed up by reasoning about how to act accordingly.

In being habituated well, the agent is not surrendering voluntariness or self-determination, but is developing them. We need to learn what to regard as worthwhile and what to love, and the virtuous agent loves the right things in a mode of knowing appreciation. Poor habituation does indeed corrupt, and it does so by misguiding desire, affect, and judgment in ways that cultivate dispositions that misrepresent their proper objects or even put them out of sight of the agent.[1] The agent then becomes the sort of person who takes pleasure in things that are not genuinely good, and may even despise things that are. It is not as though virtuous and non-virtuous agents recognize or 'take in' the same features of situations, the virtuous agent responding in one way, and the non-virtuous in another.[2] They take in different features and regard some of the same features as considerations in different ways.

While character is crucial to virtue, a virtue is a state of a *rational* agent's second nature. It includes developed capacities for attention, concern, and reasoning, as well as appetitive capacities and sensibility. For example, the compassionate agent not only has fellow feeling or certain responses to the distress or suffering of others. He also has a textured, discriminating receptivity through which he is able to perceive when compassion is appropriate, and is able to judge how to act upon it. In being compassionate the agent progressively elaborates his understanding of compassion and develops and adjusts the dispositions that move him to act compassionately. He realizes that compassion (or courage, or loyalty, or honesty, or generosity) is not simple. (There are analogies to this in an agent's developed capacity for such things as aesthetic appreciation or the enjoyment of literature or a craft that requires considerable skill.)

The virtuous agent also recognizes that his conceptions of valuative matters are incomplete. Our conceptions of justice, courage, compassion, loyalty, and so forth – and our understanding of their relations – are never complete.[3] There surely are many valid generalizations and principles concerning valuative matters, but the former do not fully register the latter. There is no 'doctrine' of virtue, if to have a doctrine means that what virtue recognizes and requires can be codified or systematized. It is not part of virtue to try to impose a simple or repeated pattern where the reality resists it. Virtue is, we might say, a type of realism about value through which the agent aspires to bring his mode of attention, discernment, and concern into alignment with a complex reality.[4] The virtuous agent has the sort of conceptual fluency and careful attention needed to 'read' facts, acts, and situations for their valuative features. That is not the same thing as having a 'grid' of principles, or a theoretical architecture to fully structure valuative judgment.

In addition, a virtue (whether moral or non-moral) often involves the willingness to find significance where it would not be found by those lacking the virtue. The virtuous agent's alertness and responsiveness to valuative considerations can enlarge and enrich his conception of goods, worthy ends, activities, and experiences. The cultivation of virtue encourages a kind of openness to, and concern for, valuative considerations of new kinds. A virtue not only enables an agent to recognize a certain type of valuative matter; it can also be part of a disposition to perceive and respond to types that are new to the agent. The person who enjoys virtue also typically enjoys the enlargement of it and has an active interest in further educating his sensitivity to value.

II

A familiar line of criticism of the Aristotelian conception of virtue is that there just is no uniquely best way to exercise human capacities. Having abandoned the philosophical anthropology and metaphysics that underwrote the view that there is, the problem of life is the problem of *meaning*, rather than *eudaimonia* in the Aristotelian sense. Moreover, meaning crucially differs from *eudaimonia* in at least the respect that it is *conferred* on an activity, a situation or a life by the way in which an agent is concerned for it or invested in it.[5] Meaning is both ultimately subjective and highly individual. In contrast to what makes for *eudaimonia*, meaning is not grounded in a common human nature and a conception of what its perfection consists in. It also does not have the moral excellences as a core.

Here we will not enter the debate about the relations between meaning and *eudaimonia* in a full-fledged way, but it should be noted that Aristotle's concern was with the excellence of a life overall. While moral virtues are essential to that, even they are not *narrowly* moral if by that we mean they are concerned primarily with duties to others. Aristotle understood virtue as a reasoned concern for, and a disposition to do, what is *fine*. His view was not restricted to what is morally obligatory. In this way he was able to present an integrated account of the agent's flourishing and his concern for others and the common good. These do not constitute competing over-all aims or motivate conflicting practical requirements (at least in general or in principle). Pursuing one's own good, and striving to live well are not life-activities distinct from being a morally sound agent. Moreover, much of the criticism of Aristotle's normative conception of human nature is deflated by taking seriously the notion that, as a general rule, certain virtues are needed in order for any person to live well, whatever the agent thinks is especially important to his happiness or his sense of a meaningful or worthwhile life. Possession of the virtues does not constrain an agent to a certain set of central projects or concerns. It enables agents to more successfully form and pursue their projects and concerns, whatever they are, within broad limits of what is needed in order for an agent to act well, just as a human agent.

The key point here is that a virtuous agent's overall mode of activity and engagement with the world is such that he is able to discern and appre-ciate value and significance of different kinds. Through development of the virtues, agents recognize and appreciate the world as valuatively rich. A healthy, expansive appreciation of value does not restrict it to the category of 'the moral.'

One reason why these features of virtue are especially important is that there is a basic respect in which we are never fully at home in the world. There are persistent, unavoidable sources of anxiety, uncertainty, fear, confusion, and suffering that we cannot control and often cannot even anticipate. Hence, it is not hard to see what might recommend Stoic apathy, for example, as a strategy for not being undone by it all. It is also not hard to see what might recommend the life of gratification, or the life of honor, recognition, and status. We each seem to need one or another strategy for making it all bearable, giving it a point and a shape and to avoid becoming deeply disaffected and demoralized. It may not be a deliberately selected or constructed strategy that we each follow, and a person may, through a combination of good fortune in regard to tempera-ment and the way of the world, escape the invitation to despair or a sense of meaninglessness. Still, each of us must try to figure out a liveable way of carrying on.

By 'being at home in the world' (by means other than consoling illusion) I mean finding worth in experience and activities that indicate to the agent that the world is significant in ways that cannot be grasped entirely and exclusively in terms of any specific category of value, such as the moral or the aesthetic (among others). Each of those values, and even their conjunction, is recognized as incomplete, but in a way that is not demoral-izing or a motive for despair. This is not a view in which meaning is grounded entirely in our desires, interests, and purposes. That would be a strategy of consolation, or at least a strategy of projecting value in con-trast to finding or encountering it, and knowing that it is, could destabilize it.[6] To the extent that an agent is genuinely at home in the world it is through meaning or significance being discerned, encountered, *found* in experience, activities, and situations.

Near the beginning of *Civilization and Its Discontents* Freud identifies a small number of approaches to dealing with the ways in which life is too hard for us. These include intoxication, illusion, intellectual activity, and turning one's back on the world.[7] Each is a strategy of living that is responsive to drives and impulses that everyone has, at least to some extent. In each person there is the basis for each of these to get some kind of grip and perhaps even become a controlling conception of how to live. Yet, if it does, it can become a way of being distracted from reality rather than being engaged to it.

In the instance of intoxication that is fairly plain, but it is also true of the others. Indeed, many strategies of living that are strongly encouraged by contemporary culture seem to be effectively (if not intentionally) aimed at practices and values that constitute consoling kinds of control. They seek to maximize certain kinds of gratification or the feelings of power or importance that come with occupying certain roles and deploying material and human resources in accordance with our desires. They are ways of making the world work for us, chiefly by it affording us pleasure or by subjecting it to technical control. Gratification and technical control can be wonderful things, but as central life projects they are *substitutes* for being at home in the world.

Even categories of value such as the moral and the aesthetic, while they are of the first importance to our engagement with reality, are limited with regard to fully appreciating the valuative richness of the world (though each may be inexhaustible in its own dimension). To see this, consider the person who values all things in one or another of these dimensions, or who only values whatever he values in one or the other of those dimen-sions. The agent with a totalizing aesthetic view is almost certainly going to be seriously (and disturbingly) distracted from considerations of moral value. The totally moralizing agent is similarly going to be blind to certain kinds of value and significance and is likely to distort significance by moralizing where it is inappropriate. Moreover, that agent may be brought to despondency by the persistent injustice of the world and the sadness and suffering in it. It is not so strange that the moralizer should be broken by the attempt to make the world just, or by the inevitably frustrated ideal that it should be so. This is not to say that we should relax moral effort because it is bound to fail to some extent. Rather, it is to say that not all value, and not even every important value, is moral value.

Any totalizing view, whether it is a moral one, a scientific one, an aesthetic one, a hedonistic one, or any other, will misrepresent and distort value, by forcing it into a single mold. As a consequence, it will probably also be demoralized, when value (inevitably) fails to fit. Totalizing views can be deep and they may make strenuous demands on us intellectually and volitionally. They can have their own dignity and integrity, and can be both interesting to examine and interesting to live. Still, they truncate meaning and significance by domesticating it to only certain categories. It is an important aspect of the spirituality I wish to characterize that it involves finding and appreciating meaning in ways that are not limited or constrained in those ways.

This spirituality also takes very seriously the fact that the world is in some basic ways inscrutable. In regard to its contingencies, its surprises, the deep ways in which it eludes our control, and in its unresponsiveness to our affect and our aspirations it can be alien and hostile. It is in many ways a hard and unforgiving place, and not just because so many people in it are hard and unforgiving. There are, of course, experiences that are particularly elevating or even rapturous, such as the birth of a long-wanted child, or success at some project that had hitherto met with failure and frustration. Those can be experiences of great joy, which is not just the same thing as spirituality. The spirituality at issue here is in large part a matter of believing, in a sustained and stable manner, that in spite of the world's inscrutability and hardness, we are suited to it, fitted for it, in such a way that we can be at home in it.

This is quite different from the conviction that the world and what we do are important because of our aims, our wants, and our feelings. Those are all ways in which the world is significant because of how we expressively or projectively 'paint' the world with meaning or value. Spirituality involves a disposition informed by the acknowledgment that there is meaning that we encounter, and kinds of value that we can learn to recognize. Spirituality is not *chosen* and is not dependent upon a stance that one might decide to adopt (or not). Rather, spirituality is attained; it is some-thing that is possible through comprehension and rationally informed activity (which is not the same thing as *exclusively* rational activity). Voluntariness has an important role in individuals becoming capable of those recognitions, because there is a substantial role for voluntariness in the development of virtues and the sorts of habits that are enabling con-ditions for spirituality. But spirituality is not itself volitional. It is a mode of engagement and appreciation informed by the realities it encounters.

Spirituality is also different from hope as a theological virtue. It is not a belief that there is a non-natural life in which we can participate, or a conviction that there is an end which transcends this life and to which we can be joined by supernatural agency. Religion involves a metaphysics that includes God, God's promises, revelation, and our duties to God. The sort of spirituality characterized here is independent of theism and does not involve the optimism that is part of religion. There can be non-redemptive spirituality.

It also differs in an important way from Stoic apathy. The latter is (among other things) a life-strategy of maintaining rational composure in the face of contingency, pain, frustration, and uncertainty. It requires detaching one's self from the agitation and disturbance they inevitably bring, and achieving tranquility through self-sufficiency. The latter depends upon having concern only for that over which one can achieve rational mastery. The defender of Stoicism could argue that this is indeed a way of being at home in the world, for the centerpiece of Stoicism is to avoid being undone by the world by not being distracted in ways that subvert one's self-determination and peace of mind. On the other hand, it can be seen as a strategy of avoidance, a way of engaging with reality in a discretionary manner, on 'one's own terms' as it were, in order not to be surprised, threatened, or defeated by the world. In that way it can cut one off from sources of significance by confining it to what can be domesticated to the sphere of self-mastery. Contrariwise, spiritual engagement with reality is not mainly a strategy of control. It involves a kind of openness that is foreign to Stoic apathy.

III

We return now to the opening suggestion about the connection of spirituality with virtue. We noted the importance of the notion of the naturally pleasing. Pleasure completes and perfects activity. Unimpeded activity is pleasing, and the character of the pleasure depends upon the character of the activity. The pleasure of virtuous activity is not a distinctive sensation, but an appreciation of the activity and the object of the activity. The agent is also motivated to further elaborate the discernment that is essential to judgments of worth. The connection to the spiritual is this: through the exercise of virtue we can know that we are able to live lives in which objective value, value that is not projected or conferred, is real and that we may enjoy it. Through the doing of justice, taking delight in beauty, in deepening our understanding, and through love and care, we realize and appreciate value. Each of those is not in itself spirituality. The spirituality enters by the way in which the virtuous agent has an awareness of the inexhaustible richness of meaning and value that is in the world and sees that through the awareness and enjoyment of it we can be most fully at home in the world. Spirituality is a knowing, active, enjoyment of goods that are accessible through virtue – and delight in the acknowledgment of how we are related to the world through it, and completed by it.

We can only live distinctively human lives by conceptualizing the world and ourselves in a rich and complex variety of ways. The virtuous agent's appreciation of that can have a spiritual dimension in finding that fact a source and a focus of wonder and delight. Virtuous activity requires honest attention to the world, in aesthetic experience, in moral activity, in learning, and in all kinds of productive and creative activity. It is a concern to respond to sources of value. The virtuous agent is able to see that in spite of its terrors, hardships, and the inevitability of suffering and death, the world is inexhaustibly rich in value, which we can enjoy for its own sake. Spirituality arises from wonder at, and enjoyment of, virtue and the way in which our own causality (across a broad spectrum of purposes, concerns, and activities) can engage us to value and can actualize it.

Spirituality is not 'a way of seeing things' if by that is meant that it is a subjective option. It *is* a way of seeing things in the sense that it reflects a general mode of understanding and receptivity, of reflective engagement with the world. It is not restricted to those who are flourishing. It is not the privilege of those who are *both* lucky and good. In that regard it is distinct from *eudaimonia*. Still, it can be an important element in *eudaimonia* because of how it sustains an agent against alienation from the world and from despair. Can spirituality survive misfortune and tragedy? The virtuous agent is less likely to be undone by adversity, because of his fortitude and his attachment to what is significant.[8] His concerns are not of the sort such that frustration of them wrecks his conception of value and meaning, even if the frustration is painful. The agent who is alive to spirituality can see that there are goods and sources of meaning that are thwarted, corrupted, or disfigured by misfortune and immorality. He is not alienated from the reality of evil and suffering, yet he still discerns and values genuine goods, even if he is not able to enjoy them. His suffering does not devolve into meaninglessness. It includes grief over what is lost or absent, though it is not despairing. (To be sure, despair may become the lot of the agent whose life is fraught with misery, powerlessness, and pain.) Spirituality may lack the basic optimism of religion, but it is still a genuine and enduring concern for values and meanings that are possible, even if unrealized.

IV

There is important two-way traffic between education and spirituality. If we understand education broadly as cultivating and informing habits and abilities that enable people to be excellent (in understanding, in action, in creativity, and so forth), we can see that it is a condition for the

full spectrum of virtues. At the same time, as we have noted, virtue moti-
vates the concern to enlarge one's education. Virtue is a disposition to
realize and to enjoy value of many kinds through recognition of sources
of value outside oneself. A culture of virtue (personal or social) requires a
culture of education, and in turn reinforces it. Education is essential as a
process of learning to be at home in the world by understanding it and
by knowing how to find significance in it. It is equally clear that poor or
misguided education disables individuals for virtue and the enjoyment of
spirituality. It misdirects and misinforms their capacities to act for reasons,
and renders their receptivity to valuative considerations callous, vulgar, or
narrow.

When people realize that value is recognized and attained through
understanding, aesthetic experience, creating and making things, and the
exercise of their own self-determination, education becomes internally
motivated because it becomes important to them to know the world and
to know value. When that motivation develops into a reflection on virtue,
it can attain to spirituality, which depends upon and contributes to a
realistic engagement with the world. Lack of education and foolish education are sure ways to distract people from reality and to disable them for
reflective enjoyment of human excellence and true values.

As pleasure completes or perfects activity, spirituality completes or perfects virtue. There are many non-virtuous pleasures, and the person who
loves them may not regret that he lacks virtue. But he lacks something
through which he would improve his life by making worthwhile things
accessible to him and enabling him to actualize and enjoy what is fine.
Similarly, a person can utterly lack spirituality or even regard it as an
affect or a crutch, and not suffer for that. He may not suffer, but he lacks.
Still, for the agent who attains spirituality, distinctive and real sources of
significance and appreciation of it are made accessible. It is an enjoyment
of our own causality when it is exercised in ways that disclose and actualize
the manifold value that can be found in the world.

NOTES

1 I present a fuller discussion of this issue of the role of character in the judgment
of value in Jacobs 2001. See especially chapters 1 and 2.
2 See the discussion of this issue, and, in particular, the perceptions of salient
facts about situations that move agents to act, and how perception is
embedded in agents' conception of how to live in McDowell 1979: 331–50.
See also McDowell 1978. He writes:

> the dictates of virtue, if properly appreciated, are not weighed with other
> reasons at all, not even on a scale which always tips on their side. If a situa-
> tion in which virtue imposes a requirement is genuinely conceived as such,

according to this view, then considerations which, in the absence of the requirement, would have constituted reasons for acting otherwise are silenced altogether – not overridden – by the requirement.

(McDowell 1978: 26)

3 See a valuable discussion of the relation between the realism of moral con-siderations and the incompleteness of our conceptions of them in Platts 1988. He writes:

> Precisely because of the realistic account given of these concepts and our grasp upon them – precisely because they are designed to pick out features of the world of indefinite complexity in ways that transcend our practical under-standing – this process of investigation through experience can, and should, proceed without end.

(Platts 1988: 298–9)

4 Murdoch writes, 'I have used the word "attention", which I borrow from Simone Weil, to express the idea of a just and loving gaze directed upon an individual reality. I believe this to be the characteristic and proper mark of the active moral agent' (Murdoch 1985: 34). Also, 'If apprehension of good is apprehension of the individual and the real, then good partakes of the infinite elusive character of reality' (Murdoch 1985: 42). My discussion has been influ-enced by Murdoch in some important ways, and I see her view as lending support for (though not itself presenting) arguments for realism with respect to value.

5 There are many recent critics of the Aristotelian notion that there is a single best life for human beings, with its basis in the distinctive capacities of human nature, the harmonious exercise of which realizes that best life. See, for example, Williams 1985, especially chapter 3. He writes: 'Aristotle saw a certain kind of ethical, cultural, and indeed political life as a harmonious culmi nation of human potentialities, recoverable from an absolute understanding of nature. We have no reason to believe in that' (Williams 1985: 52). There may be grounds for disputing whether Aristotle's ethical conceptions and overall moral anthropology depend upon 'an absolute understanding of nature' in the way Williams suggests. John McDowell is highly critical of Williams in McDowell 1998. Still, independent of that debate concerning interpretation of Aristotle, many of the sorts of skeptical concerns Williams raises could be raised. Wiggins (1991) argues that the issue of meaning in and for a life has properly displaced the question of what is the end of or for a human being. He writes:

> It might be interesting and fruitful to pick over the wreckage of defunct and discredited ethical theories and see what their negligence of the problem of life's having a meaning contributed to their ruin. I have little to report under this head. But it does seem plain that the failure of naturalistic theories, theories reductively identifying the Good or the End with some natural reality, has been bound up with the question of meaning.

(Wiggins 1991: 134)

6 Wiggins (1991) argues that non-cognitivist accounts of the meaning of life are incoherent because of the incompatibility between their 'outer view,' according to which life is objectively meaningless, and the 'inner view,' according to

which there is not only meaning, but it is grounded in the features of things in the world, and not just states of consciousness. Once we have the non-cognitivist theory, acknowledgment of the 'outer view' would seem to require abandoning the inner view, or recognizing it as shot through with falsity and misrepresentation. He says that:

> for the purposes of the validation of any given concern, the non-cognitive view always readdresses the problem to the inner perspective *without itself adopting that perspective*. It cannot adopt the inner perspective because, according to the picture that the non-cognitivist paints of these things, the inner view has to be unaware of the outer one, and has to enjoy essentially illusory notions of objectivity, importance, and significance: whereas the outer view has to hold that life is objectively meaningless.
>
> (Wiggins 1991: 99–100; italics in original)

7 Freud (1989: 23–4). See especially chapter 2, where he explains ways in which we try to cope with the fact that 'Life, as we find it, is too hard for us; it brings us too many pains, disappointments and impossible tasks' (Freud 1989: 23).
8 In regard to the way fortune affects happiness, Aristotle writes of the virtuous agent:

> if he suffers many major misfortunes, they oppress and spoil his blessedness, since they involve pain and impede many activities. And yet, even here what is fine shines through, whenever someone bears many severe misfortunes with good temper, not because he feels no distress, but because he is noble and magnanimous.
>
> (Aristotle 1999: 1100b 30–33)

REFERENCES

Aristotle (1999) [c. 330 BC] *Nicomachean Ethics*, second edition, trans. by Terence Irwin, Indianapolis: Hackett.

Freud, S. (1989) *Civilization and Its Discontents*, trans. by James Strachey, New York: Norton.

Jacobs, J. (2001) *Choosing Character: Responsibility for Virtue and Vice*, Ithaca: Cornell University Press.

McDowell, J. (1978) 'Are moral requirements hypothetical imperatives?', *Proceedings of the Aristotelian Society*, Supp. Vol. 52, Tisbury: Compton Press, pp. 13–29.

McDowell, J. (1979) 'Virtue and reason', *The Monist* 62: 331–50.

McDowell, J. (1998) 'Two sorts of naturalism', in Rosalind Hursthouse, Gavin Lawrence, and Warren Quinn (eds), *Virtues and Reasons*, Oxford: Clarendon Paperbacks, pp. 149–79.

Murdoch, I. (1985) *The Sovereignty of Good*, London: ARK Paperbacks.

Platts, M. (1988) 'Moral reality', in Geoffrey Sayre-McCord (ed.), *Essays on Moral Realism*, Ithaca: Cornell University Press.

Wiggins, D. (1991) 'Truth, invention, and the meaning of life', in *Needs, Values, Truth*, Oxford: Blackwell.

Williams, B. (1985) *Ethics and the Limits of Philosophy*, Cambridge, MA: Harvard University Press.

Chapter 5

Stoic meditations and the shaping of character

The case of educating the military[1]

Nancy Sherman

To bear the vicissitudes of life well, and most especially the prospect of death, is for many a spiritual matter, though not necessarily a religious one. It is part of psychic formation, or 'soul shaping', and this is recognisably a spiritual concern. In what follows I consider a particular sphere of action in which life and death are very much to the fore, namely the military; and I examine the contribution that Stoic thought might have to make to this. As will be clear, however, my principal conclusions have relevance for civilian life also. Stoicism has something to offer all of us, whether or not our particular stations in life involve, in the way that war routinely does, imminent threats of death. We all fashion lives to endure vicissitude and fortune. How to do this is at the core of Stoic doctrine.

In a remarkably prescient moment, James B. Stockdale, then a senior Navy pilot shot down over Vietnam, muttered to himself as he parachuted into enemy hands, 'Five years down there, at least. I'm leaving behind the world of technology and entering the world of Epictetus' (Stockdale 1994). Epictetus's famous handbook, the *Enchiridion*, was Stockdale's bedtime reading in the many carrier wardrooms he occupied as he cruised the waters off Vietnam in the mid-1960s. Stoic philosophy resonated with Stockdale's temperament and profession, and he committed many of Epictetus's pithy remarks to memory. Little did he know, on that shootdown day of September 9, 1965, that Stoic tonics would hold the key to his survival for six years of POW life. The words of Epictetus would also form the backbone of his leadership style as the senior officer in the POW chain of command.

> There are things which are within our power, and there are things which are beyond our power. Within our power are opinion, aim, desire, aversion, and in one word, whatever affairs are our own. Beyond our power are body, property, reputation, office, and in one word, whatever are not properly our own affairs. . . .
>
> Remember, then, that if you attribute freedom to things by nature dependent and take what belongs to others for your own, you will be

hindered, you will lament, you will be disturbed, your will find fault both with gods and men . . . If it concerns anything beyond our power, be prepared to say that it is nothing to you.

(Epictetus, *Enchiridion*, 11)

Epictetus is right to think that our opinions, desires, and emotions are in our power, not in the radical sense that we can produce them, instantly, at will, but in the sense that we can do things, indirectly, to shape them. And he is right to think, with the Stoics in general, that our opinions about self and others influence our desires and emotions. In contrast, we have far less control over other sorts of goods. A Marine may be killed in friendly fire that he had no way of avoiding, a sailor may be deserving of decoration and promotion, though she is overlooked because of gender prejudice that she alone cannot change, stocks may take a nose-dive however prudent one's investments. A Stoic, like Epictetus, reminds us of the line that divides what is and what is not within our control. And he reminds us that we will be miserable if our happiness itself depends too heavily upon things over which we have little dominion. The Stoic recommendation is not complacency or a retreat to a narrow circle of safety. We are to continue to meet challenges and take risks, and stretch the limits of our mastery. We are to continue to strive to the best of our efforts to achieve our ends. But we must learn greater strength in the face of what we simply cannot change.

A BRAVE NEW STOICISM

Roughly speaking, the ancient Stoics span the period from 300 BC to AD 200. They are part of the broad Hellenistic movement of philosophy that follows upon Aristotle and includes, in addition to Stoicism, ancient Scepticism and Epicureanism. The early Greek Stoics, known as the old *Stoa* (taking their name from the *stoa*, or painted colonnade near the central piazza of Athens where disciples paced back and forth), were interested in systematic philosophical thought that joined ethics together with studies in physics and logic. The works of the founders of the school – Zeno, Cleanthes, and Chrysippus – survive only in fragments, quoted by later writers. Indeed, much of what we know about Stoicism comes through Roman redactors, like Cicero, Seneca, Epictetus, and Marcus Aurelius. These Roman redactors, some writing in Greek, like Epictetus and Marcus Aurelius, others writing in Latin, like Seneca and Cicero, viewed themselves as public philosophers at the centre of public life.

Cicero (106–4 3 BC), well-known Roman political orator, consul, and ally of Pompey, turned to specifically philosophical writing at the end of his political career, after Caesar's assassination, and while in hiding from his own future assassins, Antony and the other triumvirs. Though himself not a Stoic (he identified as a member of the New Academy or school of Scepticism), he wrote extensively on Stoic views and his work, especially *On Ends* and *On Duties*, remained highly influential throughout the Renaissance and Enlightenment as statements of Stoic positions. Seneca, writing in the mid-first century AD, was the tutor and political adviser of the young emperor Nero. He wrote voluminously on, among other things, the passions, and how anger, hatred, and envy, if not understood and properly reined in, can ruin a ruler and bring down a commonwealth. And he wrote about attachment and fortune, and how we can learn to become less vulnerable to their vicissitudes. Epictetus, a Greek slave turned philosopher who also wrote in the time of Nero's reign, greatly influenced Marcus Aurelius. Epictetus's aphoristic writings, summarised in a popular handbook, teach about the power of our minds and imagination to find a measure of mastery and fulfilment even in enslavement.

Marcus Aurelius, a Roman emperor and warrior, wrote his famous *Meditations* in AD 172 in the fleeting moments of quiet he was able to snatch during the German campaigns. In contrast to Seneca's writings, which are often addressed to others, Marcus Aurelius's meditations are exhortations to himself, about his status as a 'citizen of the world' and the community of humanity and god linked through reason and law with nature. He warns how one can be lured away from reason by the attractions of 'place or wealth or pleasurable indulgence', and how a zeal for glory can pervert happiness. A repeated theme is that we live in a Heraclitean world of flux. To find happiness, we cannot hold on too tightly to what is transient and beyond our control.

The Stoics teach self-sufficiency and the importance of detaching from dependence on worldly goods that make us vulnerable. In a similar fashion, they advocate a detachment from sticky emotions that mark our investments in things beyond our control. However, full Stoic detachment from the kinds of emotions that record connection as well as loss can be too high a price to pay, even for the warrior. In particular, the capacity to grieve, to mourn one's dead, is crucial for warrior survival.

Consider Coriolanus, the legendary fifth century BC warrior who turns against his native city for banishing him. He is portrayed by Shakespeare as the paragon Stoic warrior. Physically strong and detached, more at home in the battlefield than with his wife and son, he is the military man par excellence. Fearless, he sheds few tears. And yet the play's turning point comes when Coriolanus remembers how to weep. 'It is no little thing', he concedes, 'to make mine eyes to sweat compassion.' It is Coriolanus's mother, Volumnia, who reawakens his soul. Her entreaties persuade him to quit his siege of Rome and to restore peace. In weeping, Coriolanus finds human dignity.

Coriolanus may be a loner, a mama's boy at heart, touched only by a mother's tears. But for most soldiers, combat itself nurtures a camaraderie and attachment akin to the family relationships of childhood. The friendship of Achilles and Patroclus, central to the *Iliad*, symbolises, for all time, brothers-in-arms. We cannot begin to understand Achilles' near suicidal mourning for Patroclus without appreciating the sheer intensity of that bond. Moreover, we are misled if we think, as many readers have, that a friendship so passionate must be sexual, that only warrior lovers could grieve as Achilles does for Patroclus (Shay 1994). Whether sexual partners or not, Achilles' grief for Patroclus could not be greater. The *Iliad*, like much of Greek culture, celebrates *philia*, the bond of friendship, with all its passion and shared journeys. And it recognises the dignity of grief that comes when death or separation breaks the bond.

In contemporary war, too, where soldiers put themselves at risk to defend each other, where Marines risk the living to save the dead or those with little breath left, the camaraderie of brothers- and sisters-in-arms underwrites the sacrifices. But contemporary combat soldiers do not always have time to grieve. Indeed, in missions where combat rarely stops, where pilots catapult from carriers only seconds after learning that the sorties before them will never return, where vets come home in ones and twos aboard commercial airlines (as they did from Vietnam) and not en masse with their cohorts, there is little time or place to sweat tears of compassion. And yet deferring grief has devastating psychological costs.

Of course, the orthodox Stoic might say loss is not real loss if it falls outside what we can control through our own effort and virtue. We would do better to change our habits of attachment than to pamper those whose false attachments create their losses. But we can learn from Stoicism without embracing its strict letter. And what we can learn is that in the midst of our grieving, we still have a home in the world, connected to others whose fellowship and empathy support us, that we have inner resources that allow us to stand again after we have fallen. This is the human side of Stoicism that can toughen us without robbing us of our humanity.

Other traditions, before and after Stoicism, present from the start a philosophy with softer, human lines. Aristotle emphasises throughout his ethical and political writings that the attachments of friendship are an irreducible part of a good life. To lose a beloved friend is to lose part of what counts for happiness. One's own goodness cannot make up the difference. One necessarily relies on the goodness of others to complete one's own goodness. Similarly, Judaeo-Christian traditions emphasise love and compassion and the healing power of each. In Exodus 15:26, God is portrayed as fearful and awesome, but also for the first time in the biblical narrative as a healer, ready to protect the Israelites against disease and ready to provide them with water and bread in their trek through the wilderness.

The Stoics may struggle to capture the full palette of emotional attachment, but they do recognise profoundly our cosmopolitan status in the world. They stress, in a way significant for military education, the respect and empathy required of citizens of the world. So, Seneca in *On Anger*, reminds his interlocutor, Novatus, that he is a citizen not just of his country but of that 'greater city' of his, that universal commonwealth of the cosmos (Seneca, *On Anger*, II.31). Each of us is a 'world citizen', the Stoics emphasise, following Diogenes the Cynic's notion of the human as a *kosmopolites*, literally, 'cosmic, universal citizen' (Diogenes Laertius, *Lives*, 6.63; Epictetus, *Discourses*, 2.10.3, I.9.2). We are each parts of an extended commonwealth and risk our individual integrity, our wholeness, when we sever ourselves from the fellowship of that community. Marcus Aurelius makes the point graphically in terms of a much used Stoic metaphor of the organic body:

> If you have ever seen a dismembered hand or foot or head cut off, lying somewhere apart from the rest of the trunk, you have an image of what a man makes of himself . . . when he . . . cuts himself off and does some unneighbourly act . . . For you came into the world as a part and you have cut yourself off.
>
> (Marcus Aurelius, *Meditations*, 8.34)

The Stoic, Hierocles, writing in the first century AD, adverts to the notion of cosmopolitanism in the following way: 'Each one of us' he describes as 'entirely encompassed by many circles, some smaller, others larger.' 'The first circle contains parents, siblings, wife, and children.' As we move outward, we move through grandparents, to neighbours, to fellow tribesmen and citizens, and ultimately to the whole human race. He insists that it is incumbent upon each of us 'to draw the circles together somehow towards the centre', to respect people from the outer circles as though they were from the inner. And we arc to do this 'by zealously transferring those from the enclosing circles to the enclosed ones', to bring what is far to what is near, 'to reduce the distance of the relationship with each person' (Long and Sedley 1987: 349).

Hierocles himself does not tell us exactly how we are to psychologically assimilate those in outer circles to inner ones so that we can come to identify with their circumstances. Later philosophers, themselves influenced by the Stoics, fill out the psychological story. For example, the eighteenth-century Scottish Enlightenment writer Adam Smith argues that sympathy is a cognitive transport, which involves 'trading places in fancy'. It requires an active transference of the mind on to another, a simulation or role-play of what it is like to be another in his or her circumstances. 'To beat time' to another's breast, he says, requires a projective capacity by which we imagine another's case:

As we have no immediate experience of what other men feel, we can form no idea of the manner in which they are affected, but by conceiving of what we ourselves should feel in the like situation. Though our brother is upon the rack, as long as we ourselves are at our ease our senses will never inform us of what he suffers. They never did, and never can, carry us beyond our own person, and it is by the imagination only that we can form any conception of what are his sensations. . . . It is the impressions of our own senses only, not those of his, which our imaginations copy. By the imagination we place ourselves in his situation, we conceive ourselves enduring all the same torments, we enter, as it were, into his body and become in some measure the same person with him; and thence form some idea of his sensations, and even feel something which, though weaker in degree, is not altogether unlike them.

(Smith 1759: 47–8)

The description brilliantly presages what contemporary philosophers of mind and cognitive psychologists now refer to as a 'simulation' process by which we come to identify with others, and, in some sense, 'read' their minds. But again, we do well if we go not only forward in time, but backward. Smith was an avid reader of Cicero (as were most philosophers of the Enlightenment period), and the notion of 'placing ourselves in another's situation' becomes far clearer if we bring to bear Cicero's notion, in *On Duties*, of the different personae we wear (Cicero, *On Duties*, I.96ff).[2] To read another's mind one must 'recentre' oneself on another, by imagining, as Cicero would put it, the shared personae we all have as rational, human beings, but also the personae we wear that are different from person to person. To empathise or simply understand others, we must imagine what it is like to be another with her distinctive temperaments and talents, in her situation and circumstances, living her life with her life choices. It is not just that we 'change' circumstances; we also change who we are in those circumstances. Thus, we do not simply put ourselves in others' shoes. We imagine ourselves *as others in their own shoes*. Sometimes we do this almost unconsciously. But at other times, as Hierocles says, we must 'keep zealously' working at the transference.

SOUND BODIES AND SOUND MINDS

Stoicism within the military revives another ancient Greek educational theme – namely, the belief that strong bodies and minds must be cultivated together. Even in leg irons, with a broken leg and in solitary prison, Jim Stockdale forced himself to do more than a hundred sit-ups each morning. Controlling his own body, in the face of relentless torture and deprivation, was his way of staying alive and sane. He lived and breathed the Stoic doctrine that effort and endurance, inner virtue, are major components of human goodness. And the self-endurance began with regaining control of his own body, even in shackles.

For a public obsessed with consumption and its consumer products, hungry for epicurean novelties but tired of pleats of adipose, the stripped-down life of military endurance and discipline offers an attractive tonic. Strong bodies are mission critical for the military. The military trains warriors who will have the strength to endure on the battlefield and the stamina to test human limits. As civilians, how should we view physical fitness when strong bodies are not exactly mission critical, when there are no jungles to pass through, no daily thirty-mile hikes to endure, no ammunition and persons and bodies to carry to safety? In most white-collar professions, fit bodies are simply not part of the job description. To have legs of steel and arms of iron is neither here nor there. True, how we look in our clothes might subtly matter for job success, but there is nothing like the ubiquitous (even if unwritten) military requirement to look good in a uniform.

This misses the obvious point. Civilian fitness is mission critical in the very sense that any sort of healthy living requires it. Current worries about the significant rise of child and adult obesity are not misplaced. We need weight that does not overly tax vital organs; a strong heart to pump enough oxygen, adequate release of endorphins, serotonin, and other hormones to give us vitality and zest, bones that are dense enough to bear our own weight, and so on.

Ancient Greek and Roman thought is, again, an important source. For Plato and Aristotle, the great Greek philosophers who precede the Stoics, virtue is as much a disposition toward self as toward others, where the care of self includes how we care for our bodies. So, for example, temperance, for Aristotle, is a kind of internalised control in which we no longer have excessive bodily appetites and can moderate ourselves without much internal conflict. In short, we have mastered indulgence and its impulses – lost the temptation, as one might say, to do otherwise. The prior developmental step is *enkrateia* or self-control or continence. Here we master appetite, but not without active struggle and forbearance. When we lapse from either of these forms of control, we are 'akratic', literally lacking in control or weak-willed. Appetite gets the better of judgement; we know what is best, but act against our knowledge. We avert our eyes. At times, Aristotle and before him Socrates suggest that weakness of will is a kind of ignorance (Aristotle, *Nicomachean Ethics*, VII.1–3). But we do best to think of it as *motivated* ignorance. We are ignorant only in the sense that we do not want to be reminded of what we know to be best.

Plato's dialogue, *The Republic*, has long influenced Western culture in its advocacy of an early education that includes gymnastics as well as music.

But Plato insists that in the best education 'the exercises and toils of gymnastics' are not mere 'means to muscle' (Plato, *The Republic*, Book III); like music, body building is a way of shaping the psyche as well. For it is a way of building mental discipline and spiritedness, a way of storing the general habit and procedures of control in one's mind as well as in one's muscle memory. The lessons of athletics are wasted, Plato insists, if their point is only to make a body more chiselled or agile. As Cicero remarks, strength of soul resembles 'the strength and sinews and effectiveness of the body' (Cicero, *Tusculan Disputations*, IV.13.30).

If the Stoics, too, are to offer inspiration, the lesson to celebrate is not human control in excess, but in moderation. The Stoics are constantly reminding us how and in what way we have more dominion than we might at first think, whether it be in the physical sphere or the moral or emotional arena. But no humanly plausible Stoicism can urge that we have unlimited dominion, even over our own virtue.

CONTROLLING ANGER AND RAGE

It is often said that anger is the underbelly of courage, that it mobilises us to fight, that to be warriors in our lives we need to keep the flame of anger kindled. Cicero rehearses the view: 'no stern commands' can rally ourselves or others, whether on the battlefield or off, 'without something of the keen edge of irascibility'. Irascibility is 'the whetstone of bravery' (*Tusculan Disputations*, IV.19, 21).

Both Cicero and Seneca will deny the claim. Indeed, the Stoics argue strenuously that anger and rage are, on the whole, pernicious emotions. They do more damage than good. 'No plague has cost the human race more,' Seneca says in his famous treatise, *On Anger*. A true Stoic warrior does not rely on anger to fight his battles.

Part of the problem with anger, according to the Stoics, is that it cannot easily be moderated. Once turned on, it cannot easily be turned off. It is a 'runaway passion', the Stoics will say, whose stride outpaces reason and its command. It is 'the most rabid and unbridled of all emotions,' says Seneca (*On Anger*, III.16). It perverts the body and mind, and literally disfigures the face. Seneca is graphic in his portrait. Those who are angry have:

> eyes ablaze and glitter, a deep flush over all the face as blood boils up from the vitals, quivering lips, teeth pressed together, bristling hair standing on end, breath drawn in and hissing, the crackle of writhing limbs, groans and bellowing . . . the hideous horrifying face of swollen self-degradation – you would hardly know whether to call the vice hateful or ugly (I.2).

And yet Seneca insists that we can control this hideous frenzy and rid ourselves of its corrosive effects. The method is straightforward, even if bold: let go of the attachments, to honour or reputation or victory or wealth, which when threatened make us angry. These are not real goods, he teaches, following ancient Stoic doctrine. True, the Stoics concede, they are the kinds of goods which we might like to have, which we would prefer rather than reject, but having them really does not add anything substantive to our happiness. They are not genuine parts of happiness. For happiness, on the Stoic view (which closely follows Socrates' teachings), is only a function of inner virtue. Its prosperity is the prosperity of virtue, not of wealth, fortune, or the opinions of others.

The full Stoic view may be hard to swallow. We *do* depend on others' opinions of us, and think our reputation and standing in a community matter. We would be different kinds of creatures, far less social and communal, far less able to achieve the very *Stoic* goals of community and fellowship, if we were totally indifferent to others' praise and blame, compliments or slights. We could not raise children without praise and blame from parents. Yet in holding that certain emotions, like anger, involve mistaken values, the Stoics presuppose something more fundamental and more revealing: namely, that emotions are themselves kinds of evaluations or appraisals, ways of judging the world. Aristotle too holds that emotions involve construals about the world, though on his position those construals are neither systematically false nor misleading.[3] They are part and parcel of knowing the world accurately and wisely. This view has been reappropriated by contemporary cognitive psychologists. On that view, emotions involve cognitive assessments of the environment that lead to arousal and desiderative responses. So sadness involves an appraisal that I have been hurt, or love the idea that he is attractive, or pity the thought that someone has suffered unjustly. The Stoics go the whole hog, though. Emotions are nothing but beliefs. And consequently, they hold that we can change emotions in their entirety by changing beliefs. There is no remainder. We might say they are the first to advocate a thoroughgoing cognitive therapy as a method of emotional change. Under their aegis, the particular form that cognitive therapy takes is philosophical dialectic. 'Row the oars of dialectic,' Cicero says, if you are to transform the soul.

Few of us hold, with the Stoics, that emotions are nothing but beliefs or as corrigible as them. Nor are we likely to endorse the Stoic doctrine that the kinds of beliefs emotions involve are predominantly false, embodying false values. Rather, most of us probably think, with Aristotle and current day cognitive psychologists, that emotions can often give us truthful views of the world, even if sometimes exaggerated or magnified. Also, we tend to think that the desires that lace emotions and the physiological arousals expressive of emotions make for states that are as much body as mind, and hence hard to relinquish by a sheer act of belief or will. Again, few of us are ready to embrace wholeheartedly the Stoic doctrine that all goods other than the pure goodness of our souls ought to be matters of pure indifference to us, things from which we can fully detach in a search for a meaningful life. And yet despite the harshness of some of their views, the Stoics propound a view that we might have considerable sympathy with. And this is the view that, to some degree or other, emotions embody ways of thinking about the world, ways of reading the world and evaluating it. Emotions are a form of judging the world, and when we subtly shift those ways of thinking – i.e. stop thinking that something is an offence, or a loss, or an injury, or an attraction – we make possible a shift in our emotional states. What most of us probably dispute is that the cognitive shift is itself sufficient for an emotional shift, that feeling can be reduced to believing.

But we need to return to the specific Stoic claim that we began with – that anger is an emotion that needs extirpation. Can a Stoic, who roots out all anger, be trained as a killer? Does this feature of a Stoic education make sense for a military person?

The harder conceptual problem, I suggest, is not in thinking of the possibility of a warrior who lacks anger, but the possibility of a person of virtue who is devoid of all anger. For to be a soldier, defending principle, abiding by rules of engagement, cognisant of the constraints of just war and just conduct in war embodied in such documents as the Law of Land Warfare or the Geneva Conventions, in fact, requires a principled response to the demands of warfare. To act out of frenzy or rage, to systematically dehumanise the enemy in the way that anger toward an enemy often requires, for a commander to rev up his troops by blood thirst for revenge, for a pilot to be battle-happy in a way that makes him nonchalant about the 'no-fly' zone, is to risk running afoul of the moral framework of war. Of course, no one can fight without the adrenaline rush of aggression and competitive spirit and it is a drill sergeant's job in life to push his troops to know those emotions well. But that physiological arousal may not itself be underpinned by the kinds of judgement that Seneca claims ground irascibility and rage. But even if we can conceive of a warrior who fights best because of principle rather than anger, can we conceive of a truly virtuous person who leaves behind his sense of anger, his sense of moral indignation, his sense of outrage? Consider retired Chief Warrant Officer Hugh Thompson, the man some have called the hero of My Lai. On March 16, 1968 he was flying his observation chopper when he spotted several wounded people on the ground, and a dyke where a group of GIs approached an injured, unarmed woman, about 20, and later one officer prodded the woman with his foot and then killed her. Minutes later he saw dozens of bodies in an irrigation ditch. The writhing movements suggested that some were still alive. American infantry men on the side of the ditch were taking a cigarette break from battle, and began taking off their steel helmets for a moment of respite. Several minutes later, he saw one of the sergeants shooting at people in the ditch. Thompson's worst fears were confirmed. With his side gunner, Larry Colburn, and his crew chief, Glenn Andreotta, Thompson landed the bubble, telling Colburn to 'open up' on the GIs – 'open up on 'em, blow 'em away' – if they opened fire at him as he intervened (Hilton and Sim 1992).

The Army, after some thirty years of relative silence, belatedly decorated Hugh Thompson for his valour on that day in My Lai with the prestigious Soldier's Medal. What were those moments of seeing the massacre at My Lai like? What did he feel? He remembered thinking that what he witnessed was too much like Nazi behaviour during the Holocaust. At the time he thought, American soldiers do not behave that way. We do not commit genocide. The traces of anger and disbelief were still visible on his face and audible in his voice, as he recalled approaching the GIs who were wielding weapons against the innocents. He himself did not use the words 'moral outrage', but it was clear that the judgements he made about the horrors he saw that day were the judgements of moral anger. Thirty years later, upon returning to the village of My Lai for a memorial, he was met by one of the village women who had survived the slayings. He remembered her then as a young mother. She was now a frail, ageing woman. She yanked at Thompson's sleeve and implored, 'Why did the American GIs kill my family? Why? Why were they different from you?' He could only break down in tears and say, 'I don't know, I don't know. That is not how I was taught to behave.'[4]

If we follow Seneca, are we consigned to an education that would have forced Thompson to behave differently, to look on with dispassionate disinterest, a kind of Stoic apathy, that could incite neither rage nor grief? Would we root out what was at the core of Thompson's virtue and humanity? Seneca himself is inconsistent on the point. Anger is the clear enemy in this essay, and yet he closes his piece with the following exhortation: 'While we still draw breath, while we still remain among human beings, let us cultivate our humanity' (*On Anger*, III.43).[5] A Stoicism, committed to the cultivation of humanity and human fellowship, cannot, in fact, eliminate all human anger. As frenzied and blinding as anger's outbursts, as dehumanising as rage can be, anger expressed in the right way at the right time is the sure sign of humanity. Aristotle, and not the Stoics, gets this point right: anger can be morally fine and praiseworthy. If the Stoics improve upon Aristotle on this point it is that they remind us that emotions are, more often than we think, a matter of our responsibility. The Stoics urge that the emotions are volitional states. We are not just *affected* when we suffer emotions but, as the Stoics put it, we *yield* or give *assent* to certain judgements implicit in those emotions.[6] Even if we are reluctant to embrace a notion of emotions as voluntary, it is hard to deny that, over time, we have considerable dominion over *how* we respond emotionally. We take charge of how we cultivate our humanity, including, I would add, our anger.

CONCLUSION

The Stoics offer important lessons for the military and civilians alike. They give guidance in how we might begin to shape a character education that takes seriously the values of discipline and self-mastery, at the same time recognising our dependence upon others in small communities but also more globally.

We have seen that Stoic lessons of self-sufficiency and self-mastery are crucial antidotes to the indulgences of consumerism and appetite that plague the contemporary scene. The point is not to idealise the life of deprivation or slavery (as a Stoic like Epictetus may seem sometimes to do), but rather to cultivate the inner resources and virtues that allow for a measure of control in the face of strong temptations and hard losses. The Stoic wisdom is that we have dominion in more areas of our lives than we often acknowledge. Our physical strength can often be built, our emotions 'affect' us, but we also regulate them and learn habits of mind and expression that convey what we care about.

The Stoics make the latter point by suggesting that proper emotions are forms of judgement that we openly consent to and as it were wilfully 'allow in'. In the case of an emotion like anger, we can control, they say, the judgements to which we consent and which we endorse. We have seen how this stance has both its attractions and dangers. We know without being card-carrying Stoics that reflection allows us to revise overly hasty views about what may annoy, insult, or offend, and that these revised judgements help us to change how we feel, in some cases releasing us from the grip of unreasonable anger. The Stoics, however, insist that all anger is poisoned and that the truly virtuous person is rid entirely of its venom. But we have argued against the extremism of this view. Anger can also show its face as moral outrage, indignation, and a sense of injustice. There are human moments when anger is precisely the right response, however much we may 'lose' ourselves in the reaction. Likewise, for grief, compassion, and love. Perhaps the Stoic lesson to preserve is that there are ways of *recovering* our mastery even after we have let go. There are forms of resilience and self-governance that allow for stability in the face of the strongest winds.

The Stoics also insist upon our cosmopolitan status in the world. We are citizens of the universe, not isolated individuals or isolated nations. Military and civic education must emphasise loyalty to country but also loyalty to values that extend beyond national borders. But the young civilian no less than the junior military officer needs to know that moral obligations and wider circles of allegiance must extend beyond national borders. It is not just our economy that is global but, in a pointed way, our moral community as well.

I have turned to the military as something of a case study for exploring Stoicism. I have argued that we have much to reap from the richness of Stoic texts. But I have also urged a critical attitude in the face of more orthodox, Stoic tenets. The task as moral educators is to shape a Stoicism with a human face. As Coriolanus, Shakespeare's legendary Stoic warrior, came to realise, 'it is no little thing to make mine eyes to sweat compassion.'

NOTES

1 An ancestor of this chapter appears as 'Educating the Stoic warrior' in *Bringing in a New Era in Character Education*, W. Damon (ed.) (Stanford: Hoover Institution Press, 2001), pp. 85–111. My thanks are due to Elisa Hurley for her invaluable editorial assistance with that paper.
2 For a very helpful commentary, see Gill 1988.
3 See, for example, the account of emotions in *Rhetoric II*.
4 I am remembering the gist of the conversation as it appeared on CBS's *60 Minutes*.
5 For an insightful discussion of *On Anger*, see Nussbaum 1994: chs 10 and 11.
6 For a nuanced description of the voluntary and involuntary aspects of emotional experience, see Seneca, *On Anger*, II.1–4.

REFERENCES

Aristotle [c. 335 BCE] *Nicomachean Ethics*, trans. D. Ross, Oxford: Oxford University Press, 1998.
Cicero [c. 44 BCE] *On Duties* [De Officiis], M.T. Griffin and E.M. Atkins (eds), Cambridge: Cambridge University Press, 1991.
Cicero [45 BCE] *Tusculan Disputations*, trans. J.E. King, Cambridge, MA: Harvard University Press, 1927.
Diogenes Laertius [3rd century CE] *Lives of Eminent Philosophers*, trans. R.D. Hicks, Cambridge, MA: Harvard University Press, 1972.
Epictetus [c. 100 CE] *Discourses*, trans. W.A. Oldfather, Cambridge, MA: Harvard University Press, 1925.
Epictetus [c. 100 CE] *Enchiridion*, trans. N. White, Indianapolis: Hackett, 1983.
Gill, C. (1988) 'Personhood and personality: the four-personae theory', in 'Cicero, De Officiis I', in *Oxford Studies in Ancient Philosophy*, Vol. VI, Oxford: Oxford University Press, pp. 169–99.
Hilton, M. and Sim, K. (1992) *Four Hours in My Lai*, New York: Penguin.
Long, A.A. and Sedley, D.N. (eds) (1987) *The Hellenistic Philosophers, Vol. 1*, Cambridge: Cambridge University Press.

Marcus Aurelius [c. 170 CE] *Meditations*, trans. A.S.L. Farquharson, Oxford: Oxford University Press, 1989.

Nussbaum, M. (1994) *The Therapy of Desire*, Princeton: Princeton University Press.

Plato [360 BCE] *The Republic*, trans. G. Grube, Indianapolis: Hackett, 1974.

Seneca [c. 62 CE] *On Anger* [De Ira], in *Seneca: Moral and Political Essays*, J.M. Cooper and J.F. Procopé (eds), Cambridge: Cambridge University Press, 1995, pp. 1–116.

Shay, J. (1994) *Achilles in Vietnam*, New York: Simon & Schuster.

Smith, A. (1976) [1759] *The Theory of Moral Sentiments*, Indianapolis: Liberty Classics.

Stockdale, J.B. (1994) *Courage Under Fire: Testing Epictetus's Doctrines in a Lab of Human Behavior*, Stanford: Hoover Institution Press.

Part II
Aspects of spirituality

Chapter 6

Metaphor, cognition and spiritual reality

J. Mark Halstead

When I began teaching English Literature some thirty years ago, metaphor was viewed widely as a literary technique which was ornamental, which appealed to the reader's imagination or emotions and which enriched poetic meaning. It was thought to consist of an implied comparison, in which one experience or state of affairs (the 'topic') was described in terms of another (the 'source' of the comparison), and the reader's task was to understand the 'grounds' of the comparison and thereby arrive at the meaning. Thus in L.P. Hartley's celebrated opening to *The Go-Between* (1953), we read: 'The past is a foreign country: they do things differently there.' In this case the topic is 'the past', the source is 'a foreign country' and the fact that 'they do things differently there' provides the grounds for comparison. Of course, the three elements (topic, source and grounds) are not spelled out so clearly in every metaphor, and often the reader is left to infer the topic, to identify the point, aptness and range of the comparison, and to explore the tensions as well as the similarities between the topic and the source. At the heart of this conventional, Aristotelian approach to metaphor, however, is the belief that metaphors point to some literal truth, and that it is the literal truth that matters. The metaphor simply draws attention to the literal truth by expressing it in a concise or engaging way (Davidson 1978; Searle 1993).

However, recent work in the fields of cognitive science, linguistics and the philosophy of literature has challenged this view that metaphor is merely a matter of language and emotional response. A body of theoreticians (we may call them 'experientialists') has argued that metaphor is the normal (almost automatic) way of understanding abstractions and complex phenomena. We make use of our imagination to explore complex ideas and develop our understanding in terms of more readily understood social and physical experiences, and conceptual systems are built up on these metaphorical foundations. Metaphor thus becomes a 'conceptual and experiential process that structures our world' (Johnson 1995: 157), and this process is not an arbitrary one, but is 'grounded in our most basic embodied experience' (Winter 1995: 237). Imagination operates on our shared embodied experience in a systematic, structured way, which experientialists like Lakoff (1987, 1993) have analysed closely.

This chapter brings an experientialist perspective to our understanding of spirituality. Over the past twenty years, experientialists have engaged in a series of mapping exercises setting out the use of metaphor in many areas of human thought, including science (Kuhn 1993), law (Winter 1995), social policy (Schon 1993), morality (Rethorst 1997) and even warfare (Lakoff 1991). Spirituality has been curiously neglected. Yet it is clear that metaphor pervades every aspect of our thinking about spirituality. We talk of spiritual journeys, spiritual enlightenment, spiritual health, spiritual hunger, spiritual beauty, spiritual anguish, spiritual quest. It is in the interplay between the imagination and embodied experience that we see metaphor actually structuring our conceptualisation of what the domain of the spiritual is.

The chapter falls into three sections. The first contains a rather more detailed discussion of the views of cognitive scientists and experientialist philosophers on the nature and importance of conceptual metaphor. The second section applies their arguments to spirituality and shows how the way we think about the spiritual is pervasively and inescapably structured by metaphor. The third section explores in more detail one particular example of conceptual mapping in the spiritual domain – the use of the body in the poetry of John Donne as a metaphor for the soul, and of sexual experience as a symbol for spiritual experience.

THE NATURE OF METAPHOR

According to recent theoretical research on metaphor (see, for example, Johnson 1987; Lakoff 1987, 1993; Lakoff and Johnson 1980; Lakoff and Turner 1989; Leddy 1995; Sweetser 1990; Turner 1987, 1991), metaphor involves using the imagination to relate one idea or conceptual domain (the source of the comparison, which is normally based on embodied experience or experience of the social or natural world) to another (the topic of the comparison, which is normally a more abstract concept) in order to facilitate thought and communication and to construct the meanings we give to things. There are three key elements in this definition of metaphor: the exercise of the imagination, the grounding in bodily experience, and the construction of meaning.

The first element, the exercise of the imagination, is crucial. Recent work in the fields of morality, philosophy, therapy and other disciplines (cf. Burke 1999; Johnson 1993; Novitz 1987; Warnock 1994) suggests that human thought (unlike artificial intelligence) is essentially imaginative. However, the imagination does not operate as 'a kind of cognitive wild card' (Winter 1995: 227), but rather in a regular, systematic fashion which is open to investigation and analysis (Johnson 1987; Lakoff 1987). The imagination takes a conventional conceptual metaphor and develops it in strikingly new ways. Thus, in Psalm 23, the psalmist takes two conventional root analogies ('God is our protector' and 'the spiritual life is a journey') and develops them into a beautiful and highly original train of thought:

> The Lord is my shepherd; I shall not want. He maketh me to lie down in green pastures; he leadeth me beside the still waters. He restoreth my soul; he leadeth me in the paths of righteousness for his name's sake. Yea, though I walk through the valley of the shadow of death, I will fear no evil: for thou art with me; thy rod and thy staff they comfort me.

However, the imagination can go further than merely re-expressing ideas in effective, original language. It can also use the basic stock of root analogies to construct new ways of understanding the world.

Secondly, human embodied experience provides the raw material on which the imagination works in the construction of metaphors (Winter 1995: 237f). Johnson points to a growing body of empirical research showing how core analogies 'typically come from basic-level experiences that are shared by human beings because of their shared bodily and cognitive makeup and because of the common features of the environments with which people interact' (1995: 159). To take two more biblical examples, Jesus draws on shared embodied experience when he says, 'Let not thy left hand know what thy right hand doeth' (Matthew 6:3) and on human interaction with the environment when he says, 'Enter ye in at the strait gate' (Matthew 7:13). Metaphors are both motivated and constrained by common patterns of bodily experience and experience of the social and natural environment.

Thirdly, what emerges from this fusion of the imagination and embodied experience is new meaning, new ways of structuring our experiences and looking at the world. This claim about the truth-bearing, even truth-creating, possibilities of metaphor is not a wholly new idea. Writing in 1821, Shelley argues in his 'A defence of poetry' that the language of poets 'is vitally metaphorical; that is, it marks the before unapprehended relations of things' (2002). In other words, metaphor is used by poets as a means to transform the way we perceive the world. But what the experientialists have done is to extend this claim from poetic metaphor to conceptual metaphor. They argue that there is an extensive system of metaphor used by everyone, not just poets, to understand complexities and abstractions. Indeed, the use of such metaphors is so widespread that it often occurs unreflectively. Leddy argues that the only difference between literal statements and metaphorical statements is that in the former we understand one thing in terms of something else of the same kind, whereas in the latter we understand it in terms of a different kind (1995: 207). But through this process metaphors facilitate abstract thought and understanding. For example, when Earl (2001) writes an article entitled 'Shadow and spirituality', we understand what the article is likely to be about, though we might have difficulty expressing it as a literal statement. It is not just that metaphors help us to understand the world, but that in some domains at least – and I shall argue shortly that the spiritual is one such domain – the fundamental constituents of our experienced world are accessible to us only through metaphor.

Experientialism thus hovers in the middle ground between objectivism and radical relativism. It is clearly opposed to the literalism and absolutism of objectivist theories of knowledge and meaning, and is incompatible with Hobbes' and Locke's dismissal of metaphor as an unhelpful distraction in philosophical debate. On the other hand, the fact that metaphor is grounded in human embodied experience acts as a constraint on the imagination and challenges postmodernist claims about the arbitrariness of meaning and radical relativism of our concepts. From an experientialist perspective, deep conceptual metaphor provides 'a new positive and constructive view of the embodied and imaginative character of human understanding' (Johnson 1995: 159). The ramifications of this position are still to be explored, but it seems likely that it will raise questions in many areas of philosophy, including metaphysics (cf. Leddy 1995).

Currently, however, we do not even have an accepted terminology to describe the nature of deep conceptual metaphor, though the processes by which metaphors structure our conceptualisation and reasoning are now reasonably clear. The everyday use of metaphor (which may be original or clichéd, explicit or implicit, dead or full of vitality) is the product of a more general framework of correspondences or core metaphors, which Lakoff (1993) calls 'cross-domain mappings', Johnson (1995) 'deep conceptual metaphors' and Goatly (1997) 'root analogies'. Whatever their name, they take the form x is y, where x is a conceptual domain in need of description or clarification, and y is the conceptual domain which conveys the description or clarification. Thus we say 'Kevin is a rat', or 'My love for you is an oasis in life's desert'. We elaborate on these core metaphors in a variety of ways. For example, the root analogy 'ideas are commodities that we buy and sell' may give rise to a whole cluster of everyday metaphors: 'I won't buy that idea'; 'it's not worth the paper it's written on'; 'the marketplace of ideas'; 'with the right packaging we might just be able to sell that idea'; and so on.

Metaphor, of course, is only one of a number of cognitive mechanisms. In some areas, its impact in terms of transforming our understanding might be modest. In other areas (such as the arts, for example), metaphor may be a key to the very conceptualisation of the topic, such that understanding is impossible without it. I shall argue in the next section that spirituality is one such instance.

METAPHOR AND SPIRITUALITY

Metaphor is all-pervasive in writing about spirituality: even a cursory glance at the titles of articles in the *International Journal of Children's Spirituality* shows us a language which is simply dripping with metaphors. However, the role of metaphor in our understanding of the spiritual domain has not so far been the object of much research, though interestingly Hammond *et al.* include a number of exercises based on metaphor in their textbook utilising an experiential approach to Religious Education (1990: 93–6, 118–20, 125–30, 158–9).

In fact, there is a long tradition going back to Plato which suggests that the physical world is a shadow of the spiritual, and this tradition was a major influence on the spiritual thinking of a number of seventeenth-century poets including Donne, Herbert, Crashaw, Marvell and Vaughan (cf. Halstead 1999). At the same time, the use of embodied experience as a metaphor for spiritual experience is widespread in sacred texts (cf. Levine 1999: 134–7). In the New Testament, the human body is 'the temple of the Holy Spirit' (1 Corinthians 6:19). We are told that Christ 'is the head of the body, the church' (Colossians 1:18), that the church is the bride of Christ (2 Corinthians 11:2; Revelation 19:7), and that 'we are members of his body' (Ephesians 5:30). In the Jewish scriptures, the relationship between Israel and God is described as that of an unfaithful wife and her forgiving husband (Isaiah 54:1–10; Ezekiel 16; Hosea 2:2–3:5), and the Song of Solomon famously celebrates God's love for his people through an extended metaphor of erotic love.

It is as if metaphors drawn from embodied experience are the only way of getting a grip on spiritual realities. Otherwise, the spiritual concepts may be beyond our grasp. Milton makes this point in the words Raphael addresses to Adam and Eve in Book V of *Paradise Lost*:

> . . . And what surmounts the reach
> Of human sense, I shall delineate so,
> By lik'ning spiritual to corporeal forms,
> As may express them best; though what if Earth
> Be but the shadow of Heaven . . . ?
>
> (lines 571–5)

In other words, we can most readily understand the spiritual world through the physical. Elsewhere I have called this kind of thinking an inductive form of incarnation theology, in which our understanding is led upwards from the familiar, the human, the embodied, to the unfamiliar, the divine, the spiritual (Halstead 1999; cf. Brunner 1952: 322). Under-standing and loving God (whom we cannot see) thus begins by under-standing and loving our fellow human beings (whom we can see, and who show in tangible form something of God's nature). To use more experien-tialist terminology, the conceptual systems through which we understand spirituality are constructed out of metaphors based on embodied experi-ence, and these conceptual systems in turn structure what we perceive, what we experience, and the way we define spiritual reality.

Let us consider some of the metaphors we use to refer to the spiritual domain. We find spirituality conceptualised in terms of health, healing, well-being, hunger, thirst, breath, nourishment, birth, pain, fulfilment, family relationships, movement (up, in, beyond), growth, childlike inno-cence, development, regeneration, rebirth, learning (literacy), journey, search, quest, home, stillness, opening, listening, contemplation, light, shadow, contact, narrative, intoxication, ecstasy, despair, passion, desire, struggle, battle, beauty, transformation.

Often, these spiritual metaphors take exactly the same form as the conceptual metaphors or root analogies discussed in the previous section: *x is y*. From each of the comparatively small number of core analogies may be derived a whole array of ordinary linguistic metaphors. For example, one of the most widely used core analogies takes the form 'the spiritual life is a journey'. The journey may involve persevering in the face of difficulties and temptations, overcoming obstacles, following the right signposts, discarding unnecessary baggage, passing through a particular landscape, focusing on the destination, helping others along the way, refusing to turn back. The core metaphor thus finds expression in very many variations on the theme. Scott Peck uses a quotation from Robert Frost as the title of his six million copy bestseller on the spiritual life, *The Road Less Traveled* (1978), while the seventeenth-century bestseller, Bunyan's *Pilgrim's Progress* (1984), builds the same core metaphor into a thorough-going allegory of the spiritual life, in which Christian makes his way towards the Celestial City, passing through many places including the Slough of Despond, the Valley of the Shadow of Death and Vanity Fair en route. The core analogy is also found in the Gospels, where Jesus warns his followers that 'broad is the way that leadeth to destruction' (Matthew 7:13). However, the conceptualisation of life as a journey is clearly not exclusive to the spiritual domain (cf. Lakoff and Johnson 1980; Lakoff and Turner 1989). Mrs Thatcher's 'no turning back' speech is a famous example of a non-spiritual application of the metaphor. One con-sequence of this non-distinctiveness of the core metaphor is that it is not always possible to be sure whether it carries a spiritual meaning or not: thus the 'spiritual life' may merge simply into 'life'.

On many occasions, however, the use of metaphor in the spiritual domain differs from its use in other contexts. For example, spiritual metaphors often take the form *y1 is y2*, where both *y1* and *y2* are conceptual metaphors, as in the sentences 'spiritual hunger is a desire for union with God', or 'spiritual growth is progress on the path to enlightenment'. This is not just an expansion of a core metaphor, as occurs, for example, when Jesus says '[The sheep] shall hear my voice' (John 10:16), which is just part of the conceptual mapping of the root analogy 'I am the good shepherd' (John 10:11). On the contrary, the source domain and the target domain are quite different conceptual metaphors. It is no longer a matter of a literal conceptual domain being explained by means of a metaphor, but of one metaphorical conceptual domain being explained in terms of another. It is rather like saying, instead of 'my feet are lumps of lead', 'my lumps of lead are an insoluble problem', except that the topic is abstract and intangible, not physical like feet.

There are three consequences that result from this distinctive use of metaphor in the spiritual domain. First, it becomes apparent that spiritual meaning and spiritual truth are different from other forms of meaning and truth. But this distancing of the spiritual domain from the level of ordinary literal meaning does not require us to conclude (as do Nietzsche and Derrida, for example) that the prevalence of metaphor undermines any search for timeless truth at all. Spirituality may well be an essentially contested concept (to use Gallie's term (1956)), but no more so than aesthetics, for example, with which it has much in common, and indeed, it may be through the accumulation of metaphors that spiritual truth is to be found.

A second feature of the spiritual metaphor is multiple meaning. A phrase may carry significance both literally and metaphorically at the same time, and operate at both a physical and a spiritual level. We have already seen this in the case of the Song of Solomon, which is taken simultaneously as a love poem expressing Solomon's love for a Shulamite girl and as a sustained metaphor expressing God's love for Israel or Christ's love for the Church. As Ricoeur points out (1977: 224) this characteristic generates tensions between the source domain and the topic domain, between the literal and metaphorical interpretation, and between the impulse to similarity and the impulse to difference, which may make understanding difficult. Part of the ambiguity, he suggests (p. 248), is because there is an *is not* lurking within the metaphorical *is*.

Thirdly, the distinctive use of metaphor in the spiritual domain allows much scope for the exploration of abstract spiritual ideas. Indeed, it seems likely that metaphor provides the only way through which deep spiritual concepts can be explored. Certainly, seventeenth-century metaphysical poets made full use of metaphor for this purpose. In his collection of spiritual verse entitled 'The Temple' Herbert uses striking metaphors to reflect on rebellion, doubt and fear, a sense of being unworthy of God's love, the nature of spiritual conflicts, the serenity of worship and the meaning of prayerful devotion. Marvell in 'On a drop of dew' describes the soul's longing to return to the spiritual reality of heaven in terms of a dew-drop delicately balancing on a leaf, 'trembling lest it grow impure' until it evaporates and returns to heaven. Crashaw in his 'Hymn to Sainte Teresa' uses sexual imagery to convey a compelling sense of the loss of self, of union with the transcendent and of the exultation which this sense of union brings.

In the final section of this chapter, I examine in rather more detail how Donne uses sexual metaphors in his religious poetry to explore spiritual experience, and how the sexuality of his love poetry is often a tangible, physical symbol of spiritual truth.

UNDERSTANDING SPIRITUALITY THROUGH SEXUALITY: SOME EXAMPLES FROM DONNE

Donne's poetry is not spiritual in the normal seventeenth-century sense of devotion, worship or meditation (cf. Martz 1954; Oliver 1997). Indeed, Gardner describes him as 'not remarkable for any spiritual gifts and graces', and as 'by nature arrogant, egotistical, irreverent', with a mind that is 'naturally sceptical and curious, holding little sacred' (1952: xvii). In this section, however, I shall contend that his poetry is deeply spiritual in other ways; in particular, it is much more concerned to develop spiritual understanding than to illuminate or encourage spiritual virtue (Wilcox 1994). It strives for spiritual understanding through the application of both imaginative and critical thinking to embodied experience. In fact, spiritual metaphors are used to illuminate sexuality just as much as sexual metaphors illuminate spirituality. We find examples of the former in 'Elegy VIII', where he compares his own tender love-making to the 'devoutly nice' manner of 'priests in handling reverent sacrifice' (cf. Davies 1994: 38–9), and in 'Elegy XIX', where he compares the 'full naked-ness' of his mistress once she has stripped off her last remaining garment to a soul free at last from the encumbrance of the body. Examples of the latter are found in 'Holy Sonnet XIV' where he asks God to ravish him and in 'Holy Sonnet XVIII' where he suggests that Christ's spouse (the Church) is most pleasing to her husband 'when she is embraced and open to most men'.

Sometimes Donne's metaphors take the conventional, uni-directional form *x is y*. The line near the end of 'The Extasie', 'But yet the body is his [Love's] booke', recalls the description of women in 'Elegy XIX' as 'mystick books', but what the line is saying is that the 'body' is the 'book' in which we can study the spiritual mysteries of love. We can only understand spiritual love (whether human or divine) through the body, and ultimately there is as little difference ('small change') between them (cf. Osmond

1990: 116). At other times, however, the sense flows back and forth between the sexual and the spiritual, the human and the divine in a multi-directional way. In 'A Valediction: of weeping', Donne suggests that when he weeps, it is the reflection of his mistress's face in his tears which gives them worth, just as it is the reflection of God's mercy which gives worth to his tears of repentance ('Holy Sonnet IX'). Reflection is a deep conceptual metaphor much loved of Donne (cf. Lacan 1977; Miller 1998). Woman is often presented as a mirror in which the male poet sees himself reflected. She is the 'glorious nothing' (as opposed to the male 'thing': cf. DiPasquale 2001: 211), an empty space which acquires meaning through the projection of the speaker's masculinity into her, just as the Church acquires meaning through the action of her bridegroom, Christ. In 'A Valediction: of my name in the window' the poet's mistress can see both her own reflection ('. . . and cleare reflects thee to thine eye') and his name engraved in the window ('here see you mee'): the result is both self-knowledge and knowledge of the other, and at the same time a merging of the two ('I am you') (cf. Davies 1994: 13–16). Such merging is the goal of the spiritual life. The notion of merging is most complete in 'Sapho to Philaenis', where the fusion of the two lovers is such that it is no longer clear when Sappho is responding to Philaenis and when she is responding to her own reflection in the mirror. This represents a perfect bodily union, in which the bodies of the lover and the beloved merge as if through an alchemical process into a single identity; she speaks to Philaenis, but it is her own reflection that she touches and kisses in the mirror, and the two melt into each other. Of course, this parallels the union of souls that takes place in 'The Extasie', but it also speaks symbolically on the divine level of the virtuous soul losing itself in, and attaining perfect union with, and hence becoming, God.

The movement from the human to the divine, or from the physical to the spiritual, is precisely the idea at the heart of 'Holy Sonnet XVII', in which the poet uses a number of metaphors to show how his love for his wife Ann led him to seek God, and how God's love has filled the vacuum left by her death:

> Since she whom I lov'd hath payd her last debt
> To Nature, and to hers, and my good is dead
> And her Soule early into heaven ravished,
> Wholly in heavenly things my mind is sett.
> Here th' admyring her my mind did whett
> To seeke thee God; so streames do shew their head;
> But though I have found thee, and thou my thirst hast fed,
> A holy thirsty dropsy melts me yett.
> But why should I begg more Love, when as thou
> Dost wooe my soule, for hers offring all thine:

> And dost not only fear least I allow
> My love to Saints and Angels things divine
> But in thy tender jealosy dost doubt
> Least the Worlde, Fleshe, yea Devill putt thee out.

The first four lines are much more than the conventional platitude that after the death of a beloved spouse one turns to heaven for comfort. 'Ravished' is a term used much more frequently for the carrying away of bodies than of souls, and the metaphor conveys the poet's unwillingness to see his wife wrested from him and the physical wrench he feels at her loss. Yet since the early arrival of her soul in heaven, his mind is now fixed 'wholly in heavenly things'. It is his admiration for his wife while she was on earth which now stimulates his desire to seek God; the earthly love he had for his wife leads him to the divine love. The metaphor in line six of streams being traceable back to their source suggests that since the stream is essentially the same as its source, the physical love he experienced with his wife is of the same nature as the divine love which now satisfies his thirst. While he highly values the experience of God's love, there is a sense at first that this love leaves his physical appetite unsatisfied (the 'dropsy' of line eight). But this is only a momentary glance back at the physical world that has been left behind, not a fatal attraction like Lot's wife's. For he quickly realises that God's love is all he needs, and that when God offers all his own love (which lasts for eternity) in exchange for the love of the poet's wife (which has been brought to a premature end), the poet has indeed got a good bargain. The poem's argument moves from earthly love to heavenly love: earthly love is good in itself, though it comes to an end, but it points symbolically to the eternal love of God. The last four lines describe God's love in a clever combination of the Old Testament metaphor of God as a jealous husband and the New Testament metaphor of God as a kind and self-sacrificing bridegroom: the image is of a tenderly jealous lover willing to give everything for the one he loves but worried that in the end he may lose out to any of three possible rivals.

The movement from the physical to the spiritual, and the fusion of the two, are seen as much in the love poetry as in the religious poetry. In the first verse of 'Aire and Angels', for example, we read:

> Twice or thrice had I loved thee,
> Before I knew thy face or name;
> So in a voice, so in a shapelesse flame,
> Angells affect us oft, and worship'd bee;
> Still when, to where thou wert, I came
> Some lovely glorious nothing I did see.

> But since my soule, whose child love is,
> Takes limmes of flesh, and else could nothing doe,
> More subtile then the parent is,
> Love must not be, but take a body too,
> And therefore what thou wert, and who,
> I bid Love aske, and now
> That it assume thy body, I allow,
> And fixe it selfe in thy lip, eye, and brow.

The first experience of love described in this poem is immaterial, spiritual. The narrator feels he has already loved his mistress before he has even seen her or knows her name (just as angels can be sensed and worshipped when still invisible), and even when he comes into her presence, the first impression he gets is of a delightful spiritual (loss of?) consciousness. 'Nothing', as well as symbolising a woman, implies the absence of anything physical or tangible, and also implies zero, naught, the circle, the symbol of eternity; it may thus perhaps allude to the Platonic eternal world of true realities, of which the familiar everyday world is an imperfect reflection. However, just as the soul of a human being is incomplete without a body and must therefore 'take limmes of flesh', so love (which is the 'child' of the soul) cannot be more spiritual ('subtile') than its parent, but must itself become incarnate. His love therefore comes to focus on her body and its various physical charms. Like angels, women have to 'put on' corporeality in their relations with men. Clearly, important spiritual ideas are lurking beneath the surface of this love poem. God's love, like human love, needs to 'take a body too' if it is to be understood and appreciated; because of the way that humans themselves are made (as a combination of body and soul), love, whether human or divine, is incomplete if it is purely spiritual. The Word must become flesh, and dwell among us. Thus for Donne the physical world is more than a symbol of the spiritual world, and sexual relationships are more than symbols of spiritual relationships: incarnation – the embodied world – is the *only way* in which the spiritual dimension to life can be understood. Spiritual love is a mystery and can only be explained (perhaps even experienced) through physical images and symbols, but nonetheless this kind of love is real and eternal, and elixir-like it transforms the commonplace into the divine (cf. Osmond 1990: ch. 6).

T.S. Eliot famously wrote, 'A thought to Donne was an experience; it modified his sensibility' (1932). In this section, I have argued the reverse: an experience to Donne was a thought. He took any experience – breathing, melting, dying, feeling jealousy, watching a candle, winking, studying alchemy or geography, sailing to other countries or seducing a woman – and transformed it through his imagination into new insights into love and the spiritual life. The metaphors he used were not just tools for thought, but were the actual bricks out of which he constructed the domain of the spiritual. Without them, for us as for Donne, there can be no spiritual reality.

NOTE

References to all John Donne's poems quoted in this chapter come from Patrides (1985); other references to metaphysical poetry come from Gardner (1972). All biblical references are from the Authorised Version.

REFERENCES

Brunner, E. (1952) *Dogmatics II: The Christian Doctrine of Creation and Redemption*, London: Lutterworth Press.

Bunyan, J. (1984) [1678] *Pilgrim's Progress*, Oxford: Oxford University Press.

Burke, P.A. (1999) 'The healing power of the imagination', *International Journal of Children's Spirituality* 4, 1, pp. 9–18.

Davidson, D. (1978) 'What metaphors mean', *Critical Inquiry* 5, pp. 31–47.

Davies, S. (1994) *John Donne*, Plymouth: Northcote House.

DiPasquale, T.M. (2001) *Literature and Sacrament: The Sacred and the Secular in John Donne*, Cambridge: James Clarke.

Earl, M. (2001) 'Shadow and spirituality', *International Journal of Children's Spirituality* 6, 3, pp. 277–88.

Eliot, T.S. (1932) *Selected Essays*, New York: Harcourt, Brace & World

Gallie, W.B. (1956) 'Art as an essentially contested concept', *Philosophical Quarterly* 6, 23, pp. 97–114.

Gardner, H. (ed.) (1952) *John Donne: The Divine Poems*, Oxford: Clarendon Press.

Gardner, H. (ed.) (1972) *The Metaphysical Poets*, Harmondsworth: Penguin.

Goatly, A. (1997) *The Language of Metaphors*, London: Routledge.

Halstead, J.M. (1999) 'John Donne and the theology of incarnation', in L. Gearon (ed.), *English Literature, Theology and the Curriculum*, London: Cassell.

Hammond, J., Hay, D., Moxon, J., Netto, B., Raban, K., Straugheir, G. and Williams, C. (1990) *New Methods in RE Teaching: An Experiential Approach*, Harlow: Oliver & Boyd.

Hartley, L.P. (1953) *The Go-Between*, London: Hamish Hamilton.

Johnson, M. (1987) *The Body in the Mind: The Bodily Basis of Meaning, Reason and Imagination*, Chicago: University of Chicago Press.

Johnson, M. (1993) *Moral Imagination: Implications of Cognitive Science for Ethics*, Chicago: University of Chicago Press.

Johnson, M. (1995) 'Why metaphor matters to philosophy', *Metaphor and Symbolic Activity* 10, 3, pp. 157–62.

Kuhn, T.S. (1993) 'Metaphor in science', in A. Ortony (ed.), *Metaphor and Thought*, 2nd edition, Cambridge: Cambridge University Press.

Lacan, J. (1977) 'The mirror stage', in *Ecrits: A Selection*, trans. A Sheridan, London: Tavistock Publications.

Lakoff, G. (1987) *Women, Fire and Dangerous Things: What Categories Reveal about the Mind*, Chicago: University of Chicago Press.

Lakoff, G. (1991) *Metaphor in Politics: An Open Letter to the Internet* (available from lakoff@cogsci.berkeley.edu).

Lakoff, G. (1993) 'The contemporary theory of metaphor', in A. Ortony (ed.), *Metaphor and Thought*, 2nd edition, Cambridge: Cambridge University Press.

Lakoff, G. and Johnson, M. (1980) *Metaphors We Live By*, Chicago: University of Chicago Press.

Lakoff, G. and Turner, M. (1989) *More than Cool Reason: A Field Guide to Poetic Metaphor*, Chicago: University of Chicago Press.

Leddy, T. (1995) 'Metaphor and metaphysics, *Metaphor and Symbolic Activity* 10, 3, pp. 205–22.

Levine, S. (1999) 'Children's cognition as the foundation of spirituality', *International Journal of Children's Spirituality* 4, 2, pp 121–40.

Martz, L.L. (1954) *The Poetry of Meditation: A Study in English Religious Literature of the Seventeenth Century*, New Haven, CT: Yale University Press.

Miller, J. (1998) *On Reflection*, London, National Gallery Publications.

Novitz, D. (1987) *Knowledge, Fiction and Imagination*, Philadelphia, PA: Temple University Press.

Oliver, P.M. (1997) *Donne's Religious Writing: A Discourse in Feigned Devotion*, London: Longman.

Osmond, R. (1990) *Mutual Accusation: Seventeenth-century Body and Soul Dialogues in Their Literary and Theological Context*, Toronto: University of Toronto Press.

Patrides, C.A. (ed.) (1985) *The Complete English Poems of John Donne*, London: Everyman's Library.

Peck, M.S. (1978) *The Road Less Traveled*, New York: Simon & Schuster.

Rethorst, J. (1997) *Art and Imagination: Implications of Cognitive Science for Moral Education* (available at http://www.ed.uiuc.edu/EPS/PES-yearbook/97docs).

Ricoeur, P. (1977) *The Rule of Metaphor: Multidisciplinary Studies in the Creation of Meaning in Language*, Toronto: University of Toronto Press.

Schon, D.A. (1993) 'Generative metaphor: a perspective on problem-setting in social policy', in A. Ortony (ed.), *Metaphor and Thought*, 2nd edition, Cambridge: Cambridge University Press.

Searle, J. R. (1993) 'Metaphor', in A. Ortony (ed.), *Metaphor and Thought*, 2nd edition, Cambridge: Cambridge University Press.

Shelley, P.B. (2002) [1840] 'A defence of poetry', in D.H. Reiman and N. Fraistat (eds), *Shelley's Poetry and Prose*, New York: W.W. Norton & Co.

Sweetser, E. (1990) *From Etymology to Pragmatics: Metaphorical and Cultural Aspects of Semantic Structure*, Cambridge: Cambridge University Press.

Turner, M. (1987) *Death is the Mother of Beauty: Mind, Metaphor, Criticism*, Chicago: University of Chicago Press.

Turner, M. (1991) *Reading Minds: The Study of English in the Age of Cognitive Science*, Princeton, NJ: Princeton University Press.

Warnock, M. (1994) *Imagination and Time*, Oxford: Blackwell.

Wilcox, H. (1994) 'Squaring the circle: metaphors of the divine in the work of Donne and his contemporaries', *John Donne Journal* 13, 1–2, pp. 61–79.

Winter, S.L. (1995) 'A clearing in the forest', *Metaphor and Symbolic Activity* 10, 3, pp. 223–45.

Young, F. (1977) 'A cloud of witnesses', in J. Hick (ed.), *The Myth of God Incarnate*, London: SCM Press.

Chapter 7

After philosophy and religion
Spirituality and its counterfeits

Joseph Dunne

I

Coming to philosophy by a side-door – as a student in a Catholic seminary for whom attendance at university lectures in philosophy was a required propaedeutic to the study of theology – I could not avoid being struck by its distance, indeed aversion, from spirituality. This term was one that I did not then need to define: deepening one's 'spiritual life' was a central aim of the seminary regime, with 'spiritual reading', for example, a daily discipline and engagement with 'the spiritual exercises' of St Ignatius of Loyola an early element in the formative process. I would later come to recognise the limitations of this kind of spirituality – limitations stemming not from its immersion in a particular religious tradition but from its having too heavily absorbed the very subjectivism which in some respects Catholic teaching saw itself as opposing. What seemed more obvious to me at the time, however, was the limitations of the kind of *philosophy* to which we were introduced. To be sure, there was value in being exposed to discourses in which religious convictions could be made to appear incomprehensible, weak-minded, or regressive. And there was a particular frisson in encountering Marx, Freud and Sartre, whose militant atheism connected strongly with one's own commitments; even if it contested their rightness, at least it confirmed the importance of the issue on which one was wrong (Nietzsche's star had not then risen – it was the late 1960s and postmodernism had not yet arrived to claim him as prophet). Still, these figures were heroic exceptions. What we came to recognise as 'philosophy' was dry in tenor, its posture to the world detached and defla- tionary. Determined by epistemological anxieties that seeped into its treat- ment of virtually every topic – by an Ayer, a Strawson or a Hare – it hardly spoke to the concerns of anyone seeking wisdom or existential enlighten- ment let alone a student working through the strains of a religious vocation.

Having left the seminary, and having been neither converted to militant atheism nor impressed by the then sanctioned modes of deploying the undoubted virtues of conceptual analysis, I was not, perhaps, a promising candidate for further philosophical study. And there was in succeeding years, I confess, a continuing hiatus between the expectations and conventions of the academic discipline in which I had gone on to be indentured and the 'spiritual' concerns that I had not left behind at the seminary gates. These concerns could find oblique expression, of course, even in one's philosophical work: for at least one reader, my investigation of Aristotle's concept of *phronesis* (Dunne 1993) was a context – or pretext – for bringing the archetypal empiricist and rationalist 'as far east as he can be brought'! An alternative to obliquity was marginality – which seemed to be the fate of philosophers whom I greatly admired albeit that their direct engagement with spiritual themes kept them off the superhighways of academic philosophy: for example, Martin Buber and Simone Weil, each with roots in Jewish traditions to which they reacted very differently.

What I want to notice here, however, is a distinct *change* in the registers of what counts as respectable philosophy, making the discipline more hospitable now to someone coming to it with my particular prejudices. The work of Iris Murdoch and Charles Taylor is exemplary in this regard. Murdoch's early essays were written adversarially and from the sidelines. But, not least through the subsequent reception of her work, the established moral philosophy – haunted still by Hume's strictures on deriving 'ought' from 'is' and restricted almost entirely to justifying principles of obligation – now seems less formidable: its 'far too shallow and flimsy an idea of human personality' (Murdoch 1983: 43) is more exposed. When Charles Taylor recurrently uses the phrase 'moral and spiritual sources' in *Sources of the Self* (1992), he is still writing against a 'cramping of the spirit' that he finds endemic in the naturalistic temper of a great deal of modern culture, including its philosophy; but what he calls the 'retrieval' of a whole dimension of the human now seems more assured and his own book is recognised as a major work. In a more recent essay, which is a tribute to Murdoch and an acknowledgement of his indebtedness to her, he offers three suggestive images to characterise successive horizons within which 'morality' may be conceived (even as the term itself becomes increasingly unsatisfactory). The 'corral' symbolises a restricted concern with rules of duty or of *what it is right to do*; the 'field' includes concern with human flourishing or *what kind of human life it is good to lead*; while the 'forest' symbolises a further possibility of self-transformation through openness to *what can most fully inspire one's love* where this may be a good that is irreducible to a rich or satisfying life and may call for suffering or even death (Taylor 1996). Modern philosophy has given us many articulations of the first domain, most influentially in utilitarian or Kantian terms, and of the second, mainly through accounts of the virtuous life traceable back to Aristotle. For a mapping of the third domain, however, we must turn to various religious traditions or spiritual paths – or to work such as Murdoch's, which is an attempt to give it *philosophical* articulation.

Neither Murdoch nor Taylor sets out to define or delimit the terrain of 'spirituality'. This may be as well since the very term is perhaps unfortunate: it too easily invites a specialisation similar to, though perhaps the obverse of, that undergone by 'morality'. If the latter term signifies only duty and rules, 'spirituality' is supposed to capture a higher, more discretionary type of self-cultivation to which, exceptionally, people can be lifted. But the danger here does not only arise from the reifying potential of an abstract noun; it is reinforced by a well-established tendency in contemporary culture. Whereas for Murdoch and Taylor the spiritual maps on to ordinary experience and occupies a conceptual space already densely marked by substantive ethical and religious traditions, in common parlance now 'spirituality' increasingly refers to a zone, discontinuous with the ordinary, in which the self develops special qualities or powers that are supposed to be already latent in itself or available through 'spiritual' channels to which it can gain access.

If there is work of conceptual analysis to be done here, perhaps a first important clarification is to notice what is obscured when 'spiritual' is used as a valorising term, as in 'she's a very spiritual person'. This is the fact that everyone, inescapably, is spiritual – in the sense that there is *some* overall orientation to their lives, some assumption, however implicit, of what most matters or is most worthy of care. Any concept of the spiritual, then, that simply counterposes it to the material, will not do. For, to a considerable extent, the spiritual *is* how various aspects of material life, not least the body itself as well as food and possessions, are disposed and valued. A view that ignores, or even denies, the existence of anything beyond 'this life' (i.e. life in a material body) is still not without its own spirituality – so that, for example, Taylor can refer to what he calls the 'affirmation of ordinary life' (the concern to prolong life, increase prosperity, and ameliorate suffering), even when it amounts to a claim that this is the *only* life, as 'a powerful constitutive strand of modern Western spirituality'(1996: 22). A second, related point of clarification, then, is that spirituality is not to be ascribed exclusively to individuals or confined to purely private experience. It is not only modern individualism, reinforced by liberalism as a powerful political philosophy, that tends in this direction; with the example of a Socrates, a Jesus, or a Buddha, many spiritual seekers for generations have been highly individuated, their search driven by dissatisfaction with what the immediate or dominant culture made available to them. Still, now as ever, the dominant culture carries its own spiritual energies, of whatever character. And so it is an impoverishment rather than an intensification of any particular 'spirituality' if, confined to private experiences, it does not, for example, inform political debates or help to shape the economic policies of a society.

I have been suggesting that 'spiritual' characterises not a special domain of experience but rather the overall burden and direction of any life or way of life and that, as such, it is not an honorific term: one does not dignify a person or culture by calling it spiritual. It does not follow from this, however, that evaluation has no place with respect to the spiritual; it is just that evaluation is be carried out in terms of the familiar polarities of true and false or good and bad – and not of the spiritual and unspiritual. But true and good have a peculiarly intimate, reflexive relation to spirit. It is not just that a spirituality, like much else, can be true and good or false and bad. It is also the case that *truth and goodness are themselves defining goods of the spirit* or, in Simone Weil's term, 'needs of the soul'. And so a spirituality is true or good precisely when it satisfies and furthers our pursuit of truth and goodness, and is false or bad when it frustrates, or deflects us from, that pursuit.

II

How one construes spirituality, then, will be closely bound up with how one understands our condition with respect to truth and goodness. Murdoch's understanding of this condition is a reworking (influenced by Simone Weil and taking Freud seriously) of Plato's post-lapsarian vision. The knowledge that we acquire in our default state, and formulate through the medium of public, uniformly available concepts and language, will not serve to orientate us to the good. It is not so much ignorance as illusion that puts us off track. We are caught up in a kind of phantasy – projection of the 'fat, relentless ego' – that holds us back from accurate, just perception of others, of our own motives, and of what lies before us in different situations to be acknowledged or accomplished. To possess *this* kind of knowledge is at the same time to be enabled to act – this is the truth of the Socratic equation of virtue with knowledge. But such knowledge is only acquired, against the resistance of much that entrenches us in our present ways, through a transformation of vision, a retuning of psychic energy. As Plato depicts it most vividly in the allegory of the cave, it requires a 'turning around' and 'ascent' of the soul – what we might call a spiritual awakening, or the finding and following of a spiritual path. This process is one of *askesis* – purification of the emotional springs of knowledge and action that requires alert attention and ever renewed effort. But it is also, in Plato's sense, *erotic* – driven by the desire aroused in us by a goodness and beauty that, as it is becomes more manifest, has power to delight and attract us further along the path.

This kind of understanding of the dynamics and blockages in the human psyche that condition our openness to goodness and truth frames a spirituality that is exigent and inextricably bound to ethical life. Ethical life here certainly includes that of the plain person or 'virtuous peasant'; and so it is to be distinguished from its philosophical articulation by a Murdoch, a Plato, or whomever. Still the relation of philosophy to spiritual/ethical living can be more active and internal than that of mere articulation. Or, rather, articulation may itself be more than 'mere': as well as defining what we should desire to do or be, it may also inspire or *move* us to do and be it – so that philosophy can, even if less efficaciously, have the same edifying function as stories and parables depicting the exemplary deeds and lives of real or fictional characters. It can achieve this by its particular power to elicit and direct *attention* – which for Weil (1977) is the purpose of all intellectual work. Moreover, and more radically, philosophy can be reconceived so that it is not primarily concerned with articulation. If this now seems a weird claim given the thorough professionalisation of philosophy as a discipline in the secular academy not to speak of the managerialist, instrumentally driven, contemporary university – it had a lot to recommend it to Plato, especially the Plato of the *Seventh Letter* and the *Phaedrus* and *Symposium*. And it was to become the working assumption of Hellenistic and Roman schools in later antiquity.

In recent writing nothing has more powerfully brought this historical and philosophical fact to our attention than Pierre Hadot's *Philosophy as a Way of Life*. Hadot shows how ancient philosophy did not consist in 'teaching an abstract theory much less in the exegesis of texts – but rather in the art of living', which was also of course, from Plato's *Phaedo* onwards, the art of dying. As such, it was primarily a therapeutics of the passions, especially of 'unregulated desires and exaggerated fears', aimed at a 'profound transformation of the individual's mode of seeing and being' (p. 83). This transformative intention and the practical means taken to pursue it are most evident in the Stoic and Epicurean schools. Each of these had its own spiritual tenor; while the Stoic emphasised rational sovereignty through the cultivated ability to limit one's care to matters one can affect and to contemplate those outside one's control from the perspective of an impassive cosmos, the Epicurean encouraged a more insouciant and joyful appreciation of the gift of existence in each moment. But both schools initiated students into practical disciplines designed to increase vigilance and lucid self-presence in the conduct of life. And study of the schools' theories, not least their physical doctrines, was intended to engrave them on the soul so that they came to constitute a rule of life operative in every situation. Moreover, there was no great difference between the aim of theoretical pursuits as framed in these explicitly psychagogic schools and that of classical dialectic as envisaged by Plato and even by Aristotle. The often tortuous dialectical movement can be understood not as the immanent unfolding of abstract thought but as responsive in every case to the given state and particular make-up of the individual interlocutor who at each step must be persuaded and moved.

And this engagement of the interlocutor in the actuality of his beliefs and dispositions in all their idiosyncrasy is necessary just because the aim of dialectic was to bring him beyond his individual state to participate in *Logos* and an apprehension of the Good.

The best term that Hadot finds to designate a wide array of practices in the philosophical schools of antiquity is *'spiritual* exercises' (acknowledging that this expression is 'a bit disconcerting for a contemporary reader', he considers as alternatives – only to reject them – 'psychic', 'moral', 'ethical' and 'intellectual'). And this integration of theoretical endeavour within a programme designed to bring about 'the indispensable metamorphosis of our inner self' was carried forward not only in neo-Platonism but also in the new Christian *philosophia* of early church fathers such as Origen, Clement of Alexandria and Augustine. It began to fall apart, so Hadot suggests, only with the rise of scholasticism, when:

> [t]heology became conscious of its autonomy *qua* supreme science, while philosophy was emptied of its spiritual exercises which, from now on, were relegated to Christian mysticism and ethics. Reduced to the rank of 'handmaiden of theology', philosophy's role was henceforth to furnish theology with conceptual – and hence purely theoretical – material. When, in the modern age, philosophy regained its autonomy, it still retained many features inherited from this medieval conception. In particular, it maintained its purely theoretical character, which evolved in the direction of a more and more thorough systematization.
>
> (Hadot 1995: 107–8)

This characterisation of philosophy's evacuation of spiritual substance – or abandonment of any designs on students' souls – whatever its warrant as a historical judgement on scholasticism, captures well my first experience of philosophy in the seminary (though it was *analysis* perhaps, rather than sytematisation, that had now become 'more and more thorough').

III

Philosophy's loss in the transition from antiquity is one issue. The more important one here, however, is the fate of spirituality when it is separated from philosophy – *and* when the religion within which it had come to be articulated and practised itself goes through its modern decline. It might be expected that spirituality would now align with ethics – an ethics of ordinary life largely uninstructed by philosophy and increasingly unbound from religion. But what if ethics undergoes its own crisis? Here Alasdair MacIntyre's diagnosis in *After Virtue* seems apposite. The crisis of ethics that MacIntyre depicts in that book is related to the philosophical feebleness of emotivism. But, more consequentially, it is related to a wider cultural milieu in which the figures of the 'aesthete', the 'therapist' and the 'manager' have become leading character types. These types are the cultural embodiments of emotivism: their prominence on the social scene is evidence of its now being not so much one moral theory among others as an accurate formulation of the dominant assumptions of an entire society and culture. The chief assumption is that there is no longer 'any genuine distinction between manipulative and non-manipulative social relations' (MacIntyre 1984: 22). It is MacIntyre's thesis that the culture in which this assumption is in place, and of which these three 'characters' are representative figures, undermines the enabling conditions for reliable acquisition and exercise of virtue (for him, the cardinal concept of ethics). But one might also argue that, despite or perhaps rather because of this fact, it has provided hospitable ground for many ersatz versions of 'spirituality'.

MacIntyre draws his figure of the aesthete by reference to the characters of Ralph Touchett and Gilbert Osmond in Henry James's *The Portrait of a Lady*, and what he sees as their forerunners in the characters of the young Rameau in Diderot's *Rameau's Nephew* and 'A' in Kierkegaard's *Either/Or* (the classic account of the aesthetic as altogether unmoored from both the ethical and the religious). Aesthetes are people who see in the social world

> nothing but a meeting place for individual wills, each with its own set of attitudes and preferences and who understand that world solely as an arena for the achievement of their own satisfaction, who interpret reality as a series of opportunities for their enjoyment and for whom the last enemy is boredom.
>
> (MacIntyre 1984: 25)

Their social world being one in which 'large sums of money have created some social distance from the necessity of work', they are people 'with a plethora of means [who must search] restlessly for ends on which . . . [to] employ them' (MacIntyre 1984: 25). Since this search is of its nature both indeterminate and desperate, it can lead to surprising places – some with a 'spiritual' character – while at the same time ensuring that they are not engaged with seriously. As MacIntyre observes:

> [S]o great can the burden of enjoying oneself become, so clearly can the emptiness and boredom of pleasure appear as a threat, that the aesthete sometimes has to resort to even more elaborate devices than were available to the younger Rameau or to 'A'. He may even become an addicted reader of Kierkegaard and make of that despair which Kierkegaard saw as the aesthete's fate a new form of self-indulgence.

And if over-indulgence in despair seems to be injuring his capacities for enjoyment, he will take himself to the therapist, just as he would for over-indulgence in alcohol, and make of his therapy one more aesthetic experience.

(MacIntyre 1984: 73)

With the animus in these remarks, MacIntyre may seem an unreliable, because excessively unsympathetic, witness regarding our current spiritual condition. However, in fastening on the aesthete and the therapist, and on the link between them, he identifies, I believe, a crucially important feature of contemporary culture in our 'advanced' western societies. Indeed, in presenting these as archetypal characters he perhaps understates the case. For they have long since migrated from the fictions of great writers, where their appearance is still layered with irony, to the 'Living' and 'Life-style' sections of our 'quality' newspapers, where they appear not as an especially privileged élite but as within range of easy emulation by the average reader. Rather than speak of *the* aesthete and *the* therapist as iconic figures, representing specialised zones of experience or expertise, we can speak of a whole contemporary sensibility that is pervasively aesthetic and of an entire culture that has absorbed and naturalised the therapeutic mode. All this is, of course, closely related to greater and more widely diffused levels of affluence and to the consumer culture thereby spawned. But consumption now is not just a matter of material goods; connoisseurship has shifted focus from objects to experiences – experiences that somehow enhance, intensify or express the self. And the kind of sublimation involved in this shift creates a receptivity to, indeed a vogue for, a wide array of spiritualities. If religion was once the opium of the impoverished proletariat, spirituality is now the opium of the affluent middle classes.

So far from acting as a critical check on the aesthetic, then, spirituality is recruited as one more form of aesthetic consumption (a recent article in a 'Home and Interiors' magazine recommends setting up a 'spirituality corner', as well as a 'career corner', in one's house). It is sought out as a special zone of elevating or refining experiences that open up a higher dimension of selfhood. Or it is seen as a kind of psychological virtuosity enabling one to negotiate the whole gamut of experiences, adroitly avoid-ing or transmuting negative ones, while maintaining a harmonious and mobile sense of self. It is here that therapy becomes a conspicuous medium of the spiritual. For therapy is no longer just a healing art predi-cated on psychological ailment or pathology; in service to the aesthetic, its goal is to optimise functioning, bringing power and fluency to one's external transactions and tranquillity and ease to one's inner experi-ences. Freud himself was famously hostile to any notion of the spiritual, with the irrationalism and mysticism that he assumed to be its natural accompaniment. But, already in the first generation of psychoanalysis, Jung valorised 'soul', construing the work of 'individuation' which therapy was designed to serve as an inward journey or spiritual quest. And since the 1960s, humanistic and transpersonal psychologies have combined with a burgeoning interest in eastern and 'new age' thinking to create a whole scene – replete with workshops and retreats as well as books, magazines and journals in the 'self-help' or 'mind-body-spirit' sections of bookshops – in which therapy and spirituality have become virtually indistinguishable.

The orientation of this kind of spirituality seems very different from that of the third character in MacIntyre's trinity of modern characters, the 'manager' whose governing norm is *effectiveness* especially as underwritten by scientifically accredited knowledge of human functioning. But, as MacIntyre himself observes, the hallmark of the therapeutic is the way in which 'truth has been displaced as a value and replaced by psychological effectiveness' (1984: 30–31). And effectiveness – largely, though not exclusively, psychological – is also the driving motivation of much contemporary spirituality. To be sure, the means to effectiveness in a great deal of this spirituality are paranormal, embracing such diverse phenomena as crystals, channelling, near-death experiences, miracles, and angels (see Wuthnow 1998: ch. 5); and therapy and management, if their basis is supposed to lie in the reliably predictive knowledge of the new human sciences, may seem at a safe distance from all this. But for MacIntyre there is no such scientific basis for either management or therapy – so that, in both cases, effectiveness is more a masquerade than a reality. Moreover, 'spirituality' itself is not slow to co-opt science to its cause. Thus, for example, a recent book on 'spiritual intelligence' informs us that researchers at the University of California have discovered 'a built-in spiritual centre . . . located among neural connections in the temporal lobes of the brain', which they have named the 'God spot' (Zohar and Marshall 2000).

MacIntyre's account of what is inimical to ethical life, I have tried to show, also gets purchase on what distorts many contemporary approaches to spirituality. It doing so, it illustrates something that I take as essential to the spiritual – the fact that it must not be divorced from the ethical. In place of a cultural landscape dominated by the figures of the aesthete, the therapist and the manager, MacIntyre goes on to depict 'practices', the 'narrative unity of a life' and 'tradition' as together providing the context within which virtues can be realised and made intelligible. However, his reconstruction of these concepts does not, I believe, provide resources for a rich articulation of spirituality. And if this is the case, it illustrates another essential fact about the spiritual: that, though inseparable from, it is also irreducible to, the ethical – even to the relatively expansive conception of the latter (as 'field' rather than 'corral') entertained by MacIntyre.[1]

Practices, as he understands them, provide for MacIntyre the most sub-stantial sites where virtues are acquired and exercised. While 'practice' has a wide denotative range, in every case – architecture, farming, chess, chemistry, and so on – there are standards and goods internal to that particular practice which, if the practitioner succeeds in meeting and achieving them reliably, lead to her acquiring (in addition to specific com-petencies and technical skills) *virtues* such as, according to the context, patience, courage, truthfulness or justice. Now one might point out that this notion of practice does not accommodate the kind of exercise that a Buddhist undertakes in her practice (as she calls it) of *zazen* – the act of sitting in stillness and silence with no intention other than the cultivation of mindfulness, including compassionate apprehension of the suffering and impermanence of human life and lucid, deeply embodied attentive-ness in all one's activities and comportment (and even *this* intention is renounced in the mere sitting). Or one might notice that MacIntyrean 'practice' makes no gesture to the idea that simple things can be done wholeheartedly in a spirit of service or of reverence (as suggested in the Benedictine motto, *laborare est orare* or in the beautiful Puritan saying that 'God loveth adverbs').[2] But these points, even if valid, do not indicate the full distance between the ethical as construed by MacIntyre and the spiritual.

IV

There is a kind of internality that this notion of practice – despite its valu-able insistence on the priority of internal goods to external goods and the all too easy corruption of the former by the latter – does not capture and that, as I shall argue, is crucial to any adequate articulation of the spiritual dimension of human life. Here I want to return to and elaborate on some-thing I said at the end of section I: that truth and goodness are themselves defining goods of the spirit or 'needs of the soul'. I follow Raimond Gaita in using soul here in the ordinary sense conveyed by such expressions as 'soul-destroying work' or 'suffering that lacerates the soul', or even 'soul music'. 'Man that is born of a woman hath but a short time to live, and is full of misery.' Having quoted these words, Gaita immediately goes on: 'Life conceived in these accents of sorrow and pity is the natural home for talk of the soul' (Gaita 2000: 239). But in an earlier chapter he had also quoted Pablo Casals' words about his beginning every day by playing some preludes and fugues of Bach:

> It is a sort of benediction on the house . . . It is a re-discovery of the
> world of which I have the joy of being a part. It fills me with awareness

of the wonder of life, with a feeling of the incredible marvel of being a human being.

(Gaita 2000: 219)

Our vulnerability to suffering and our inevitable journey towards death, our exposure to sadness and grief – not least through our often unfathomable attachments to others – *and* our capacity to be moved to joy and gratitude by the goodness and beauty of the world reveal the spiritual dimension of life. 'Soul' or 'spirit' here owes nothing to metaphysical argument about immaterial substances nor does it presuppose religious faith. Rather, religion itself would scarcely be intelligible were human beings not spiritual in the sense just specified. To say this is not to undercut religious claims or to suggest that for sophisticated people religion ought to be replaced by 'spirituality' (much as for Hegel it is to be properly sublated into art and philosophy). But it is to agree with Gaita when, with particular reference to Casals' words, he suggests that people who associate the spiritual only with the religious are left with 'a barren conception of what is honestly available to someone who is not religious, by which I mean, to someone who cannot speak God's name in prayer or in worship' (pp. 220–21).

If I have correctly identified what we point to with the language of 'spirit' and 'soul', it still remains to specify more adequately its particular character. Disordered passions can interfere with the kind of selfless exercise of intelligence needed to achieve the internal goods of a practice such as chemistry or chess; hence, acquisition of the virtues that order these passions – for example patience or temperance – may be a necessary condition of such achievement. Although the good to be achieved is internal to the practice, it is *qua external cause* that the virtue is its necessary condition. It is otherwise, however, if we consider the relationship between cognition and passion in the kind of experience that better reveals the properly spiritual character of human beings. Consider the case of a person grieving a friend's death, or being moved to compassion by someone's affliction, or being inspired with admiration and gratitude by some epiphany of goodness or beauty. In each of these cases there is knowledge and emotion. The knowledge, however, is not of the kind that can be assembled within the framework of natural science (as in chemistry) or programmed in a computer (as in chess). And the emotion is not just a potential contaminant of or aid to knowledge; rather, it is itself a form of knowledge. Grief or sympathy or joy or gratitude can be rightly or wrongly related to their respective objects, just as propositional beliefs can be rightly or wrongly related to *their* objects. In both cases, then, we properly invoke the notion of truth and falsity. But there is a crucial difference between the two cases. Whereas one may get it wrong in one's belief without thereby being *untruthful,* to be wrongly related in one's grief or joy is *ipso facto* to be untruthful – to deserve the imputation of sentimentality, shallowness or banality.

Such failure is a *spiritual* fault – and not merely (or perhaps not at all) a psychological one. Carl Rogers esteems as 'realness' in a person 'congruence' between what one 'is experiencing at an organismic level', one's 'awareness at the conscious level', and what one expresses in 'words and communications'; and he understands psychological disturbance as failure to achieve such congruence (Rogers 1961: 283–4). What is notable in this core construct of a psychologist who has hugely influenced both the development of psychotherapy itself and its outreach into the terrain of 'spirituality' is that all the salient relationships are *intra*psychic. Experience, awareness and expression are to be well attuned to each other; but none of them needs to be rightly related to a reality outside or beyond the psyche or self. A properly critical notion of the spiritual, I argue, need not dispense with this psychological construction;[3] but it would have to incorporate it into a fuller and more exigent framework where each of the different psychic levels is answerable for the adequacy of its response to the reality of the situation in which the person finds herself. This response does not just come naturally to us as a biological species; it is beyond the capability of other animals, and also beyond the compass of psychology considered as a natural science. In animals' emotional responses there is a certain infallibility; without reflection, getting it right or wrong does not arise. And if science is essentially fallibilist, it makes a virtue of its very fallibility by building reliable control of error into its defining methodology. In our responses to humanly significant situations, however, our fallibility is of a different order. When we get it wrong there is, as it were, a wrongness, an untruthfulness, in ourselves. The kind of truthfulness that we have yet to attain includes the capacity for attunement to the objective reality of an event or another person; but this attunement is itself inseparable from a quality of our own being that cannot be adequately specified without recourse to a vocabulary of critical terms such as purity and depth, or self-indulgence and superficiality. The quality which is subject to the discipline expressed by these terms is love. This is a quality of our own being only insofar as we are drawn by the good. Truth arises here as a form of the good which is the object of our love, and the love itself is already informed by the spirit of truth.

It is right to see the work of spiritual purification and deepening as objective and impersonal; love burns away the elements of particular subjectivity that are the source of our phantasy and projection. And yet nothing is more personal than this working of the spirit; it is no less individuated than a face or a voice in both of which it is expressed. An apt analogy here is with a work of art, which exists only in its utterly concrete embodiment. 'You can't say Cézanne painted apples and a tablecloth and have said what Cézanne painted' (quoted in O'Connor 1969); and the impossibility of this re-saying holds no less for literary than for plastic arts. Literature, indeed, is the most indispensable exploration of our spiritual nature – which includes our inclination to evil no less than our responsiveness to good, and the ways in which we are made vulnerable by the world to suffering as well as to joy. Because they sound the spiritual depths, great works of literature are food for the soul – much more so than 'self-help' books with their attempts at instant uplift. (Gaita refers to Primo Levi's telling of how, when he sometimes forgot much-loved lines of Dante in Auschwitz, he 'would give today's soup' to remember them (Gaita 2000: 225).) But this reference to literature should serve not only to illustrate the inextinguishably individual character of spiritual life but also to reinforce a quite different point I made earlier: the extent to which the spirituality available to individuals depends on the given resources of their culture. The existence, gratuitous and contingent, of great works of literature is a reminder of what the human spirit can be moved to – though it is also a reflection of our spiritual nature that this reminder can run dead. The most ambitious task of education is to enable students to read such literature in the spirit in which it demands to be read; but given its immersion in the kind of culture that I have depicted earlier in this essay, what are the chances that our education can rise to this challenge? Might our new busyness with importing 'spirituality' into the curriculum be only the clearest sign that it can*not*?

The reality to which we are opened as spiritual beings is unconfined; cutting deeply into us, suffering can seem bottomless, and goodness and beauty, too, have no obvious bounds. This makes it sensible to say that the work of purification or of deepening is an endless task; there is no point at which the human spirit is complete, either in comprehension of all that is given to it or in self-transparency (it is our fate, rather, to 'live and travel between truth and falsehood, good and evil, appearance and reality' (Murdoch 1992: 166)). And this is surely one reason why the idea of God has played such a large part in the history of spirituality; if our spirit must always elude our own grasp – and, in a different way, that of other human beings – it might still be searchable and knowable by God. Hence the power of St Augustine's *'tu autem eras interior intimo meo'* or of the lines of St Paul: 'For the word of God is living and active, sharper than any two-edged sword, piercing to the division of soul and spirit, of joints and marrow, and discerning the thoughts and intentions of the heart' (Hebrews 4:12). For the religious believer, God exists; but even for the unbeliever, the idea of God can gesture to the limit of our attainments and the limitlessness of our aspirations as spiritual beings.

NOTES

1 Emmanuel Levinas's reconstruction of ethics is perhaps sufficiently radical to make it an exception to my claim here about the irreducibility of the spiritual to the ethical. But to show this would require a separate essay.

2 The two ideas that supplement 'practice' in MacIntyre's elaboration of virtue, the narrative unity of a life and tradition, are helpful in safeguarding the spiritual character of human life: the former as counter to the 'psychological polytheism' (Moore 1992: 66–7)) of the 'dispersed self', and the latter as counter to the dilettantism of much contemporary spirituality. Still, they do not provide sufficient resources to characterise, as I attempt in the final section, what is most intimate to our nature as spiritual beings.

3 I say this to indicate that I am not hostile to psychotherapy *tout court* or to a *rapprochement* between it and spirituality. *Psyches therapeia* was, after all, Socrates' way of characterising his conversational style as 'care of the soul'; and the 'therapy of desire' remained integral to the ancient schools to which I referred in section II. The extraordinary recent expansion of psychotherapy is one aspect of the whole post-Romantic move towards expressive individualism as a key constitutive source of modern selfhood. This move is indeed vulnerable to multiple debasements (with regard to therapy, specifically, the classic critiques are those of Rieff (1966) and Lasch (1979)). But I am in sympathy with Taylor's (1991) attempt, against both 'boosters' and 'knockers' of this new culture, to disclose a genuine moral ideal – an 'ethics of authenticity' – at its core. As to a rapprochement, we should understand therapy as an intrinsically spiritual practice; difficulty arises only when we do the reverse, reducing 'spirituality' to 'therapy', often of the most banal kind.

REFERENCES

Dunne, Joseph (1993) *Back to the Rough Ground: 'Phronesis' and 'Techne' in Modern Philosophy and in Aristotle*, Notre Dame and London: University of Notre Dame Press.

Gaita, Raimond (2000) *A Common Humanity: Thinking about Love and Truth and Justice*, London: Routledge.

Hadot, Pierre (1995) *Philosophy as a Way of Life*, ed. Arnold I. Davidson, Oxford: Blackwell.

Lasch, Christopher (1979) *The Culture of Narcissism: American Life in an Age of Diminishing Expectations*, New York: Norton.

MacIntyre, Alasdair (1984) *After Virtue*, 2nd edition, Notre Dame: University of Notre Dame Press.

Moore, Thomas (1992) *Care of the Soul: A Guide for Cultivating Depth and Sacredness in Everyday Life*, New York: HarperCollins.

Murdoch, Iris (1983; 1961) 'Against dryness: a polemical sketch', in Stanley Hauerwas and Alasdair MacIntyre (eds), *Revisions: Changing Perspectives in Moral Philosophy*, Notre Dame: University of Notre Dame Press.

Murdoch, Iris (1992) *Metaphysics as a Guide to Morals*, London: Chatto & Windus.

O'Connor, Flannery (1969) *Mystery and Manners*, New York: Farrar, Straus & Giroux.

Rieff, Philip (1966) *The Triumph of the Therapeutic: Uses of Faith after Freud*, New York: Harper & Row.

Rogers, Carl (1961) *On Becoming a Person*, London: Constable.

Taylor, Charles (1991) *The Ethics of Authenticity*, Cambridge, MA: Harvard University Press.

Taylor, Charles (1992) *Sources of the Self: The Making of the Modern Identity*, Cambridge, MA: Harvard University Press.

Taylor, Charles (1996) 'Iris Murdoch and moral philosophy', in Maria Antonaccio and William Schweiker (eds), *Iris Murdoch and the Search for Human Goodness*, Chicago and London: University of Chicago Press.

Weil, Simone (1977) *Waiting on God*, trans. Emma Crauford, London: Harper-Collins.

Wuthnow, Robert (1998) *After Heaven: Spirituality in America since the 1950s*, Berkeley: University of California Press.

Zohar, D. and Marshall, I. (2000) *Spiritual Intelligence: The Ultimate Intelligence*, London: Bloomsbury.

Chapter 8

Images of spirituality

Traditional and contemporary

Iris M. Yob

'Spirituality' is another of those words that Nelson Goodman might well have called 'promiscuous' (Goodman 1976: 171). It is the kind of term that is handed around in many different contexts and takes on many different meanings. It is as though common usage has not agreed on whether spirituality is congruent with religion, a feature of religion, independent of religion, or counter to religion; whether it indicates a human quality or an extra-human incursion; whether it denotes a real or imagined event, something natural or contrived, has a subjective or objective focus, is collectively or privately experienced; or whether it is only a psychological event.

However, simply offering a definition for spirituality, even if it were to be generally accepted (which is unlikely given the range of vested interests and passionate commitments involved with particular meanings), is not necessarily the most helpful way to clear up the confusion surrounding the term. By its reductionist nature, a literal definition is at most the starting point to worlds of meaning constructed around the defined term. Cultural and other contextual influences, personal and collective histories, specific applications and extensions of the term give colour and depth and particularity to the way individuals understand it. If one is really to know a term, one needs to grapple with it at the level of these enriched meanings. In other words, a definitive answer to the question, 'What is spirituality?', is likely to rob spirituality of its power to inspire and guide educational practice by casting it too narrowly, too poorly, whereas an imaginative exploration permits both critical analysis and the search for appropriate applications. Here we shall examine traditional western constructions of spirituality, especially their most problematic features, and appraise some contemporary images to discover to what extent they have addressed these past problems.

TRADITIONAL CONSTRUCTIONS

In western thought, the notion of spirituality has had a long career embedded in the triad, physical–mental–spiritual, and the equally prevalent dyad, material–spiritual. With this heritage, finding a place for spirituality in the public school arena is threatened on two fronts: the fragmented nature of human being it assumes and the ostensibly religious connotations it conjures up. However, while these two potentially damaging features of 'spirituality' are entrenched, they are not necessarily intransigent and may possibly serve as starting points for a more inclusive and more potent understanding of the life of the spirit and its role in schooling.

THE MIND–BODY–SPIRIT SPLIT

Spirit comes from the Latin, *spiritus*, literally denoting 'breath' or 'the breath of life'. The Greek equivalent was *psyche*, generally understood to be a subtle, breath-like principle that animates the living person and survives the death of the body to exist eternally as a shade or shadow. The distinction of spirit and matter and the consequent superiority of the soul to the material body were early explored by the Pythagoreans and Orphics, most clearly delineated in Platonic thought (see *Phaedo*, for instance), and inform an Idealist understanding of the nature of human being and human destiny. The Platonic account has a great deal of imagery that eventually found its restatement in Christian theology – especially the notion of the soul departing the body at death for another world where it is judged and if necessary purified. Such a dualistic conception had been largely foreign to Jewish thought that also formed a backdrop to Christian anthropology (Robinson 1926 [1911]: 12–21).

Through a slow process of syncretism, conscious or unconscious, however, Greek ideas increasingly came to temper later developments in Christian theology and some branches of Jewish thought, culminating in Augustine, whose contributions to theological anthropology have been among the most influential. Swayed by Platonic thought, he distinguished body and soul but, more definitively than his predecessors, he redirected metaphysical dualism toward ethical and religious dualism. Body now was clearly aligned with sin; soul with grace (Robinson 1926 [1911]: 158–61).

The dualism introduced in the Patristic era continued to be influential in the development of Christian doctrine and western thought right through to the Protestant reformers. However, the doctrine of the separation of soul and body finds its modern reprisal most notably with René Descartes (1596–1650), who maintained the existence of two different kinds of substance: physical, extended substance, which has dimensions and so can be measured; and thinking substance, which is unextended and indivisible. The body belongs to the first category; the soul or mind to the second. With these assumptions in place, he devoted considerable effort to addressing some of the consequent philosophical problems; chiefly, how do soul and body interact? An antagonistic division between spirit or mind and body has continued under various guises and modifications, with the accompanying elevation of mind forming the foundational assumption about human being that undergirded Enlightenment self-understanding.[1]

Quite clearly, from the beginning, dualism has done more than simply divide human nature into distinct parts. It has also assigned values to each of the parts and hierarchically arranged them. Without exception, spirit has been regarded as higher and nobler, usually immortal, invariably aligned with light, the good, the pure; body as lower, baser, mortal, corrupt, evil, dark. As such, body has usually been regarded as an impediment to soul, to be denied (through celibacy, fasting, poverty, and so on) and punished (through flagellation and penance, for example), or, in some views, treated as irrelevant, so that one could indulge any appetite one desired without affecting the soul, which remained bright and true like a diamond even though it had been cast into the muck of bodiliness.

Strictly dualistic constructions of spirit and matter have shortchanged both spirit and matter. The perceived gulf between the two prohibits conceiving of spirit drawing its energy and inspiration from the rest of life's experiences or finding expression or development in otherwise secular or bodily activity. Instead the focus of the spirit is on the transcendent and the hereafter. The legacy of 'other-worldliness', the goal and destiny of the soul, and a corresponding devaluing of the 'this-worldliness', the home of the body, has paradoxically also undergirded an exploitation and/or disregard for the earth and its resources, its women and their children, and its poorer and 'undeveloped' people. The challenge for contemporary constructions of spirituality is to address this tension between spirit and matter in such a way that both are given their rightful due as parts of the whole of what we know as human life in its fullness.

RELIGIOUS CONNOTATIONS

Inseparable from spirit–body dualism are the traditionally religious connotations of spirituality. The spirit, separately considered and independently nurtured, became the domain of religious organisations, schooling took charge of the mind, and common life claimed the body. Across times and cultures, the soul has essentially been a religious term, an entity that has been the focus of priestly endeavour, the subject of religious exhortation, and the object of religious discipline. Even today, the term spirituality does not easily shake off an accumulation of religious glosses, which can serve as a powerful disincentive to state-run schools to engage in spiritual education.

The conceptual advantage of distinguishing religion and spirituality is that it allows one to speak of an individual as spiritual who does not profess any religion at all. This prompted, at least in part, Robert Coles' choice of spiritual over religious in his *The Spiritual Life of Children* (Coles 1990: xvii). As one reads through his record of conversations with children who had no formal connection with organised religion, however, it is apparent that many use religious terms ('God-talk') to talk about their views on untimely deaths, fate, human origins and destiny, the natural world, poverty, good fortune, sin, the soul, the meaning of life, beauty and mystery, and the supernatural. It seems that when non-religious children borrow religious terms to name the realities they are wrestling with, the labels are not without some of their original content (Coles 1990: 292). Even if all that religion offers non-religious thinkers are categories and concepts to structure and concretise the field on which they grapple with spiritual matters, this narrows the gap between religion and spirituality.

And yet, there is also a sense in which the two terms are not wholly interchangeable. On one dimension, 'religion' indicates more than spirituality. It refers also to the accoutrements designed to nurture and promote spirituality: systematised beliefs, prescribed behaviours, a community of followers, supported by specific sacred texts, rituals, art, music, architecture, authorities, and traditions. 'Spirituality', along another dimension, indicates more than religion. While it may be sustained and stimulated by religion, it may also be prompted by or nurtured from other sources – secular works of art, natural phenomena, dreams, the experience of an accident, illness, or death of a loved one, for instance.

Yet again, even in these different dimensions, the distinction between religion and spirituality is not absolute. Both can be comprehended by the same metaphors (for instance, both are pictured as a pilgrimage)[2] of transformation (both imply the transcendence of one's narrow self-interests). Additionally, the meanings sought by both religious and spiritual persons are prompted by the same kinds of questions: Where do I come from? Who am I? What is my purpose and destiny? The search for answers in either case is not only a cognitive activity. It is informed by and informs affective response as well – hope, *angst*, awe, wonder, feelings of dependency, interdependency, or independency, and so on. It is expressed in similar behaviours – how one relates to others, to oneself, to the exigencies and crises of life, and to the future. Since the generative questions, the available vocabulary, the accompanying emotional life, and the resultant behaviours of both religion and spirituality are often indistinguishable, it is not surprising that the two concepts may appear somewhat synonymous.

The contemporary educational challenge, then, is to construct a notion of spirituality that encompasses the full range of personal spiritualities, including those that draw on a foundation of religious beliefs as well as those that are agnostic and atheistic, and those that may be independent of or contrary to a prevailing religious or non-religious view. In other words, contemporary images of spiritual education need to be responsive to the pluralism that reflects the broader spectrum of religiously and non-religiously based spiritual perspectives in the larger community.

CONTEMPORARY METAPHORS

So far, 'spirituality' has been pictured mostly in terms of what it is not: it is not located in an isolatable part of the human personality, and while it is not reducible to religion, neither is it necessarily either religious or non-religious. In contemporary thought, including current Christian thinking, new images of spirituality are emerging that reflect at some level both a rejection and development of traditional constructions. Here our discussion focuses on some fresh Christian images because historically Christian thought has been the dominant force shaping state-run education in much of the West. In the context of today's classroom, two questions will be addressed: To what extent have these images overcome the dualism of traditional notions of spirituality? and, How inclusively have they dealt with the religious/non-religious manifestations of spirituality?

PAUL TILLICH'S 'ULTIMATE CONCERN'

Tillich may seem a little outdated in this context: 'ultimate concern' was popularised in *Dynamics of Faith*, published eight years before his death in 1965 and had been lurking in his written work for a number of years before that. However, 'ultimate concern' still remains a stock metaphor in many recent discussions of spirituality and spiritual education (see, for instance, Eck 1993: 54, 55, 91; Myers 1997: 95; Purpel 1989: 82, 111–12) and is one of the most fully elaborated in current usage.

In his analysis of the human situation, Tillich identified what he considered to be inescapable – the certain awareness of one's own finitude and the anxiety and fear that this produces. Describing the human situation as one of existential *angst*, since human beings live under the threat of non-being – death, meaninglessness, and condemnation – Tillich concluded that they are driven to ask 'the ontological question' (1955a: 9). This could be in the form: Why am I going to die? or Can I escape dying? or What is the meaning of my death? Existential *angst* may not be as popular a characterisation of the present mind-set as it was in mid-twentieth century but, expressed positively, the question might be restated, 'What is the meaning of life?', and that has a very contemporary ring. The asking and the answering of these kinds of questions Tillich described as manifestations of 'ultimate concern' (1967a 1: 14).

The *ultimacy* of the concern refers to the nature of what the concern is about – it is about that which is ultimately significant, 'the ground of all that is' (1967b: 80–82). Expressing this ultimate as *concern*, Tillich intended to direct attention to its experiential and personal character in that it refers to an inner human posture and as such is a matter of infinite passion and interest (1967a 1: 12). Deliberately ambiguous, 'ultimate concern' refers both to one's being ultimately concerned, a subjective experience, and it also refers to the focus of one's ultimate concern, the objective element in that experience (1965: 7, 11). Ultimate concern is what is known, felt, and striven for, as well as the knowing, feeling, and striving itself. And so in typical tautology, he says: 'Ultimate concern is concern about the ultimate' (1957: 12).[3]

This description reflects something of a wholistic understanding of human being. In Tillich's words, being ultimately concerned is 'the most centered act of the human mind', integrating all the disrupted elements within the individual and, for that matter, the community, brought about by humankind's estrangement from the power of being, giving 'depth, direction, and unity' to all other concerns and the human personality itself (1957: 4–8, ch. IV).

This notion of ultimate concern, however, does have its limitations. In today's harried world, people have many and varied concerns which occupy them in turn. If they can find a unifying foundation that gives meaning to all these concerns, it might be argued, their energies would be better directed and even renewed. Unfortunately, many would not be able to articulate or identify a defining ultimate in their experience and might even regard such a notion as irrelevant or merely an intellectual tour de force. It seems most at home in the Jerusalem faiths (Judaism, Christianity, and Islam) with their focus on a Holy Other, somewhat forced in Hinduism with its pantheon of gods, possibly recognisable in Buddhism enlightenment but inapplicable in many indigenous forms of meaning making, and counter-intuitive in the eclectism of many of the New Age movements. Fundamentally, it assumes a particularly rationalistic base to spiritual experience that is not universally applicable.

Notions of ultimacy, moreover, imply hierarchies and a hierarchy implies a split between upper and lower levels. Tillich describes ultimate concern as the sense of the 'entirely other', that which is 'apart from the ordinary realm of things'. For him, ultimacy is transcendent, concern for which directs one above and beyond the messiness of everydayness. But since humanity, by its very nature, is caught up in everydayness, this ultimacy demands a reaching beyond and dissociation from immediate reality.

In fact, the more closely one's 'ultimate concern' is connected with the ordinary, the more Tillich condemns it as unworthy and prone to become a mere idol. What is immediate can at most serve as a symbol pointing to the ultimate,[4] so spirituality is focused not on the material world but on that to which its symbols may point. The old dualism has not totally disappeared: the immanent world we occupy with its needs, challenges, responsibilities, relationships, joys, and occupations, fades in significance and meaning in the light of higher considerations. 'Ultimate concern' goes only part way toward resolving the spirit–matter dichotomy.

One of the appeals of the metaphor 'ultimate concern' is that it includes non-religious experience along with religious (1963: 3–12), although, as earlier noted, not all forms of religion are equally well represented by the image. In interfaith dialogue (and interfaith classrooms), 'God' is not a universally appropriate label for the object of faith but the notion of 'ultimate concern' provides some common language by which to communicate and articulate different faiths.[5] In treating the religious–nonreligious tension by employing 'ultimate concern', in place of notions such as 'God', Tillich, however, intends to do more than provide an inclusive term. By his definition, ultimate concern is religious experience. It is a matter of faith, a coming into awareness of the holy and whatever becomes a matter of ultimate concern is made into a god (1957: 44). This makes ultimate concern a universal human phenomenon (e.g. 1967a 2: 9, 3: 130; 1965: 7, 8) which 'everybody experiences . . . at some time or place', although it may not always be recognised as such (1965: 27, 28, 44, 183).

In describing religion in ontological terms and thus making it universal and inevitable, however, he is giving the term 'religion' a very wide meaning. As Sidney Hook has pointed out, Tillich 'has converted "erring souls" by arbitrary definition' (Hook 1984: 133, 134)! Religion is so broadly defined that it covers a vast array of human concerns, however non-religious these things are otherwise judged to be. Addressing the issue of religious versus non-religious expressions of spirituality by eliminating the non-religious category in this way treats the presence or absence of formal religion as an irrelevancy when for many it is anything but that. Despite this rather dubious reformulation, his notion of 'ultimate concern' lingers in discussions of spirituality because it remains one of the most inclusive terms currently available to cover the realm of talk about the foci, purposes, and experiences of spirituality.

PARKER PALMER'S 'TROTHFULNESS'

Where Tillich wrote primarily as a theologian and philosopher, in *To Know as We are Known: A Spirituality of Education*, Palmer writes as an educator and for educators, casting his understanding of spirituality within the classroom. Knowing that is prompted by the desire to exercise control over what is known is characterised by its attention to facts, theories, objectivity, and reality, which is approached through the head while the heart is kept out of it (Palmer 1983: 22–4). He argues that this view of knowing is the legacy of dualistic views of human being, producing knowers who are alienated from the world they know and what is known is alienated from them.[6] Spiritual knowing, by contrast, is driven by compassion and love that 'implicates the learner in the web of life' so that he or she and whatever is known are called to 'involvement, mutuality, and accountability' (pp. 8, 9). The grounding metaphor of this understanding of spirituality and knowledge is 'troth', or 'covenant', as reflected in the word 'betrothed', and root meaning for the word 'truth'. The significance of this metaphor is summarised thus: 'To know in truth is to become betrothed, to engage the known with one's whole self, an engagement one enters with attentiveness, care, and goodwill' (p. 31).

One of the implications of this metaphor is that troth involves the active participation of two parties – the knower and the known. This suggests that what is known brings with it something that can impact on the knower, some demand for response, the possibility of a meaningful relationship. Parker even speaks of it as having a transcendent centre, something beyond the self and the world around us, which reaches for the learner as the learner seeks it (1983: 11–13). He describes transcendence in the Christian sense, that is, in terms of God, who created both the world and the self in love. His views are clearly shaped by his own tradition, but he hopes that his talking about these ideas from within his own religious heritage does not make them inaccessible to others with different spiritual legacies (p. xii) and in fact he encourages their wider applicability by preferring to describe transcendence in terms of love rather than of God (p. 13). This manoeuvre, however, still maintains a thoroughly Christian flavour for 'God is love' is pre-eminently a Christian construction.

Like Tillich before him, Palmer sees spirit not as an independent aspect of human being, but something thoroughly human and fully implicated in being and knowing. Nevertheless, paradoxically, he still pictures spirituality as dependent on connection with a source (God) outside of human beings. One wonders how Buddhist conceptions of 'enlightenment', or Taoist conceptions of the impersonal 'Way', or humanistic constructions would interpret this relationship.[7]

Although 'troth' is the root of 'truth', Palmer does not subscribe to an entirely cognitive kind of spirituality. Rather, troth suggests that a passionate commitment to knowing is like a passionate commitment to loving – every capacity of the learner to receive knowledge is engaged: sensation, rationality, intuition, empathy, emotion, and faith, which when combined, he believes, can move the knower beyond perception and theory into relationship with the world to be known (Palmer 1983: 52, 53).

He adds that truth, like a lover, withdraws when students fail to enter into troth wholeheartedly as well as wholeheadedly (p. 42). He urges teachers to evoke joy, awe, and wonder, address *angst*, fear, and despair, and admit faith, hope, and love into their courses of study and in so doing they may make greater progress towards developing trustworthy knowledge, appropriate attitudes, and essential skills.

Another characteristic of covenant or troth is its ethical dimension, which further serves as a corrective to an entirely 'other-worldly' focus of knowing. As betrothal demands faithfulness, trust, and responsibility, so trothful knowing is manifest in responses that are also faithful, true, and responsible to the knowledge. When 'I not only grasp truth but truth grasps me' (Palmer 1983: 58), he argues, the classroom has become an integral, interactive part of reality and students relate to this reality in purposeful, active ways. This element of Palmer's argument goes beyond the pragmatic dictum that we really believe only what we are willing to act on in that he incorporates also the moral imperative to act in ways that establish community, freedom, and the good. The picture he develops is one of interactive, constructive learning contributing to personal integrity, honesty, candidness, and sincere action.

In this account, many features that characterise the old dualism are undermined. While there lingers the sense of a divide between the spiritual person and the source, motive, and focus of spirituality, the distinct division between mind and spirit is weakened by envisioning knowing as a spiritual act played out in the real world of the knower. Likewise, spirit and body are brought together: first, by seeing the physically experienced emotions as formative influences on spiritual development and, second, by embedding the spiritual life in the rational, ethical, and behavioural aspects of being. The distance between the knower and what is known is narrowed by the claim that the two are intimately related, constructing and being constructed by the other.

MARIA HARRIS'S 'DANCE OF THE SPIRIT'

Harris begins where traditional views of spirituality falter – with the body. 'Too much spirituality from the past, both in the Eastern and Western worlds', she suggests, 'has taught withdrawal from and denial of the body, and even doing violence to the body' (1989: 8). In *Dance of the Spirit: Seven Steps to Women's Spirituality*, she participates in a project to claim the major issues and elements in women's experiences as shapers of the 'innerness' or spirituality of their lives, a process she describes in terms of a dance (p. xi). The dance metaphor, according to Harris, suggests primarily rhythm, reminiscent of the bodily rhythms natural to women, and movement, calling up images of steps, 'backward and forward, turn and return, bending and bowing, circling and spiraling' (p. xii). Connecting spirituality and dance is not original with Harris, but, wherever it occurs, dance is clearly a challenge to the traditional view of spirituality that separates spirit from body, sensuality, and passion, and spirituality from the common life.

Although Harris does not fully explicate how 'dance' overcomes the dualism that characterises most other images of spirituality, the idea is implicit in the image itself. Dance is a physical activity, involving a range of bodily movements from vigorous leaping, pirouetting, and rapid steps to balanced rest and graceful swaying. In this art, the body becomes both an instrument to express something felt or known deep within the soul and a provocation or stimulation to new insights and understandings for performers and audience. Like all artistic 'languages' or symbol systems, the meaning of a particular dance can be described, discussed, evaluated, improved on, and explained within its own cultural conventions.

In her account of the dance, Harris does not explore the full richness of the cognitive component in spiritual experience. Reflection is the primary mental capacity she encourages, along with some analysis and critique directed primarily at dominant spiritual conceptions. While she is not opposed to an intelligent spirituality, and in fact endorses it and lists a range of cognitive capacities that should be brought to bear when one is handing on spirituality especially to the young (1989: 158, 159), this feature of spirituality is only lightly explicated or otherwise left implicit in her account. Herein lies a common critique of feminist spirituality: it is judged to be too sensuous, too emotional, lacking balance from the intellect. This proclivity to the feelingful rather than the rational side of spirituality is understandable when it is seen as an antidote to the overwhelming rationalistic focus in many traditional forms of spirituality, but feminist deconstruction of patriarchal spiritualities is incomplete without a reconstruction of spirituality that is thoroughly wholistic.

The main focus of Harris's treatment of the 'dance of the spirit' is on the steps that she sees comprising its total movement: awakening, discovering, creating, dwelling, nourishing, traditioning, and transforming, each one leading to the next and extending what was begun in the previous one, so that the whole has a natural flow or progression. The first step, Awakening, is a time of heightened awareness and attending, that may be instigated by a sensuous focus on bodily reality, induced possibly by giving birth, nursing, caring for another, or sexual encounter, and that serves as a marker to a moment that 'rearranges [one's] normal perceptions and patterns, enabling newness to break in' (1989: ch. 1, especially p. 13). This, however, is simply the first step. A dance of many steps suggests that spirituality is not merely an ecstatic moment in time but a way of being, a progress of the life, including both its high and low points, concurrent with the whole history of mind and body.

An element of the dance image that Harris explicates is its communal nature. Where traditional spirituality has usually been 'synonymous with withdrawal from the world, with separating ourselves from what we love, and with severing connections', in this image, spirituality involves the 'revelation, born out of the power of our connectedness, that we are part of everyone and everything that exists'(1989: 41). She invites a more inclusive view of community than one's own religious or non-religious tradition, although this does not entail dismissing that tradition and its call on one. So while spirituality is broad in its reach, the individual remains grounded in her particular faith. At times, she admits, a dancer's insights and understandings will be uniquely her own. For example, they may be so woman-specific that men may feel alienated from them. Yet she also encourages a sharing of insights for the mutual benefit of all. This contextualising of spirituality serves both as a reminder that one form of spirituality does not fit every individual or every occasion and also as an invitation to make space for the diversity that characterises today's world of spiritual expressions. While this encourages an appreciation of both religious and non-religious spiritual communities, when it comes down to it, there is also something of a self-defeating element in this view. If the community remains intact and the individual remains part of the community, how is it possible to instate a woman-friendly spirituality when that community, its theology, and organisational forms are an entrenched patriarchy?

Harris is clearly working within a Christian world-view. The dancer has a partner, and the partner is Someone who awakens her, seeks her, dwells in her, nourishes her, traditions her, and transforms her. Envisioning God as her dance partner is certainly a major revision of the altogether Other that is featured in traditional Judaeo-Christian-Muslim constructions and represents a breaking down of the dualistic hierarchy that has created a greater remove from God for women than men. As a development of the notion of an incarnate divinity, God is pictured as physically close, an intimate partner, although still mysterious, all-powerful, the source and goal of spirituality. And possibly still gendered. Certainly still anthropomorphic. However, the dance image is sufficiently rich that one might wonder whether non-theistic faiths might prefer to focus more specifically on the choreography, or the music, or the creative, artistic energy of the dancers than on 'the partner' as the representation of what their community offers the individual as spiritual source and inspiration.

IMPLICATIONS

From this brief analysis, a number of features emerge that reflect how spirituality is understood in the present context, each feature rich with implications. First, the fact that spirituality is primarily comprehended in imagery rather than in literal and prosaic claims is again worth underlining. Although assertions may be made on the basis of grounding images, there remains something of the esoteric and mysterious, if not mystical, at the core of conceptions of spirituality. The writers examined here have grappled with language for the transcendent and ultimate, for true knowledge, and for a sense of physicality as an aesthetic conduit for the human spirit. The import of this process is enormous. Spirituality conceived imaginatively and claims made suggestively on the basis of its grounding metaphors imply that spiritual education at least begins with a corresponding aesthetic suggestiveness and imaginative construction.

Second, the images for comprehending spirituality, even in long established traditions of faith, are not static but organic. That is, they grow and re-form to meet current needs and understandings, sometimes in ways radically different from the parent image. Each of the writers discussed here begins at a different point: Tillich with transcendence and ultimacy; Palmer with knowing; and Harris with the body, and yet each in his or her own way describes the meaning and nature of contemporary spirituality for them. To varying degrees they have each addressed the untenable aspects of traditional constructions of spirituality, endeavouring to articulate a more inclusive understanding among different perspectives and incorporating all the dimensions of human experience. The implication for schools is that conscious analysis and critique of present images coupled with creative construction of corrective alternatives are skills and opportunities that inhere in spiritual ways of thinking and can be fostered for spiritual growth.[8]

Third, even the radical reformulations of spirituality by these writers have not severed them from their faith traditions even as they have adjusted to accommodate insights gained from alternative visions. At the very least, they have each dealt with the problem of absolute claims and concertedly reached out for and invited dialogue with others of different spiritual visions. In these three accounts, some predominant Judaeo-Christian categories and assumptions are questioned and criticised while at the same time serving as starting points for acknowledging other religious and non-religious constructions of meaning and value. In the public sphere, discussions about spirituality, including discussions with an educative purpose, do not depend on the kind of agreement that abandons particularity in favour of consensus. That is to say, the school's task is not to propose a common spirituality to which all can subscribe but to permit the flourishing of faith in all its forms.

Fourth, in these images the knower takes on a new wholeness. Where mind and body and soul were once seen to comprise human being, something of the old Jewish and former Christian sense of the unity, body–soul, is being reclaimed. While this bipartite formulation might appear initially weak, providing again a foundation for dualistic constructions, its primary value lies in its identification of different aspects of human wholeness which, once identified, can each be given their rightful due, both in human experience and in education. The spiritual life in its fullness is both embodied and mindful. It follows, then, that neglect of any aspect of human wholeness impacts the whole. Conversely, if human beings are understood to be a unity of different aspects, including the physical, mental, and spiritual, then wholeness is revealed, experienced, and expressed through each of them. In spiritual terms, this suggests that if spirituality were to be embraced as a domain for nurture, it may very well have an impact on mental and physical thriving. In discovering and claiming human spirit not as something apart from and opposed to human body and mind, but as part of and mutually interdependent with body and mind, nurturing spirituality would be regarded not only as an imperative but as an inevitable responsibility of educators.

Fifth, the 'promiscuity' of the term 'spirituality' that initially seemed at best challenging, at worst problematic, emerges as its most enduring and enriching feature. Clearly, spirituality takes many forms, derives its inspiration from many sources, and finds expression in many ways. The greatest strength of Tillich's image of 'ultimate concern' has been its demonstrable capacity to provide a language for people of many different faiths, religious and non-religious, to name and communicate the central essence of their spiritual experience and to dialogue across the boundaries of their own belief systems. Palmer and Harris, embedded in their respective Christian heritages, nevertheless turn their faces towards other traditions and offer their spiritual insights for dialogue with them. Harris's image of the 'dance' squarely places body back within the meaning and compass of spirituality. Her approach is clearly less cognitive than Palmer's and much less rationalistic than Tillich's, but while Tillich's image may be over-rationalised, Harris's may be under-rationalised, and a point of balance might be found somewhere between them. Palmer represents one such point with his image of 'trothfulness' – a commitment to living out the truths that one knows. The other-worldliness that is apparent in Tillich's and to some extent in Palmer's explanations is compensated for in the this-worldliness that can be found in significant parts of Harris's account, especially in the image she offers of God not as a distant Other but as a dance partner and in the role she claims for bodily experience. Considered together, each image resonates with the other images, completing, correcting, enlarging them. In the variety of metaphors that seek to capture the inspiration and understanding of spirituality at specific times and places, spirituality in its richness is more fully comprehended. That is to say, in the multi-faith classrooms of today, spiritual education is best guided by multiple visions.

NOTES

1 It should be noted that a similar separation of spirit and body has also been a predominant theme in some non-Christian and non-Western thought traditions as well. In Hindu thought, reincarnation is the belief that the soul is reborn in successive life forms, depending on the accumulation of good and bad karma during the previous incarnation. Buddhism rejects the notion of an unchanging and immortal soul, but a 'self', bearing the consequences of actions and intentions, determines consecutive lives. Jains conceive of a soul separate from body although coextensive with the body it occupies where it is the repository of good and bad karma and susceptible to pain. In shamanistic religions, the soul is understood to have the capacity to leave the body during sickness, death, dreams, or even sneezing, or it can be stolen away by sorcery. The shaman's role is to restore it to the body where it belongs.

2 Compare Coles' chapter 13, 'The Child as Pilgrim', with literal and metaphorical uses of 'pilgrim' in religious writings.

3 Using 'ultimate concern' in this dual sense to refer to both an objective and a subjective experience creates a number of difficulties. See Alston (1961) and Rowe (1968: 20), but Tillich claimed that it is beyond and subsumes simple object–subject differentiations.

4 Examples of the 'material of our daily encounter' which he suggests can be symbols in this fashion are social standing, economic power, one's parentage, the nation, an ideology (such as nationalism or socialism or the 'American way'), religion, or the God of religion. See Tillich 1957: 2–4; 1955b: 192; 1965: 29, 83.

5 Even the notion of 'God' falls short of the mark for theists, Tillich argued, if it is couched about with qualifiers and qualities which necessarily rob it of its ultimacy, so religion is not necessarily privileged as a medium for spirituality. See, for instance, Tillich 1967a 1: 14; 1957: 44–8.

6 Palmer illustrates this alienation by describing among other things the responses of the scientists who produced the first atomic bomb. Even though there had been speculation that the shot might explode the atmosphere and destroy the world, the experiment still went ahead. See Palmer 1983: 1–2.

7 In fact, Palmer criticises secular humanism for not centring on transcendence. See Palmer 1983: 12.

8 This is Nel Noddings' basic argument in *Educating for Intelligent Belief or Unbelief* (1993). See also Nord 1995.

REFERENCES

Alston, W.P. (1961) 'Tillich's conception of the religious symbol', in S. Hook (ed.), *Religious Experience and Truth*, New York: New York University Press, pp. 12–26.

Coles, R. (1990) *The Spiritual Life of Children*, Boston: Houghton Mifflin Co.

Eck, D.L. (1993) *Encountering God: A Spiritual Journey from Bozeman to Banaras*, Boston: Beacon Press.

Goodman, N. (1976) *Languages of Art*, Indianapolis: Hackett Publishing Co.

Harris, M. (1989) *Dance of the Spirit: Seven Steps to Women's Spirituality*, New York: Bantam Books.

Hook, S. (1984) *The Quest for Being*, New York: St Martin's Press.

Myers, B.K. (1997) *Young Children and Spirituality*, New York: Routledge.

Noddings, N. (1993) *Educating for Intelligent Belief or Unbelief*, New York: Teachers College Press.

Nord, W.A. (1995) *Religion and American Education: Rethinking a National Dilemma*, Chapel Hill: University of North Carolina Press.

Palmer, P. (1983) *To Know as We are Known: A Spirituality of Education*, San Francisco: Harper & Row.

Purpel, D.E. (1989) *The Moral and Spiritual Crisis in Education: A Curriculum for Justice and Passion in Education*, New York: Bergin & Garvey.

Robinson, H.W. (1926) [1911] *The Christian Doctrine of Man*, Edinburgh: T. & T. Clark.

Rowe, W.L. (1968) *Religious Symbols and our Knowledge of God: A Philosophical Study of Tillich's Theology*, Chicago: University of Chicago Press.

Tillich, P. (1955a) *Biblical Religion and the Search for Ultimate Reality*, Chicago: University of Chicago Press.

Tillich, P. (1955b) 'Religious symbols and our knowledge of God', *Christian Scholar* 38, September.

Tillich, P. (1957) *Dynamics of Faith*, New York: Harper & Row.

Tillich, P. (1963) *Christianity and the Encounter of the World Religions*, New York: Columbia University Press.

Tillich, P. (1965) *Ultimate Concern: Tillich in Dialogue*, D. Mackenzie Brown (ed.), New York: Harper & Row.

Tillich, P. (1967a) *Systematic Theology, Three Volumes in One*, Chicago: University of Chicago Press.

Tillich, P. (1967b) *My Search for Absolutes*, New York: Simon & Schuster.

Chapter 9

Scholarship and spirituality

John Sullivan

I wish to defend the following two claims: first, scholarship and spirituality are intimately connected; second, a better understanding of this connection could assist researchers and scholars in rising above inadequate frameworks and impoverishing assumptions for academic work. There are two different kinds of challenge to what I see as the optimal interaction between scholarship and spirituality, one secular, the other religious. With regard to the first challenge, secular assumptions and frameworks for academic work frequently fail to do justice to the connection between the development of personal virtues, both moral and spiritual, and the attainment of knowledge. With regard to the second challenge, some religious believers fail to do justice to the constructive and creative part played by the enquiring and critical intellect in its engagement with received, even revealed truth. They neglect the important part played by criticism, creativity and controversy in the communication of a religious tradition. Since I have addressed the second challenge elsewhere (Sullivan 2001), it is not considered here.

In revisiting a very traditional view, namely that scholarship and spirituality are intimately connected, I intend to draw attention to something that is often inadequately appreciated. The primary 'tools' of the scholar are neither the sources (or media) through which s/he works, nor the methods s/he employs in interrogating these. While the nature of the material one studies and the reliability of the methods one uses are crucial, what determines the effectiveness of scholarship are the 'inner tools,' the personal qualities, moral and spiritual, of the scholar.

There are two main steps in my argument. First, some deficiencies, from a Christian perspective, in the current academic 'climate' will be spotlighted. Here I face the threat posed by inappropriate or unduly limiting secular assumptions about scholarship. Then I shall draw from the Christian spiritual tradition some indications of how the spiritual and the intellectual are related to one another. Here I suggest ways of viewing the interaction between spirituality and scholarship that are more in keeping with Christian faith.

CURRENT DEFICIENCIES IN THE CLIMATE FOR SCHOLARSHIP

The Research Assessment Exercise (RAE) carried out every five years in UK universities seems to be a technicist task that threatens to constrain scholarly activity. Ostensibly its purpose is to promote research by rewarding researchers and facilitating further research. The RAE is a mechanism for distributing public funds made available through taxation to academic institutions that promote research efficiently according to certain limited criteria. The focus is on outcomes, the published products of research. These outcomes are assessed by panels of peers working in the principal subject areas taught in UK universities.

In the RAE, the 'rules of enagagement' press scholars to present some kinds of work and to suppress others that may be equally valuable (but not eligible). Furthermore, the focus on measurable outcomes, closely linked to a formula for future grant aid, attends insufficiently to the (legitimately varied) purposes of research and how these relate to the other purposes of an educational institution. It also pays insufficient attention to the processes involved in research, the conditions in which it is carried out, the applications to which it is deployed and the effects it has, not least upon the researchers. The emphasis on productivity, interpreted according to fairly restrictive criteria, operates in such a way as to distract attention from persons. The development of personal qualities among researchers is neglected, thereby undermining scholarship; at the same time questions about the potential significance of research for others is also neglected, thereby undermining the growth of wisdom and depth of understanding.

At a different academic level, the Department for Education and Employment (DfEE) in England and Wales recently launched a new project called Best Practice Research Scholarships. This is aimed at schoolteachers and it is intended to promote small-scale research relating to school improvement. Teachers who are successful in their applications to this project receive grant aid that supports research training, software, travel, consultancy and covers costs incurred in carrying out research during the school day. Such opportunities for teachers to reflect critically on practices that contribute to school improvement are admirable. However, once again this project slips into a technicist exercise. The topics that can be researched are tightly prescribed in advance. They operate in a vacuum; that is, no reference is made to the purposes of education. Philosophical, moral and spiritual considerations are absent. A very narrow interpretation of school improvement is at work. For example, examining the effects of an after-school homework club for pupils is considered a satisfactory topic, worthy of receiving grant aid, whereas examining the effectiveness of a programme of induction for new teachers is not. In the context of a church school, research that examines the implementation of the mission would not be eligible, nor would an investigation into the impact of liturgy on school ethos. These kinds of 'improvements' cannot contribute to league tables and so apparently do not merit attention. While many worthwhile areas for study are included, too many are excluded because of the impoverished yet unarticulated assumptions about education (and research) that lie behind the introduction of the project.

Apparently neutral ground rules can often serve to import into an activity assumptions that are, at worst, incompatible with and alien to religious principles and priorities, or, at least, inhospitable to the flourishing of such principles and priorities. In the long run, the operation of such ground rules serves to undermine and to restrict unnecessarily the development of the qualities required for effective scholarship.

In *The Outrageous Idea of Christian Scholarship* the American (Protestant) historian of education, George Marsden, has defended the legitimacy of scholars establishing connections between their religious commitments and their scholarly pursuits. He argues that the disconnection between these two 'parts' of persons, a disconnection that is often taken as mandatory in many higher educational institutions, is damaging, both for religion and for scholarship (Marsden 1997). According to Marsden, scholars often have to keep quiet about their faith in order to be accepted in their academic community (p. 7). Faith perspectives are marginalised (p. 20). Religiously based belief is considered parochial, sectarian and divisive (p. 21). In the name of multiculturalism subcultures are silenced (p. 32). Out of a fear of a resurgent Christian imperialism many groups, including gays, feminists, Jews and secularists, display a vigilant and suspicious watch over any expression of Christian faith in the academy, although, owing to the manifest, constant and self-destructive divisions among Christians, such resurgence is highly unlikely ever to materialise (pp. 32, 34). Marsden believes that the neutrality espoused by liberalism, as between different world-views or 'thick' interpretations of the good, is in reality a pretence: 'the self-appointed referee turns out to be a contestant in disguise' (p. 73). Reductionism, relativism and methodological atheism pervade academic ways of working (pp. 75, 84, 86). Given this scenario, it is not surprising that Marsden advocates the need (and right) for the maintenance of some institutional bases for Christian scholarship, centres where the implications of Christian faith for the academy can be addressed and where the pressures to conform to secular assumptions can be counteracted (pp. 101–6).

In contrast to prevailing secular expectations, Marsden argues that religious beliefs (inevitably and appropriately) shape our values and priorities, our assumptions and questions. They have a bearing on our motivation for scholarship, the particular fields of study we select and the questions we pose in them. They change how we see that field of study and the assumptions that appear to govern it. They help us to fit our academic projects into a larger framework of meaning (pp. 63–4). As examples of key Christian beliefs that potentially influence scholarship in these ways, Marsden cites the doctrines of creation, incarnation and the Holy Spirit. Each of these doctrines can shape how we interpret the data available to us in our particular field of study, how we seek connections and how we weigh different hypotheses to account for the data. Both separately and cumulatively they will affect our understanding about what kind of world we are in, what kind of people we are, and what kind of relationship we can have with God.

This connection, between our theoretical presuppositions and the way we observe, interpret and respond to the realities we encounter, holds for all of us, since we cannot help but see things from a particular position and for a particular purpose. We assimilate knowledge 'in a complex web of connections, distinctions, inferences, and applications' (Anderson 1993: 80). Not only is it the case that the data in any particular field does not speak for itself; even the rigorous and systematic employment of a particular method of research does not lead inevitably to unambiguous results. What the data yields depends very much on the kind of interrogation to which it is subjected, by whom, for what purpose, and according to which guiding principles. The most fertile kinds of research are far from being merely a series of isolated exercises of some approved methodology, which could in principle be carried out by anyone with the requisite training and competencies. Rather they are seen as cumulative and component practices that both draw upon and in turn contribute to, a wider whole, some overarching 'story' or framework or set of principles, as well as to a way of life, with an integrated set of values and principles.

Insofar as universities 'screen out' from explicit consideration the passions, prejudices, personal commitments and qualities of scholars, they undermine, rather than purify, the practice of individual research. As I shall argue below, the apparently internal and private features of personal qualities or virtues exert a powerful influence on the external or public outcomes of scholarship, but one that is insufficiently acknowledged. Our fundamental commitments cannot fail to colour the way we see our particular academic discipline, the questions it asks, the methods it employs, the qualities it develops and its understanding of education, teaching, learning and virtue.

If universities fail to encourage institution-wide reflection on the big questions of life that connect with our fundamental commitments, they undermine at least part of the potential of particular disciplines. I refer here to two things: first, the contribution that each discipline can make to a wider whole, to a community beyond the membership of its own specialists; and, second, the opportunity for one discipline's development to be enriched by encounter with others. When specialisation, fragmentation and isolation pervade the university, this damages the potential of traditions to provide an appropriate context, one that combines challenge and support for scholarship. Traditions of enquiry share a common language, a set of common values and a canon of texts that exemplify landmark studies and breakthroughs in the relevant field. They offer commonly accepted methods of investigation and criteria for evaluating these. They create the conditions where a sustained conversation can be carried out, not only about the findings of scholars in that field, but also self-reflexively, with regard to the principles governing the tradition, its provisional and porous boundaries, its relationship with other traditions, its significant unresolved questions. The quality of this self-reflective dimension is enhanced by institution-wide fostering of hospitable spaces for spirited cross-disciplinary exchanges on the questions and issues that transcend particular departments. At the moment the university often functions as 'a holding company for the set of organised disciplines – itself empty of philosophy . . . it does not consider the big picture . . . [and] there is no prevailing sense of necessary relation or priority among the fields' (Anderson 1993: 29).

I have indicated several different deficiencies in the current climate for scholarship. These include a privileging of outcomes over the processes that lead up to them, a neglect of the personal dimension in study and an attempt to ignore the bearing of fundamental commitments on research. Inadequate attention given to philosophy and to the architectonic leads to insufficient effort being expended on establishing connections between different areas of knowledge. As a result of these limitations both virtue and wisdom are undermined. This situation applies to theology and religious studies as much as to other academic areas.

Paul Griffiths distinguishes religious from consumerist reading, claiming that academic life encourages the latter, while neglecting the former (Griffiths 1999). He claims (p. 182) that 'the study of religion in universities makes it impossible to understand what is studied.' Religious reading depends on a certain kind of relationship between the reader and what is read, a relationship that allows the text to address, to question and to challenge the reader, and at the same time it adopts an attitude of reverence and obedience towards the text. Rather than standing in authority *over* the text, interrogating it with critical tools, deferring commitment, questioning its authenticity, the religious reader stands *under* or in the light of such a text. This kind of understanding entails a willingness to be vulnerable to the message contained in a text, submitting to its power, allowing it time to penetrate one's thinking and feeling and appreciating its resonance. By trusting its source, inhabiting its ambience and participating in the community which is the proper location for its interpretation, religious readers find themselves able to attain a depth of understanding that cannot be reached by consumerist reading and the detached use of critical methodologies. Religious reading, seen in this light, requires relations between readers and texts that are simultaneously 'attitudinal, cognitive, and moral; [such relations] imply an ontology, an epistemology and an ethic' (Griffiths 1999: 41).

It will already be apparent that the climate in which much academic work is conducted is inhospitable to religious ways of reading texts and the world in general. A religious way of reading does not treat the individual as the basic unit; it gives priority to the religious community. It does not adopt a detached and distant perspective; it expects engagement, participation and commitment. It does not divorce the personal qualities of the seeker from the public methods and outcomes of the search; it expects conversion and transformation of life as the price – and the key – for unlocking the doors to the treasures held within the tradition. Religious accounts of the world are learned in a social, linguistic and institutional context (Griffiths 1999: 13) though this does not mean that there is a deterministic relation between relevant practice and religious accounts. There is an expectation in religious learning that the personal life of the student will be modified, redirected and brought into line with the object of study. The will must be ordered and the appetites harnessed, away from self-centred gratification and toward God and other people (Griffiths 1993: 17). The transformational practices enjoined on us as essential elements in religious reading give us a new identity, one that changes us intellectually as well as morally and spiritually.

For Griffiths the predicament of the scholar in many departments of religion is like being imprisoned in an iron cage, where there is the 'desire to mention (but never to *use*) the vocabulary, the conceptual tools, and the practices of what they study' (Griffiths 1993: 184; my emphasis). The constant separation of the seeker from what is being studied, in the name of critical detachment, leads eventually to a distance that entirely disconnects the students from what is studied. This is especially damaging for students who already have religious commitments. 'If your vocabulary and your purposes are the consistent and repeated object of mention by those whose purposes are not yours . . . you will be at first marginalised, then forced into a museum' (Griffiths 1999: 184).

CONNECTIONS BETWEEN THE SPIRITUAL AND THE INTELLECTUAL

If salvation and sanctity are the goals of religious life, understanding and wisdom are the goals of intellectual enquiry. Insiders from any religious faith would contend that these religious and intellectual goals are intimately related. There are two general aspects to claims about this relationship which can be stated before looking at some of its detailed features. First, scholarship cannot be fully what it ought to be without the aid of spirituality. Second, one cannot achieve a wise holiness if one neglects to take care about one's intellectual integrity.

With regard to the first of these two aspects, David Schindler (1996) strongly urges that it is crucial for a Catholic world-view that there should be connections between the religious and the intellectual order. It is an integral feature of a Catholic university that it seeks to promote the development of a Christian mind, not merely Christian behaviour outside the classroom. For this to happen, one must recognise that 'there is an inherent mutual relation between fidelity to [Church] teaching, participation in the sacramental life of the Church, prayer, and social service, on the one hand, and the formation of a truly Catholic mind on the other' (Schindler 1996: 147). Faith should have an influence on classrooms, conversion from sin and the development of moral qualities will facilitate the proper functioning of our intellectual powers, and participation in the life of the Church will enhance our capacity to benefit from and to contribute to traditions that support and challenge intellectual enquiry. This would be the line taken by those who claim a strong connection between scholarship and spirituality.

With regard to the second aspect, realising the universal call to holiness includes, rather than bypasses, the development of mind and the deployment of our intellect. There is an 'objective-meaning-and-truth' dimension as well as a 'subjective-volitional' dimension to holiness (Schindler 1996: 148). Our spiritual life and our capacity to exercise wisdom are not helped by uncritical and naïve thinking or by passive acceptance of the assumptions, metaphors and methods of others. Nor are they nourished if one is unwilling to apply reason rigorously to questions of significance or if one refuses to seek ways to co-ordinate and to integrate coherently the different aspects of life. Furthermore, the notion of 'taking every thought captive for Christ' or 'putting on the mind of Christ' (2 Corinthians 10:5; Philippians 2:5; 1 Corinthians 2:16) does not entail the suppression of the natural use of intelligence, but rather its full employment.

From a Christian perspective, scholarship and spirituality must enter into a reciprocal relationship: a compenetration of faith, understanding and life is required. The kinds of persons we are and the different purposes we have enter into our intellectual activity. According to Christian belief, we have a design and a destiny. To ignore this is to fly in the face of reality, to defy 'gravity', to damage the apparatus through which we discern, penetrate and understand things, events, situations, decisions and principles. Scholarly endeavour is not made up of isolated acts of calculation, analysis or synthesis; it is a cumulative and coherent set of activities carried out by multi-dimensional persons who address multi-dimensional realities. The different 'parts' of a person, for example, the cognitional, affective, corporeal, intellectual and social, interact both with each other and with the different 'parts' of the reality that we engage with and reflect upon. Our intellectual acts are inextricably embedded in and influenced by the life that accompanies them. The particular and complex combination of attitudes we bring to observation, critique, reflection and scholarship will colour, even to some extent condition, our discoveries, insights and reconstructions of reality.

To try to cut off the other dimensions of our life from our intellectual endeavours is a form of vivisection carried out on the self, rather than a guarantee of academic purity. We need to bring into play and to discipline the various dimensions of our lives, so that they can be co-ordinated with and appropriately related to the focus, nature, purpose, scope, implications and wider significance of our studies. Attempts to ignore or to leave behind our passions, prejudices and commitments fall into one of two possible traps. On the one hand, we simply fail to be aware of their powerful and pervasive effects on our perspectives and findings, our scholarship is hampered by blindness and ignorance and we confuse inspection with a self-aware reflectivity. Or, on the other hand, in seeking to suppress all that seems to represent what is outside the scope of a purely intellectual approach, we castrate ourselves intellectually in the name of a distorted understanding of academic 'chastity', once again diminishing the effectiveness of our studies.

For a Christian, scholarship is a part, not the whole, of a person's life; it needs to be incorporated into their broader spiritual development, rather than left outside it. In this respect the relationship between scholarship and spirituality is similar to the relationship between other 'parts' of our lives – for example, sexual, familial, business, leisure – and our spiritual growth. Furthermore, scholarship requires many of the same virtues as spirituality: persistence, perseverance, patience, waiting, accepting 'darkness' and difficulties and enduring trials.

In the discipline of studying a religion, there is bound to be some tension between the total engagement and allegiance of the self called for by that religion, and the detachment and objectivity demanded of scholars. Yet, inescapably, the cognitive and the conative mutually influence one another: our concepts and our understanding are intertwined with our feelings and convictions (Smith 1974: 116, 103, 107). We do not treat each new piece of information in isolation from what we have already accepted and rejected. Data does not come to us as completely new and ready for some pure and presuppositionless inspection. Instead it is filtered by the discriminations and interpretations of a receiving subject, one who has already developed habits of recognition and a way of life that simultaneously privileges some features of the world while suppressing others. In this process, our moral and spiritual qualities (and their ensuing commitments) have a bearing on our scientific findings.

In the preceding paragraph I used the phrase 'the habits of recognition'. I am referring here to the notion that we operate out of a 'habitat' or a *habitus*, a personal environment from which we think and act. This environment is gradually built up from a cumulative series of decisions and patterns of behaviour that shape our intelligence as well as ordering our emotional responses to our experiences. Here our will and our affections are, in religious terms, illuminated by faith as they are surrendered to God. In the relationship with the divine that develops through the obedience of faith we find that our discipleship and our knowledge mutually penetrate one another. The moral theologian Cessario speaks of 'the sanctification of the intellect that the *habitus* of faith accomplishes' (Cessario 1996: 138). Christians have traditionally considered the following as gifts of the Holy Spirit: wisdom, understanding, counsel, fortitude, knowledge, piety and fear of the Lord. These gifts are believed to have the capacity to shape the moral and intellectual character of the Christian. When taken together, they 'conform the different capacities of the person to their proper object, so that the person chooses what is good in a "natural" way – promptly, joyfully and easily' (Cessario 1996: 168).

Choosing what is good does not come automatically to the person whose reason is wounded and weakened by sin. 'How will you manage to think rightly with a sick soul, a heart ravaged by vice, pulled this way and that by passion, dragged astray by violent or guilty love?' (Sertillanges 1946: 24). Studiousness, or the qualities of effective study, requires many different contributing aspects. These include avoidance of negligence and of vain curiosity: students must exercise care and they have to take their studies seriously. There has to be some proportion between their powers and the particular task of study selected. There also has to be a sense of proportion with regard to the amount of time and effort devoted to study as compared with our other responsibilities in life. A proper sense of priorities allows us to allocate sufficient time for study, to avoid distractions, but not to neglect our other duties. One of these other duties is worship. Full access to the truth requires the perspectives opened up through worship. Devotion and enquiry are mutually reinforcing.

In addition to exercising care and developing a sense of proportion, students need to be vigilant as to their motivating ambitions, for these can injure effective study. We should study, not to impress, nor for material gain, but out of love for truth. St Bernard of Clairvaux (quoted by Schwehn 1993: 60) wrote:

> There are many who seek knowledge for the sake of knowledge: that is curiosity. There are others who desire to know in order that they may themselves be known: that is vanity. Others seek knowledge in order to sell it: that is dishonourable. But there are some who seek knowledge in order to edify others: that is love.

Seen in this light, scholarship is the fruit of both purity and love, a pure love of some aspect of truth. We have to develop an affinity for, even a kind of friendship for, the object of our study. If we come to teach this, our friendship or affinity with the topic of our teaching should bring out how we have been changed by it, its significance for us and the difference it now makes in our lives. But we only arrive at a pure love with the aid of a discipline that separates us 'from the swirl of sensible images designed to attract our attention and desire' (Cary 1999: 65). Traditional religious *ascesis* helps us to turn away from selfish pleasure and to direct our attention beyond appearances and towards reality.

In order for us to pursue and to reach truth, there has to be an ardent search for it, combined with strength of character. Self-control allows us to focus our energies, to be attentive and to concentrate our minds on a topic. The virtue of courage enhances our ability to persevere in the face of difficulties; it prevents our will from flagging in the face of opposition. Humility, on the other hand, makes us sufficiently docile or teachable; it allows us to adopt a positive attitude towards the authority of the teacher, which, in the case of research, may be the material of study itself, rather than a particular person who is guiding us. Of course, humility does not entail naïvety; it should be combined with vigilance with regard to the sources of instruction and knowledge (Reichberg 1999: 145, 149). A sense of belonging to and of acceptance by the community of faith (and the community of faithful scholars) can provide the necessary ambience of security and of collaboration that further facilitates our study (Sertillanges 1946: 160, 84).

I end this section by referring to two writers who have contributed significantly to our understanding of the connections between scholarship and spirituality. The first of these is the mediaeval Franciscan, Bonaventure (1217–1274). This spiritual writer, theologian and administrator is, for me, one the best representatives of the synthesis between faith and learning achieved by Christian scholars. Able to read the book of nature, the sacred scriptures, the lives of the saints and the tradition of the Church, he was able to find God in all aspects of creation as well as in the Christian life. According to his teaching, thinking, caring and praying were all intimately interrelated to one another. For Bonaventure, faith capacitates human reason for correct thinking, our willingness to play a receptive role conforms our minds to the demands of God's reality, and the life of study challenges us to harmonise our own labour with God's assistance (Carpenter 1999: ix, 9, 187).

None of this can happen without the workings of grace. Grace re-creates and reforms us. It fills us up with life. It illuminates the objects of our study. It helps us both to assimilate these and to become united with them. It makes us acceptable to God and raises up our souls to Him. It lays the groundwork for ever greater willingness on our part to receive the supernatural gifts offered by God (Bonaventure, in Carpenter 1999: 36). God's grace can urge us on and remove obstacles to the effectiveness of our studies. It can empower, liberate and fortify us, by helping us to recognise our interior defects, by assisting in the mortification of our passions, by ordering our thoughts and by raising up the desire to know more and better (Carpenter 1999: 126, 171). Without an acknowledgement of our sinfulness and openness to the help of grace, our studies would be fruitless. We must have no exaggerated confidence in human reason.

> Reading is insufficient without unction, speculation without devotion, investigation without wonder, observation without joy, work without piety, knowledge without love, understanding without humility, endeavour without divine grace, reflection as a mirror without divinely inspired wisdom.
>
> (Bonaventure 1978: 55–6)

Scripture, for example, could only be understood by those with clean minds (Carpenter 1999: 41). But, reciprocally, our spiritual obligations should never be divorced from our intellectual pursuits (Carpenter 1999: 51).

The second writer who has reaffirmed the essential connections between spirituality and learning in his treatment of philosophy as a way of *life*, not just as a sphere of intellectual enquiry, is the twentieth-century historian of antiquity, Pierre Hadot. According to Hadot (Hadot 1995: 21, 59, 82), philosophy in ancient times was treated as a set of exercises intended to have comparable effects on the mind as athletic exercises were meant to have on the body. That is, philosophy should discipline the mind, turn it away from damaging habits, cure it of weaknesses, perfect it, focus it on its proper ends, transform the personality and enlighten the eyes of the soul. Readers would be made to traverse a certain itinerary in order to enable them to spend a long time in the company of important questions and to facilitate their spiritual progress (Hadot 1995: 64, 92). In this view, the fruit of such spiritual itineraries, wisdom, would combine peace of mind, inner freedom and a cosmic consciousness (Hadot 1995: 265). Four particular kinds of learning are identified by Hadot as central to philosophy as a way of life, and, by extension, to other forms of scholarship: learning to die trustingly, to live truly, to dialogue honestly and to read correctly. The goal then is to transform ourselves, for, as Aristotle said in the *Ethics*, as we *are*, so shall we *see*. 'In every sphere of conduct people develop qualities corresponding to the activities that they pursue . . . How the end appears to each individual depends on the nature of his character' (Aristotle 1979: 123, 125). This is a far cry from the bypassing of personal qualities and the failure to connect methodologies with overarching philosophical purposes that I criticised earlier.

CONCLUSION

Several aspects of the relationship between scholarship and spirituality, as seen from a Christian perspective, have been identified. One theme has been the stress on conversion from sin, the need for grace, the gifts of the Holy Spirit and the process of sanctification in our lives, all necessary elements in strengthening our capacity to know truth. (On the connections between intellectual, moral and religious conversion, see Sullivan 1983.) Another theme has been the need for faithful participation in the life and worship of the Church as a necessary 'external' accompaniment to the development *within* us of an appropriate *habitus* or personal environment for the recognition and reception of religious truth. As we act and as we live, so shall we see; our being affects our perception. This *habitus* facilitates the inculcation of a philosophical mentality or habit that is conducive to the growth within us of wisdom, an intellectual achievement that depends on character. Third, I have suggested that our spiritual life influences our commitments and our capacities to engage in scholarship. It does this in several ways. It opens us up to the transcendent. It orients us to the self-involving nature of religious study. It encourages a proper ordering of our lives, so that they are not at the mercy of impulse, temptation, distraction, false goals, erratic choices, self-contradiction and internal incoherence. Its emphasis on the role of purity, humility, patience, perseverance and discipline deepens our capacity to 'travel' the scholarly 'journey' without unnecessary personal 'baggage', with a willingness to learn and be able to keep 'on track'.

If the defects in the current climate and institutional arrangements for research, as outlined in the second section (above), are to be addressed, it will be imperative for Christian thinkers to articulate afresh how their religious faith either can or should influence their scholarship. Can there be a spirituality of research that promotes a discerning Christian response, for example, to the Research Assessment Exercise? John Haughey makes a valuable contribution to such a task (Haughey 1997). Haughey (1997: 146–9) picks out six features of such a spirituality which separately and conjointly modify how one might envisage scholarly endeavours from a Christian perspective. Each of the notions he identifies is described briefly, but they could profitably be the basis for reflection by Christian scholars. First, there is the notion of call, which opens up the question of my motivation for studying in a particular field. Second, there is the importance of interiority, of research drawing on the inner life, some features of which have been treated in this paper. Third, Haughey turns our attention to the disciplines of study, interpreted as principalities (in the scriptural sense). Fourth, the potential contribution of research to the common good is emphasised. Fifth, Haughey speaks of responsible scholarship as entailing the notion of being stewards of the goods of information. Finally, the place of discernment, not least about the effect of one's studies on oneself and one's relationships with others, is brought into focus.

In this paper I have not addressed many of Haughey's provisional categories for developing a spirituality of research, since I focus principally on the potential importance for scholarship of personal qualities and commitments promoted by the spiritual life. However, his essay does indicate how my agenda could be taken further forward.

NOTE

This chapter is a revised and shortened version of an article which was first published in *The Downside Review* in July 2002 (Vol. 120, No. 420) and it appears here with the kind permission of the editor of that journal.

REFERENCES

Anderson, Charles (1993) *Prescribing the Life of the Mind*, Madison: University of Wisconsin Press.

Aristotle, (1979) *Nicomachean Ethics*, trans. J.A.K. Thomson, London: Penguin.

Bonaventure (1978) *The Soul's Journey into God, The Tree of Life, and The Life of St Francis*, translated and introduced by Ewart Cousins, London: SPCK.

Carpenter, Charles (1999) *Theology as the Road to Holiness in St Bonaventure*, New York: Paulist Press.

Cary, Philip (1999) 'Study as love: Augustinian vision and Catholic education', in Kim Paffenroth and Kevin Hughes (eds), Aldershot: Ashgate.

Cessario, Romanus (1996) *Christian Faith and the Theological Life*, Washington, DC: Catholic University of America Press.

Griffiths, Paul (1999) *Religious Reading*, New York: Oxford University Press.

Hadot, Pierre (1995) *Philosophy as a Way of Life*, edited by Arnold Davidson, 1st edition, Oxford: Blackwell.

Haughey, John (1997) 'Faculty research and Catholic identity', in Patrick Carey and Earl Muller (eds), *Theological Education in the Catholic Tradition*, New York: Crossroad.

Marsden, George (1997) *The Outrageous Idea of Christian Scholarship*, New York: Oxford University Press.

Reichberg, Gregory (1999) 'Studiositas, the virtue of attention', in Daniel McInerny (ed.), *The Common Things: Essays on Thomism and Education*, Washington, DC: Catholic University of America Press, for the American Mariain Association.

Schindler, David (1996) *Heart of the World, Centre of the Church*, Edinburgh: T. & T. Clark.

Schwehn, Mark (1993) *Exiles From Eden*, New York: Oxford University Press.

Sertillanges, A.D. (1946) *The Intellectual Life*, trans. Mary Ryan, Cork: Mercier Press.

Smith, John E. (1974) *Experience and God*, New York: Oxford University Press.

Sullivan, John (1983) 'Lonergan, conversion and objectivity', *Theology*, LXXXVI, September, 713, pp. 345–53.

Sullivan, John (2001) 'Plasticity, piety and polemics', *Journal of Religious Education* 49, 2, pp. 16–25.

Chapter 10

Spiritual learning
Good for nothing?

Jeff Astley

HORIZONTAL AND VERTICAL SPIRITUALITY

We may discern two functions or dimensions of spirituality. First, there is a set of attitudes and values, and of undergirding beliefs and practices, on the *'human-horizontal' level*. These give rise to, and partly constitute, human psychological well-being, although they may extend beyond this category. This dimension may be understood in terms of James Fowler's concept of a universal human faith, which he defines as an activity of creating or finding meaning, and of knowing, valuing and relating to that which is taken to be ultimately meaningful, in commitment and trust. Faith, for Fowler, is understood as a disposition or stance, 'a way of moving into and giving form and coherence to life' (Fowler and Keen 1978: 24). *Religious* faith differs from other forms of faith only because it has specifically religious 'centres of value' and 'images of power' in which we believe, and religious 'master stories' by which we live our lives (Fowler 1981: 276–7).

This spiritual disposition or demeanour (cf. Haldane 2000: 62) is often patently good for us, as it helps us to cope with and triumph over the vicissitudes of our life, and to find fulfilment, purpose and direction within that life. Insofar as this is so, public education should encourage the development of this horizontal dimension of spirituality.

But what of the *'vertical' dimension* or function of spirituality? I use this metaphor to include the sense in which spiritual virtues go beyond their moral counterparts in a way that relates to their being 'orientated towards the extra-mundane dimension of human aspiration to what lies beyond the purely temporal' (Carr 1995: 92). John Hick refers to a 'fifth dimension of our nature which enables us to respond to a fifth dimension of the universe', 'the transcendent within us' that answers to 'the transcendent without' (Hick 1999: 2, 8). Theists usually speak more specifically of the goal of spiritual development as 'experience of God' or 'union with God', distinguishing this from a deeper understanding of reality or 'becoming a certain kind of person' (Haldane 1999: 200). This is the dimension that best fits a definition of (say) holiness as a spiritual orientation derived from a relation with God (Hebblethwaite 1997: 51). Such an essentially religious dimension of spirituality (cf. Carr 1996) is more problematic in secular education, of course, particularly for those who reject confessional religious education on educational grounds. Many would doubt whether it is a proper task of the common or secular school to get children to reach out to any 'super-sensible realities' (cf. Wakefield 1983).

In *Struggle and Fulfillment* (1979), Donald Evans identifies certain fundamental attitudes that are expressed in, and give rise to, both beliefs and worship in religion, and beliefs and conduct in ethics, and designates them *attitude-virtues*. He describes them as pervasive stances for living or 'modes of being in the world'. They are thus existential categories as well as dispositions to act in certain ways, and they constitute the 'style' or 'timbre' of a person's behaviour and personality (Evans 1979: 15, 186–7). The attitudes are pervasive both internally and externally, in that they influence all of a person and all of that person's situations. They are unifying in that they unify all of a person's being and all of his or her experiences and environments. Emotional/feeling tone seems to be an essential aspect of all of them.

The eight intrinsically valuable states identified by Evans are: *basic trust* (the most fundamental and foundational), *humility, self-acceptance, responsibility* and *self-commitment,* and three that together constitute love – *friendliness, concern* and *contemplation*. They were proposed in a working party of Humanists and Christians as common ground for spiritual formation in schools back in the 1980s (Lealman 1986).

Evans notes not only that these attitude-virtues are the main constituents of both religion and morality (1979: 4–5), but also that they encompass the main constituents of human fulfilment. Such fulfilment involves 'a steady predominance of the attitude-virtues over the [corresponding] attitude-vices', a state that enables people to love freely and spontaneously in harmony with themselves, others and ultimate reality.

In his *Spirituality and Human Nature* (1993), Evans defines spirituality as 'a basic transformative process' in which each of us uncovers, and lets go of or transforms, our inherent 'narcissism' (my 'self-centred preoccupation with my own comparative status and power'), so as to surrender our whole selves 'into the Mystery out of which everything continually arises' (1993: 3–4; cf. 91–2, 195, 217). Unlike the self-preoccupied concerns of much Christian spirituality, this self-surrender makes it possible 'for God to live *as us*' (pp. 250–1), in a realisation of ourselves as 'arising from God and in God: being God and being lived by God'. Evans describes this transfiguring surrender as 'the ultimate in human fulfillment' (pp. 176–7), and as a 'moral-spiritual transformation' that is broadly religious (p. 195). As I understand him, all the attitude-virtues may be said to contribute to this overcoming of narcissism or self-preoccupation (cf. 1979: 133–4), and also to a reverence for and participation in the ultimate divine reality (p. 150).

Much of Evans' perceptive account in his earlier book may be categorised under my human-horizontal dimension of spirituality. But he also recognises the vertical dimension in two claims. The first is that the attitude-virtues are necessary conditions for the discernment of the divine in religious experience, with our trust in God enabling us to discern God (1979: 171, 179–84; cf. Price 1969: 455–88); the second is a 'neo-Kantian' argument for belief in God. Basic trust is an *attitude* or *stance* directed towards something real, usually a person. This has logical implications, for believing that a trusted reality exists is a logical implication of the correct use of the word 'trust' (Evans 1979: 172–9). If the one who trusts does not accept this implication, he or she has only an untargeted *mood* rather than a stance. For Evans, the 'cosmic focus' of the 'pervasive and unifying' attitude of basic trust is God. Since this attitude is necessary to human fulfilment, he argues that it ought to be cultivated and that the theistic belief it implies is therefore to be viewed as rational.

Evans does, however, recognise that reality may not accord with human fulfilment: 'maybe we have to believe what is false in order to be fulfilled' (1979: 179). Even though the pursuit of truth and the pursuit and enhancement of life may both be fundamental to us, 'we cannot count on the first invariably to further the second' (Hepburn 1992: 140). Educators should take note. It is possible that we may best flourish by being deceived

My vertical dimension of spirituality is only one sense in which spirituality can transcend or go beyond. Transcendence is already a feature of those accounts of spirituality that speak of the true, mature self reaching out to what is beyond itself, beyond what Iris Murdoch calls 'the fat relentless ego' (Murdoch 1970: 52). By letting go of security and defensiveness in order to truly live and fully love, we become ourselves by losing ourselves (cf. Mark 8:35–7).

I wonder how far this might take us beyond 'the balanced sense of moderate self-esteem that is necessary for a fulfilled human life', which John Cottingham advocated in his interesting paper on the ethics of self-concern. He argues there that extreme self-sacrifice, as a permanent disposition of character, cannot be part of a worthwhile human life; while acknowledging that it does lead to praiseworthy actions on occasions (Cottingham 1991: 811). This is consistent with Aristotle's doctrine of the mean. Educators may be happy to join a debate over the precise range of behaviour that should be allowed as a virtuous mean (*mesotes*) between the extremities of the excess of universal agape and the deficiency of chronic, self-absorbed stinginess. They may also have a view about which of these extremes, to adopt Aristotle's words, is 'more erroneous' and which 'less so'. They should also be willing to consider the empirical realities of the practice of moral and spiritual education, and to try to discover the *actual effects* on the lives of their pupils of their portrayal of moral and spiritual ideals. But should they go any further? Should they agree with so many of their students that Mother Teresa and even Jesus, in their apparently cavalier disregard of the virtue of moderate self-preference, were just 'sad'? Must morality and spirituality *always* be good for our health?

Many 'virtues of attachment', such as kindness, generosity and humility, are not 'happy compromises between states of excess and defect'; there is no 'specifiable [vice] associated with being too considerate' (Carr 1991: 207). This is a matter of some religious significance. Thomas Aquinas rejects Aristotle's insistence on a mean when he turns to consider the theological virtues whose object is God. 'Here is no virtuous moderation', Thomas writes, 'no reasonable mean; the more extreme our activity, the better we are.' He also recognises that we should derivatively exercise one such virtue, charity, in our love for our neighbours (*Summa Theologiae* 1a, 2ae, lxiv, 4; 2a, 2ae, clxxiv, 3). When Jesus makes the radical demands of his hearers that are appropriate to the generosity of the exceeding God (Matthew 5:43–8; 18:21–2; Luke 10:29–37), and when Paul sets the wisdom of God, as revealed in the cross, over against the wisdom of the world (1 Corinthians 1:18 to 2:16), they offer what is in principle a critique – even a crucifixion – of the human values of security, power and status, and of much else that contributes to our worldly well-being. These are extreme values, marking out an exceeding spirituality (cf. Astley 2000: 27–9, 116–18).

Reflecting on Kierkegaard's distinction between the 'imitators of Christ', who must anticipate suffering evil and being shunned, and those mere detached 'admirers' who do not strive in the same way to be what they admire, Philip Quinn comments that although the imitators will have true *teleological* meaning, 'there is a problem in supposing that every such life will also have true *axiological* meaning if it terminates in bodily death, because some such lives appear not to be good on the whole for those who lead them' (Quinn 2000: 64). He concludes that 'survival of bodily death seems required to secure positive axiological meaning and thus true complete meaning.' Here the vertical dimension is clearly assumed, with a reference to a condition that is very much 'beyond' this life. Many philosophers, of course, would reject such a move (e.g. Nagel 1986: ch. XI), as would some more radical theologians. But then so would the overwhelming majority of Old Testament writers, who expressed and developed a profound religious faith without having any positive conception of an afterlife.

SPIRITUAL FLOURISHING

On the persuasive definition of education that includes a value-condition of *worthwhile* learning, education may properly include the development of attitudes, values, skills and capacities that are regarded as intrinsically valuable (or at least as instrumentally valuable) outcomes. Insofar as an agreement can be brokered concerning the range of such outcomes and the acceptability of our methods of developing them, some sort of spiritual education may readily be justified. I agree that much of the spiritual life, like much of the moral life, may be justified in terms of its (instrumental or constitutive) contribution to the good life, interpreted in terms of human flourishing. Many of the spiritual virtues fit this model, and the very language of spiritual 'health', 'salvation' or 'liberation' suggests it. But I also have some reservations.

In one of Charles Schulz's 'Peanuts' cartoons, the dog Snoopy bounces jovially through several frames under the scowling gaze of the formidable Lucy. 'Happiness isn't everything, you know!', she shouts after him. 'It will never bring you peace of mind!' (Schulz 1970). Lucy's sour remarks seem typical of a certain sort of advocate of a certain sort of spiritual education. 'There is more to your life than this', he scolds; or, more accurately, 'There ought to be more to your life than this.' Unfortunately, very many learners – like Snoopy – seem quite happy as they are.

There is an empirical element to spirituality that demands to be taken seriously in educational practice. We must 'taste and see' (cf. Psalm 34:8). Yet many of the rewards that come from spiritual development will not seem rewarding at all until they have been developed to some considerable extent. Furthermore, (i) these gains are often only won through painful changes, and (ii) the successful negotiation of the spiritual journey towards them cannot be guaranteed. Such factors should warn us against a simplistic comparison of the learner's present well-being against a future state a long way down some spiritual road. To change the metaphor from a journey to a 'leap of self-transcendence', this bound from one state to the other may seem to a person 'like a terrible sacrifice or even a form of self-immolation . . . by the standards of a good life as defined by his pre-converted condition' (Nagel 1986: 206). We can, indeed, be harmed if some spiritual states are not developed (McGhee 2000: 249), but we may also be differently harmed *as they develop*. Further, because of the sort of people we shall still be in other respects after the development of these states, some of us may even regard our final state itself as harmful. All of which makes a straightforward 'taste and see' imperative in spiritual education rather problematic.

The metaphor of taste suggests further pedagogical difficulties. Much spiritual education involves creating a sense of discontent with our contentedness and dis-ease with our present sense of fulfilment. 'Wretched taste' is 'gratified with mediocrity' even in the face of the excellent, according to Isaac D'Israeli (1823); 'happiness is a wine of the rarest vintage, and seems insipid to a vulgar taste', writes Logan Pearsall Smith (1931). That sort of taste might be quite fulfilled, however, by lower ranking drinks. Taste varies, and some gustatory goods are very definitely 'acquired tastes' that can be acquired only as people are changed through the tasting of them. To adopt Wordsworth's phrase, the spiritual educator may strive, along with the 'great and original writer', to 'create the taste by which he is to be relished'. But if he fails, then we shall remain content to do without his wares. If I still prefer Coca-Cola despite having sampled the best malts of the Highlands and Islands for thirty years, shouldn't I be encouraged to give up ordering whisky?

But this loose talk of taste is dangerous: the relativist bogey-man ever lurks at the doors. It would be better if we had some agreed criterion for adjudicating between visions of the good life. We may therefore welcome an Aristotelian analysis of human nature and human welfare in terms of common 'grounding experiences' (spheres of experience common to all human life) and the virtues that we develop in response to them. The examples given by Martha Nussbaum include fear of death (to which Aristotle's corresponding virtue is courage) and attitudes to slights (corresponding to 'mildness of temper'). There are, however, different – *spiritual* – virtues that correspond to these same experiences. Spiritual acceptance, 'self-abandonment to divine providence', hope or faith may confront the fear of death; forgiveness is the appropriate spiritual response to slights. These surely represent rival accounts of 'the proper behaviour' towards ourselves and our experience (Nussbaum 1988: 38).

But are such spiritual virtues constitutive of human flourishing *as such*, or is there a distinctively spiritual sort of flourishing that has more of a minority status? My view is that while some people need to behave, think and act in spiritual ways in order to flourish, others have no such requirements. (People are different, as well as being the same.) Although some universal elements are therefore required for a satisfactory human life, there may be other needs and conditions for well-being that are not so widely shared (cf. Haydon 1999: 26–9).

While defending 'self-concern and self-preference', and rejecting the standard view that such things are an obstacle to ethical development, John Cottingham seems to allow that agapeistic sainthood, although it is not possible and not desirable for all, may be permissible and desirable for a tiny few ('ought' implying 'can'). He thus seems willing 'to accept the possibility of more than one viable blueprint for human flourishing' (Cottingham 1991: 815). Are these alternatives – a limited self-preference, on the one hand, and a more radical and extreme self-sacrificial agape on the other – simply a function of different human psychological types? Is the (occasional) saint just someone who feels more fulfilled and satisfied by extreme self-giving than do the rest of us? Religious and spiritual traditions encourage a conversion to an ideal, which may be understood as a species of 'falling in love' with a type of character (even of 'the character of God') or a way of being in the world. Such a response expresses a *personal* appraisal that is a function of our particular psychology, and is not based on 'reasons' that would necessarily count for others (cf. Lyons 1980: 80). 'If I were pressed to say why I love him', wrote Montaigne in his essay 'On friendship', 'I feel that my only reply could be, "Because it was he, because it was I"'(De Montaigne 1958: 97).

But perhaps there is a still more excellent way. If Aristotle's *eudaimonia* may be translated as 'success', as Austin suggested, the question arises as to what *should* count as success in a human life. Aristotle's own account of it is 'certainly quite an unchristian ideal' (Austin 1968: 281), and his great-souled man has been described as one to whom 'the notion of a crucified God would have been abhorrent' (Copleston 1962: 80; cf. Cottingham 1998: 98–9). Although Alasdair MacIntyre defends 'uncalculated giving' as a virtue, along with many other virtue ethicists he declares self-sacrifice a vice (MacIntyre 1999: 160; cf. Slote 1999). Admittedly, such self-renunciatory ends are unlikely ever to emerge from a value-neutral study of human nature, or even from some underlying agreement about the good between members of different value traditions. They are dependent on some – hardly naturalistic – *re-definition* of what counts as flourishing, which is consonant with the claim that truly to flourish may involve losing one's life in order to gain it.

Gareth Moore's powerful account of Christian spirituality wrestles with the problem of rewards. In the New Testament, he argues, the depth grammar of reward language is that 'to seek a reward from God is not to seek a reward at all' (Moore 1988: 143; cf. Kierkegaard 1948: 68–78). The language of reward is used by Jesus only 'in order to encourage people to forget all about rewards' (Moore 1988: 145). The Christian life is an end in itself, not a means to something further. True spirituality is therefore not a good bet; it is a matter of the sort of person one should be, *regardless*.

Moore himself not only rejects the promise of earthly rewards for pious living, he also appears to dismiss the usual understanding of heavenly rewards. He writes, 'heavenly success is not another form of success I might try to achieve *in addition* to any other goals I might have' (1988: 172) and 'treasure in heaven is the treasure you acquire by not being interested in acquiring any treasure' (1988: 165). This interpretation is reminiscent of the vigorous defence of the virtue of *disinterestedness* in religion mounted by another radical theologian, Don Cupitt. 'We must be good for nothing', Cupitt insists, 'good without reward or consolation' (Cupitt 1986: 164; cf. 2000: 141). Cupitt's own stress on disinterestedness has become less austere over the years, better to complement his developing sense of the spiritual life as more therapeutic, aesthetic, productive, social, embodied and quietistic – and, frankly, less macho. His radical appeal to unselfing is now accompanied by an account of a love that is realised, paradoxically, through radical self-expression. He calls this 'solar ethics', as the self 'burns out, pours out and passes away' like the sun. It is only in such 'objective self-expression', he writes, 'that we succeed in making anything of ourselves' (1995: 41). But this is still a matter of becoming 'fully disinterested and objective' (1995: 45). Cupitt would there-fore presumably continue to endorse his claim, on behalf of a 'spirituality of world-transcendence' (which need not necessarily involve supernatural beliefs), that 'the essence of the matter is that you are not fully human unless there is something that is dearer to you than your own life' (Cupitt 1985: 170).

My concern is how far this principle of disinterestedness in morality and spirituality can be accommodated by a naturalistic focus on human well-being, which Cupitt himself adopts (1995: 2, 57, 98). Does self-renunciation *always* lead to 'the highest happiness', and is this result its *only* justification? Even after we have agreed about what makes human beings 'well', there may still be rational disagreements about what is the right life for them to follow and what sort of people they ought to be. *Pace* many accounts of virtue ethics, these questions may be (at least in part) independent of claims about what is non-morally and non-spiritually good for them.

The merchant banker confronted by the charity collector in the Monty Python sketch was at a loss to see the point of the transaction. 'I don't follow this at all . . . it looks to me as though I'm a pound down on the whole deal' (Chapman *et al.* 1989: 93–4). True morality will often seem 'pointless' if the only justification allowed is the agent's own enhance-ment; morality is perverted when it is made to fit this mistaken view of the moral life. Spiritual endeavour is equally open to perversion. It can become 'an instrument for self-enhancement' (Spohn 1999: 13) and a sophisticated form of self-preoccupation, a 'glorified narcissism' (Evans 1979: 150). This is equally bizarre, as the spiritually virtuous life should shift attention from the self and its spiritual or eudaemonic progress to what is outside it. Just as doing the morally right thing 'may cost more in terms of other aspects of the good life than it contributes to the good life in its own right' (Nagel 1986: 197), so may doing the 'spiritually right thing', at least sometimes. This is true even though spirituality mostly does serve our needs, and although our well-being may be defined in part by our spiritual and moral virtue.

The crucial question is whether, in the end, our natural, human well-being *exhausts* the spiritual dimension. Can we really give a satisfactory account that shows that such behaviour is virtuous on account of the rewards it brings us, especially in the hard areas of self-denial and unself-ing? There is surely not always a causal relationship between virtue and well-being, and a thorough-going constitutive account of that relationship can only make the value of the virtuous disposition dependent on its relationship to human well-being by means of a conceptual claim that many would simply reject (cf. Barrow 1980: 25–6).

The question about the way in which the unspiritual or immoral person is 'worse off' demands a more radical answer. Perhaps the sinner's – or the unspiritual person's – only penalty is simply 'being like that, being someone who acts like that', since 'it is better and lovelier to be moral' (or spiritual). On this view, the sanction of immorality or of unspirituality is a 'value sanction' (Nozick 1981: 410, 414). This may be why we are often struck by the obverse – 'the seemingly self-justifying character of the life of the saint' (Mackinnon 1957: 59). To argue in this way is to advocate the spiritual life because it captures the truth of what being human is really about, where that truth is not exhausted by states of affairs that are in our long-term interest.

George Sher adopts the term *perfectionism* for the view that spiritual and moral values are good in themselves: things of intrinsic value or worth that are good independently of the flourishing of the person who holds them (Sher 1992: 93). The goal of life, on this account, is to pursue an ideal of conduct and character. Sher has argued that 'our conception of human flourishing is itself rooted in perfectionism' (1992: 104). As parents and as teachers we often want our children to be formed in and by, and eventually to embrace and inhabit, a particular character ideal. We want them to be certain sorts of persons (while retaining, of course, their own unique qualities). Such a process does not always sit easily with talk about the benefits that will accrue should they 'adopt' this commitment or 'choose' this value. Yet pointing out the instrumental benefits to people of their morality or spirituality might seem to be the educational implication – or do I mean 'temptation'? – of the empirical justification of virtue in terms of well-being. On a more radical, intrinsic value approach, however, unbelief is not to be argued with but preached at, as Karl Barth recommends. In practice, the preaching takes a subtle form. The value-unbelievers are courted, goaded and displayed to, until they become captivated by the account of goodness and spirituality that is before them and confess, 'Yes, I want to be like that.' The saints are to be portrayed so that we may be converted: 'Be imitators of me, as I am of Christ' (1 Corinthians 11:1).

WHO DO YOU THINK YOU ARE?

I turn finally to spirituality's concern with *meaning*. This has found its way into many curriculum documents and classroom materials; it is a dimension that also fits rather comfortably with a well-being analysis, at least up to a point.

Being decently human to others, and satisfyingly human to ourselves, is highly dependent on our striking a balance between two things: (a) the subjective standpoint, in which we are not just something but everything – not just someone but *the* one; and (b) the detached, alienating objective standpoint in which our significance diminishes to but one-of-far-too-many, and we can hardly believe that we are 'anyone' at all. The subjective standpoint is prominent in one redaction of religion (e.g. Isaiah 44:1–5); but the view of our life *sub specie aeternitatis* is also powerfully represented there (e.g. Isaiah 40:21–4). As Nagel recognises in his profound, although entirely secular, account of the clash between these two standpoints, 'the objective standpoint can't really be domesticated . . . it gives us more than we can take on in real life' (Nagel 1986: 231). This is particularly the case as we face the certainty of our own death. Spiritual education, even in schools, must help us to face it.

Nagel commends two responses to this existential situation. I would label them both as spiritual responses, and argue that we might do well to encourage them in our children. One is a form of humility that allows us to reckon with the objective stance by taking a more realistic sense of ourselves. This should lie somewhere 'between nihilistic detachment and blind self-importance', avoiding 'the familiar excesses of envy, vanity, conceit, competitiveness, and pride'. The other response is the 'nonegocentric respect for the particular' which is such a conspicuous element in aesthetic responses. Spiritual education should teach *humility*, then, and *respect*.

Both these spiritual virtues were dear to Iris Murdoch. She valued them as assisting 'unselfing': a shift of perspective to a concern for what is outside the self, a process that makes us more human (Murdoch 1970: 34–43, 59–67, 85–9, 103–4; cf. Kerr 1997: ch. 4). They are also prominent in Donald Evans' work. His comments on humility include a commendation of *humour*, since laughing kindly at ourselves helps greatly in sustaining this attitude-virtue (Evans 1979: 116). He also associates different forms of the practice of *meditation* with the stance of contemplation, including the 'cultivation of a capacity to celebrate the sheer existence of people and things in their uniqueness and their togetherness' (1979: 149). I would argue that these two additional elements should also find a place in spiritual education, broadly conceived.

But Evans presents another, and more contentious, theme that is of signal importance for a fully spiritual education. He writes of *assurance* as the most fundamental constituent of trust (itself the most fundamental of the attitude-virtues), arguing that it has two components: reality-assurance and satisfaction-assurance. He defines reality-assurance as 'the assurance that life is worth living because it has already received the meaning and reality which are necessary for human fulfillment' (Evans 1979: 23). In this context, he quotes a spiritual insight reported by Sam Keen from the time of his father's death:

In the face of the uncertainty of life and the certainty of death no human act or project could render existence meaningful or secure. Nothing I could *do* would result in my being saved, ontologically grounded against tragedy and death. Either dignity and meaningfulness come with the territory or they must forever be absent. Sanctity is given with being. It is not earned.

(Keen 1971: 17; emphasis in original)

(Keen adds that, before this revelation, 'I had been riding on an ox looking for an ox.') The focus here on grace is specific to devotional religion. I would wish instead to underscore the more universal spiritual theme of 'letting go', and the recognition that meaning and value are in some sense 'given'.

'Satisfaction-assurance', which is something we receive both through the caring concern of others and from the (apparently impersonal) environment, is subordinated by Evans to reality-assurance on the grounds that when 'bodily satisfactions are not met, a man has recourse to reality-assurance as the most fundamental kind of assurance' (Evans 1979: 40). Evans reinterprets Jesus' words about anxiety in the Sermon on the Mount (Matthew 6:25–7) to uncover this deeper level of assurance:

There is no need to be anxious about food and clothing. It's all right to sow seed and to weave cloth, but don't worry about the outcome. You matter to God, and so your bodily needs matter to God. He provides the means to satisfy them, like a good shepherd or a [loving] parent. But *even if* you should turn out to be suffering from hunger and cold, what matters is the assurance of worth (and reality and meaning) which you have from God. You are absolutely safe in that reality-assurance, whatever happens to your body.

(Evans 1979: 39; emphasis in original)

This is also, of course, a theistic redaction. It therefore fits with the sort of appeal to a life after death that Quinn employs (see above, p. 144). But it could be expressed differently. For Cupitt, who rejects the traditional accounts of both God and the afterlife, our dithering in the face of life's sheer contingency needs a courage that comes from 'trusting Be-ing' in its finitude and transience. 'What we really need is a personal habit of attending to and becoming easy and familiar with the purely contingent kind of Be-ing in and by which we do in fact have to live' (Cupitt 2000: 151). 'Faith is saying an easy Yes to life. Faith lets Be-ing be' (Cupitt 2001: 72).

I would argue that what 'comes with the territory' for the spiritually mature woman or man is an assurance of worth, and an assurance that 'life is worth living' and that 'life is meaningful', which are so fundamental that they are not dependent on *any* further facts, not even facts about our flourishing – or our survival. The spiritually mature just recognise the value of their existence, unique and irreplaceable. This is an assurance that is not extinguished even by the diminishing of our flourishing: by the fading of the assurance of the satisfaction of our needs. In my view, a fully spiritual education must above all sow the seeds of this sort of perception. And it must help to root them *very* deep: deeper than can be justified by any appeal to our well-being.

REFERENCES

Astley, J. (2000) *Choosing Life? Christianity and Moral Problems,* London: Darton, Longman & Todd.

Austin, J.L. (1968) '*Agathon* and *eudaimonia* in the Ethics of Aristotle', in J.M.E. Moravcsik (ed.), *Aristotle: A Collection of Critical Essays,* London: Macmillan, pp. 261–96.

Barrow, R. (1980) *Happiness,* Oxford: Martin Robertson.

Carr, D. (1991) *Educating the Virtues: An Essay on the Philosophical Psychology of Moral Development and Education,* London: Routledge.

Carr, D. (1995) 'Towards a distinctive conception of spiritual education', *Oxford Review of Education* 21, 1: 83–98.

Carr, D. (1996) 'Rival conceptions of spiritual education', *Journal of Philosophy of Education* 30, 2: 159–78.

Chapman, G. *et al.* (1989) *Monty Python's Flying Circus, Vol. 2,* London: Methuen.

Copleston, F. (1962) *A History of Philosophy: Vol. I Greece and Rome, Part II,* New York: Doubleday.

Cottingham, J. (1991) 'The ethics of self-concern', *Ethics* 101, 4: 798–817.

Cottingham, J. (1998) *Philosophy and the Good Life: Reason and the Passions in Greek, Cartesian and Psychoanalytic Ethics,* Cambridge: Cambridge University Press.

Cupitt, D. (1985) *Only Human,* London: SCM.

Cupitt, D. (1986) *Life Lines,* London: SCM.

Cupitt, D. (1995) *Solar Ethics,* London: SCM.

Cupitt, D. (2000) *Philosophy's Own Religion,* London: SCM.

Cupitt, D. (2001) *Emptiness and Brightness,* Santa Rosa, CA: Polebridge.

De Montaigne, M. (1958) *Essays,* Harmondsworth: Penguin.

Evans, D. (1979) *Struggle and Fulfillment: The Inner Dynamics of Religion and Morality,* Cleveland: Collins.

Evans, D. (1993) *Spirituality and Human Nature,* New York: SUNY.

Fowler, J.W. (1981) *Stages of Faith: The Psychology of Human Development and the Quest for Meaning,* San Francisco: Harper & Row.

Fowler, J. and Keen, S. (1978) *Life Maps: Conversations on the Journey of Faith,* Waco, Texas: Word Books.

Haldane, J. (1999) 'The need of spirituality in Catholic education', in J.C. Conroy (ed.), *Catholic Education: Inside-Out/Outside-In,* Dublin: Veritas, pp. 188–206.

Haldane, J. (2000) 'On the very idea of spiritual values', in A. O'Hear (ed.), *Philosophy, the Good, the True and the Beautiful*, Cambridge: Cambridge University Press, pp. 53–71.

Haydon, G. (1999) 'Values, virtues and violence: education and the public understanding of morality', *Journal of Philosophy of Education* 33, 1: v–156.

Hebblethwaite, B. (1997) *Ethics and Religion in a Pluralistic Age*, Edinburgh: T. & T. Clark.

Hepburn, R.W. (1992) 'Religious imagination', in M. McGhee (ed.), *Philosophy, Religion and the Spiritual Life*, Cambridge: Cambridge University Press, pp. 127–43.

Hick, J. (1999) *The Fifth Dimension: An Exploration of the Spiritual Realm*, Oxford: Oneworld.

Keen, S. (1971) *To a Dancing God*, Glasgow: Collins.

Kerr, F. (1997) *Immortal Longings: Versions of a Transcending Humanity*, London: SPCK.

Kierkegaard, S. (1948) *Purity of Heart is to Will One Thing*, New York: Harper & Row.

Lealman, B. (1986) 'Grottos, ghettos and city of glass: conversations about spirituality', *British Journal of Religious Education* 8, 2: 65–71.

Lyons, W. (1980) *Emotion*, Cambridge: Cambridge University Press.

McGhee, M. (2000) *Transformations of Mind: Philosophy as Spiritual Practice*, Cambridge: Cambridge University Press.

MacIntyre, A. (1999) *Dependent Rational Animals: Why Human Beings Need the Virtues*, London: Duckworth.

Mackinnon, D. (1957) *A Study in Ethical Theory*, London: A. & C. Black.

Moore, G. (1988) *Believing in God: A Philosophical Essay*, Edinburgh: T. & T. Clark.

Murdoch, I. (1970) *The Sovereignty of Good*, London: Routledge & Kegan Paul.

Nagel, T. (1986) *The View from Nowhere*, Oxford: Oxford University Press.

Nozick, R. (1981) *Philosophical Explanations*, Oxford: Oxford University Press.

Nussbaum, M.C. (1988) 'Non-relative virtues: an Aristotelian approach', in P.A. French, T.E. Uehling and H.K. Wiettsein (eds), *Midwest Studies in Philosophy, Volume XIII*, Notre Dame, Ind.: University of Notre Dame Press, pp. 32–53.

Price, H.H. (1969) *Belief*, London: Allen & Unwin.

Quinn, P.L. (2000) 'How Christianity secures life's meanings', in J. Runzo and N.M. Smith (eds), *The Meaning of Life in the World Religions*, Oxford: Oneworld, pp. 187–201.

Schulz, C.M. (1970) *Here Comes Charlie Brown!*, London: Hodder Fawcett.

Sher, G. (1992) 'Knowing about virtue', in J.W. Chapman and W.A. Galstan (eds), *Nomos: XXXIV, Virtue*, New York: New York University Press, pp. 91–116.

Slote, M. (1999) 'Self-regarding and other-regarding virtues', in D. Carr and J. Steutel (eds), *Virtue Ethics and Moral Education*, London: Routledge, pp. 95–105.

Spohn, W.C. (1999) *Go and Do Likewise: Jesus and Ethics*, New York: Continuum.

Wakefield, G.S. (1983) 'Spirituality', in A. Richardson and J. Bowden (eds), *A New Dictionary of Christian Theology*, London: SCM, pp. 549–50.

Part III

Spirituality and education

Chapter 11

Spiritual development and the Qualifications and Curriculum Authority

John Keast

INTRODUCTION

1. The Qualifications and Curriculum Authority (QCA) is the British government's agency responsible for guaranteeing the standards and regulating the operation of qualifications, and for advising, developing and supporting the school curriculum in England. I shall begin with a historical view of the involvement of the QCA with spiritual development, then draw out some issues that I think arise from that development. Whilst this chapter is basically about the English experience of trying to identify the spiritual in the curriculum, I hope it will cast some light on the experiences of other education systems, for I believe the issues which the story is about are universal.

HISTORY

2. My history begins with the 1944 Education Act. Its preamble stated: 'It shall be the duty of the LEA (Local Education Authority) for every area, so far as their powers extend, to contribute towards the spiritual, moral, mental and physical development of the community.' It is interesting to note that the LEA is made responsible, and the target of development is the community.

3. The term 'spiritual' appeared in some official documents in the 1970s and the 1980s. For example, in 1977 the then Department of Education and Science (DES) issued *The Curriculum 11–16*, which listed areas of experience to be addressed in the school curriculum. These included (separately) the ethical and the spiritual. In 1985 *The Curriculum from 5–16* also included the spiritual and (separately) the moral. Descriptions of what the spiritual area is concerned with were given in 1977. The first said that the spiritual is concerned with:

the awareness a person has of those elements in existence and experience which may be defined in terms of inner feelings and beliefs; they affect the way people see themselves and throw light on the purpose and meaning of life itself. Often these feelings and beliefs lead people to claim to know God and to glimpse the transcendent . . . always they are concerned with matters at the heart and root of existence.

The second referred to the spiritual as concerned with 'everything in human knowledge or experience that is connected with or derives from a sense of God or Gods. Spiritual is a meaningless adjective for the atheist and of dubious use to the agnostic' (DES 1977).

The 1985 document gave a broader but more succinct description. It

points at its most general to feelings and convictions about the significance of human life and the world as a whole which pupils may experience within themselves and meet at second hand in their study of the works and the way of life of other people.

(DES 1985)

4. More recently and importantly the Education Reform Act 1988 stated that the school curriculum must 'promote the spiritual, moral, cultural, mental and physical development of pupils and society, and prepare such pupils for the opportunities, responsibilities and experiences of adult life'. This Act also introduced the subjects of the National Curriculum (NC), the introduction of which occupied all time and attention centrally and in schools. The statutory orders for each subject were followed by cross-curricular themes (non-statutory) that widened the scope of the curriculum by including health, environment and citizenship (aspects of what might have been found in school personal and social education (PSE) courses at that time). However, no real attention was paid to the promotion of spiritual development until the National Curriculum Council (NCC) published a *NCC Discussion Paper* in 1993. This did not give a neat definition but suggested that spiritual development 'needs to be seen as applying to something fundamental in the human condition'. It has to do with 'relationships, a search for identity, meaning, purpose and values, and our response to challenging experiences such as suffering and death'. Of the many aspects of spiritual development included were 'the development of beliefs and the appreciation of the beliefs of others, the capacity to experience awe and wonder and to be moved by beauty and injustice, a sense of transcendence, self-knowledge, self-acceptance and self-respect, and the capacity for creativity' (SCAA 1996).

5. Such discussion would probably have meant little in practice, except that in 1992 the Office of Standards in Education (OFSTED) was established. The 1992 Schools Act required OFSTED to inspect spiritual develop-

ment, alongside moral, social and cultural development. This really forced the issue of describing what spiritual development was, and how it might be seen in schools. Projects, research and academic articles began to be written in profusion. Schools paid more attention to the spiritual because they were now inspected on it, though the process is not nearly as rigorous as for, say, literacy or established subjects.

6. Among the most concerned to get a clear description were OFSTED's own inspectors. The first OFSTED Her Majesty's Chief Inspector, Professor Stewart Sutherland, set the ball in motion at a conference at Westhill College, Birmingham. Spiritual development included consideration of helping pupils to see the unity and significance of their knowledge and understanding, to extend their horizon and to see beyond the immediate. In the *Handbook for Inspection* of 1993 the focus for inspection was on the outcomes of the school's provision for spiritual development. This was to be judged by the extent to which pupils displayed 'a system of beliefs, the ability to communicate, a willingness to reflect on experience, and a sense of awe and wonder' (OFSTED 1993). It was expected that religious education (RE) would play a major role in this but that other subjects would also contribute.

7. In the following year OFSTED published a Discussion Paper of their own in which the desire was expressed to inspect not only provision of spiritual development but also the pupils' response to that provision. It suggested that some cognitive outcomes could be assessed including knowledge of the beliefs and practices of the world's major religions. The role of RE was further underlined. There was an emphasis on 'seeking to answer life's great questions'. The OFSTED *Handbook* (1994) did not introduce the inspection of outcomes but directed its attention at opportunities for provision, and specific reference was made to the important place of collective worship in schools. Two new statements also made their appearance: spiritual development could be understood as 'valuing a non-material dimension to life and intimations of an enduring reality' and 'Spiritual should not be seen as synonymous with religious' (OFSTED 1994).

8. The OFSTED *Handbook* (1995) added little that was new. However, the School Curriculum and Assessment Authority (SCAA), which had replaced the NCC, republished the NCC work in its *Discussion Paper No. 3* in September 1995. This helped to keep the discussion of these issues alive. In July 1996 the SCAA published a Discussion Paper (No. 6) called *Education for Adult Life: The Spiritual and Moral Development of Young People*. This linked spiritual to moral development. It offered its own views of what constitutes spirituality, which included

the development of the inner life, an inclination to believe in ideals, a propensity to foster particular attributes such as love and goodness, the quest for meaning, truth and values, and a capacity to respond to the 'ultimate' or God. The essential factor in cultivating spirituality is reflection and learning from experience.

(SCAA 1996)

9. Following the review of education and training for 16–19 year olds in 1996 Sir Ron Dearing (now Lord Dearing) recommended that the criteria for all qualifications for this age group include a new requirement. This was that syllabuses identify ways, if appropriate, in which the qualification promotes understanding of spiritual, moral, ethical, social and cultural issues. Whilst this requirement is little known, it is currently being put into practice. The impact of this is still unknown.

10. More significantly, in 1996–97 the SCAA established the National Forum on Values in Education and the Community (commonly known as the Values Forum). This has a long story. There were many debates about the purpose and membership of the Forum, the nature and validity of the exercise, and its alleged results. For example, Professor Adrian Thatcher accused the QCA, which replaced the SCAA in 1997, of the destruction of theology through the vacuous nature of the values, accusing them of being empty of religious meaning and content. Professor Ron Best has also criticised the process of promoting spiritual and other forms of development by identifying common values. The statement focuses on the values of self, relationships, society and the environment, and the actions they mean we should take.

11. Some work was also done by Marianne Talbot of Oxford University, acting as consultant to the QCA for the Values Forum, to cross-relate these to spiritual, moral, social and cultural development. A rather elaborate matrix and series of six steps by which schools could establish, articulate, promote and celebrate their values were published for a trial in 150 pilot schools in 1998, under the title *The Promotion of Pupils' Spiritual, Moral, Social and Cultural Development*. The pilot was not a success for a variety of reasons. In the pilot material there was a description of spiritual development, which some viewed as inadequate.

Spiritual development is concerned with the *essence* of human beings, both as human beings, and as unique individuals. This essence or spirit, when it is strong, enables us to survive hardship, exercise fortitude and overcome difficulties and temptations: it is our essential *self*.

(Original emphases)

It goes on to talk about loss of spirit, high spirits and low spirits, linking spiritual development with, in effect, self-esteem. 'Spiritual growth is the key to human motivation.'

'People who are developing spiritually will be:

- increasingly open and responsive, aware of themselves and of life's challenges;
- trusting, in themselves and in others (and for some God);
- willing to engage, to take responsibility and to do what is right with courage and hope;
- able to love others, be generous in spirit and respond well to hardship.'

This material was not published.

12. This line of development was overtaken by the review of the NC by the Labour Government in 1999. The statement of values was appended to the new NC statutory orders in the revised NC handbooks for schools, published in 1999 by the DfEE and the QCA and sent to all schools. A preamble to the NC was also written, entitled *Values Aims and Purposes.* This gave a clear steer on some issues of values and underlined the importance of (*inter alia*) spiritual development. The preamble also included two aims for the school curriculum, the second of which includes spiritual development, thus reinforcing the intent of the 1988 Act.

13. Discussion of these issues now at the QCA tends to be set in the context of the introduction of citizenship and PSHE into the NC. The QCA's involvement in this work described above was a direct result of the interest in these areas of Nick Tate, then chief executive of the QCA and Sir Ron (now Lord) Dearing, the QCA's Chairman from 1994 to 1998. They were encouraged by the government of the day and by public concern over the values of young people, most clearly evidenced by the horror at the murder of Jamie Bulger and the head teacher Philip Lawrence in the mid-1990s.

14. The development of citizenship education and its introduction as a statutory subject into the secondary school curriculum from the autumn of 2002 is another story in itself. It does mean that the English school curriculum now has a little more in common with other curricula internationally. Much of the credit for this goes to Sir Bernard Crick and his advisory group established by David Blunkett, Secretary of State for Education, in 1998 and to David Kerr of the National Foundation for Educational Research (NFER). Citizenship education will raise many issues of a spiritual and moral kind if it is taken seriously by schools, teachers and pupils (see paragraph 36 below).

15. Spiritual and moral development is still regarded as important in educational theory though there is now less work being done on it at the QCA. OFSTED, however, still have the responsibility for inspecting these forms of development. They are about to publish new guidance for their

inspectors, which will also be made available to schools to help them make a self-evaluation of such development. The story continues.

ISSUES

16. A first set of issues concern the fact that government, not to say bureaucracy, is so closely involved in describing if not defining spiritual development. The question has been asked, 'Since when have such theoretical and abstract concepts, which are mainly regarded as the subject of philosophical and theological debate and contention associated with academia, been the province of legislators, officials and inspectors?' There was a trend in the 1990s for government guidance to enter new waters. This is seen, for example, in the description of what religious education should be about and what it comprises. Perhaps even more contentiously it is also seen in guidance on what worship is and what worship which is wholly or mainly of a broadly Christian character is. Many feel that a trend of this kind is a cul de sac at best. Ron Best and Paul Yates, for example, have been very critical of the 'bureaucratisation' of the curriculum and of spiritual and moral development in particular. Paul Yates characterised 'the current culture of school as a bureaucratized vehicle for the continuing restorationist agendas that have alienated the organization from its social and political contexts and from the urgent needs of pupils facing the continuing impact of globalization' (Yates 1999: 191).

17. Associated with this is the extent to which academic research has played a part in such official approaches. Many would argue that its role had been only indirect to say the least, if not often clearly ignored. Whilst their reading has probably influenced those who have written official documents, there is still a noticeable gulf between academic papers on this subject and official guidance.

18. A second set of issues concern the nature of the work undertaken by government departments, their agencies, civil servants and officials. I have several observations here.

19. [a] One obvious comment is the enormous lack of confidence and familiarity with concepts of the spiritual among teachers (and many officials). A massive task would be needed to re-establish a vocabulary, a capacity to understand, think about and discuss the categories, and the relevance of what we call spiritual development. Questions and issues of personal commitment (or lack of it) are felt to be problematic by teachers. Such lack of awareness, capacity and confidence has, I believe, been regarded as necessitating the work that agencies like the QCA have undertaken.

20. [b] The work by agencies such as the QCA, described above, has not so much described spiritual development as such as marked out the 'space'

that spiritual development might occupy in school life and the curriculum: the form rather than the filling, the shape rather than the content. It has focused on what spiritual development is concerned with rather than what it is in itself, and where it fits in school life, the curriculum and the community. Attempts to describe this are of a rather different order from producing official descriptions of what spiritual development actually is. It is possible to argue that in all the descriptions, definitions, statements of values, what is missing is that which only particular and real institutions themselves can provide – the actual values, beliefs and their applications of them, where the source, nature, authority and prescription of values is articulated and practised. I may be able to define climate but only real weather can exist. Spirituality may constitute certain kinds of things, but which actual things are not for governments and civil servants to say. Jacqueline Watson stresses how important it is in the common school that no particular model of spiritual development should prevail.

> The naturalistic model of spirituality currently used in education is only one of a number of models of spirituality . . . Whose model should we use? In a pluralist society the answer should be none. State education cannot take sides with one particular model . . . This does not have to mean the end of spirituality in schools . . . Schools should encourage children and young people to explore different models of spirituality so that they can make their own sense of life and of the challenging world around them.
>
> (Watson 2000: 100)

21. [c] The distinction and connection between spirituality and religion is either lost on or inadequately articulated by many people. Evidence indicates that when teachers are asked about both these concepts, spirituality is described rather positively and religion is described rather negatively. Many teachers believe that there is an important distinction and that there are important connections. Spirituality and religion each have some particular characteristics that enable us to make a distinction. I think that I too would want to argue for the primacy of spirituality and the secondary nature of religion. As some of the intangible and elusive nature of spirit becomes articulated, rationalised, codified and contextualised in belief and practice, in order to be able to conceptualise, express and develop the sense of spirit, so religion emerges as a system of belief and practice encapsulating a set of spiritual experiences.

22. Some, however, would reverse this view, relying on the primacy of religious revelation and the derivation of spirituality from it, arguing that the view above is a distortion of both religion and spirituality. The sense of spirit comes from a set of beliefs about life and the universe. I would not want totally to deny this either, because I think that the relationship

of the spiritual and the religious is often mutual; each feeds the other. The relationship is dynamic and creative. The expression and practice of the spiritual does require language, community, formulae, etc., which are characteristics of religions. Religious beliefs and practice evoke a spiritual journey.

23. The reason why I hold to the primacy of the spiritual is to do with the experience of searching for meaning, the seeing beyond, through and across the mundane, the quest for the unity of things, which I believe are fundamental characteristics of all religions. I should say that I use religion here to mean systems of beliefs (coherent or incoherent) about ultimate questions. This entails that I think there can be humanist spirituality as well as religious spirituality, which I would also subdivide into theistic and non-theistic. (This is, of course, a very oversimplified statement, which needs much further explanation, and there are all kinds of assumptions here about the definition of religion that people may not agree on.)

24. In the context of schools, the discussion of the kind I have just entered rarely takes place, because, on the whole, education policy-makers, trainers, teachers, etc., do not have the inclination, capacity or time for it. They tend to equate spiritual with religious, religious with the religions, religions with the faith communities (especially the churches) and end up talking about faith schools, RE and school worship. Spiritual development often ends up as the responsibility of the RE teacher in a school or the RE officer at the QCA.

25. [d] Another assumption often made is that the spiritual (whether the same as religious or not) is easier to discuss when linked with morality. Many people's line of thought seems to be this. Religion is optional, having been privatised – it is only for the few who are so inclined. The spiritual is nebulous and incapable of further meaningful definition. But the moral cannot be avoided because it is so obviously to do with difficult social issues that do not just not go away but seem to increase in number, difficulty and complexity. Judgements involving values are there-fore inescapable.

26. This line of thinking is not, however, without its complexity either. Because values themselves are hard to define, may be private or relative, they must be connected with opinions, beliefs, arguments about and experiences of right and wrong, codes and authorities. This is getting very closely back to philosophies, ideologies and religion, and thus the spiritual. How and why values are connected with beliefs is rarely fully pursued, but their connection means that educationalists and politicians cannot avoid the spiritual and religious when talking of morality, if only because they sense some connection.

27. A last observation at this point is the difficulty with the word 'devel-opment'. In other educational areas and subjects, development is usually measured against a predetermined line of progress and observable out-

comes. No such neat line of development for spirituality in an educational context exists, as far as I know. The work that Fowler did on faith development is not easy to transfer to spiritual development in schools. The QCA has published some work in RE on tracking progress through eight levels in 'learning from religion' and in 'learning about religions' (QCA 2000) which is stimulating similar work in other places. Whilst the full validity of such work has not yet been fully tested, I am confident that much can be done to promote development of this kind within the context of RE as a subject. Whether this could or should (and if so, how) be developed more widely in terms of spiritual development I very much doubt, in which case 'development' here is a much less precise term than in other areas.

EFFECTS

28. It is not easy to be precise about the effect on schools of the episodes of the story I have related either. As will be evident, there is much confusion about spiritual development on the part of many. This may turn to some type of anxiety when an OFSTED inspection looms, for no school likes to do badly in its report. Most schools would probably worry less about getting a poor OFSTED report for spiritual development, however, than they would about literacy. Some schools might see spiritual development as a distraction from their main task of promoting the three Rs. Other schools, however, especially faith schools, see the emphasis given to spiritual, moral, social and cultural development as a safeguard against the over-prescriptive centralised subject curriculum, believing these forms of development to be central to their ethos, relationships and goals; and therefore as necessary ingredients to academic success. It is this connection of ethos with success that lies behind the fascination which the general success of church schools has for many politicians and parents.

29. Some schools have therefore tried to look at their ethos and promote a cross-curricular approach to spiritual and other forms of development. This may have involved considering different subjects and their contribution. You need only look at the current NC documents to see how this may be done. Each subject has its own rationale, and links between it and learning across the curriculum have been highlighted. This is true of RE as much as the NC. Some schools have taken spiritual development into their thinking as they work out their policies and practices for assemblies, where again a rationale for the nature and practice of collective worship might be developed.

30. It is hard to generalise about current practice. OFSTED reports that across the board spiritual development is least effectively promoted, provided and successful. Moral and social development are much more

successful. Cultural development is somewhere in between. There are no data on provision, standards or outcomes in these areas. Some would say that spiritual development is aspirational rather than actual.

31. Of the subjects, RE is regarded as having the most positive contribution to make to spiritual development. This is particularly so where opportunities are given to pupils to 'learn from religion' as well as to 'learn about religions'. However, it is clear that literature, the arts and humanities are also major contributors. Collective worship requirements are largely met in primary schools and largely unmet in secondary schools.

32. Where good practice is observed, it is often the result of guidance which the school has received either from its own seeking or given to it from a variety of sources. Many LEAs have produced guidance documents on spiritual and other forms of development, sometimes as part of the work of the local Standing Advisory Council for Religious Education (SACRE), which is often tasked with evaluating schools' OFSTED reports on spiritual, moral, social and cultural (SMSC) development. Such guidance often gives a brief account of requirements and previous initiatives, a discussion of the issues that arise, and advice on how the whole school, its ethos, worship and curriculum can contribute to such development. Sometimes these publications are followed by opportunities for training.

33. In a document published in 1999 by the Stapleford Centre, generally regarded as Church of England evangelical Christian in character, David Smith identifies four areas on which current discussion tends to focus, and goes through each in turn. These are:

- spiritual capacities – human abilities which make us the kind of creatures capable of spiritual growth (such as empathy, reflection, imagination);
- spiritual experiences – ways in which we experience different aspects of living (such as sense of curiosity, mystery, worship, awe and wonder);
- spiritual understanding – knowledge and understanding of beliefs, people, ideas and frameworks involving cognitive development (such as takes place in RE);
- spiritual responses – how we live and the connections between belief and practice (such as our commitments).

(Smith 1999)

The document goes on to discuss faith and spirituality, and makes the point that, while we should be open to and affirm spirituality as something human, we should be wary of assuming that all that is spiritual is good. This is an important point in my view, especially for schools.

34. I use this example of guidance to introduce two final reflections.

There are debates about whether the spiritual is essentially to do with the transcendent, and whether the transcendent is about a form of spiritual experience or an object/authority. In an article in the *International Journal of Children's Spirituality* (Vol 5. No. 2, 2000) Jonathan Long writes: 'It is a feature of recent attempts to define spiritual development in an educational context that they are concerned with the importance of encouraging experiences of transcendence without any exploration of the metaphysical frameworks which may be used to interpret them' (Long 2000: 152–3). The epistemic value of spiritual experiences needs to be explored alongside the experience itself. He cites Nigel Blake who argues against including spiritual education in schools because spiritual experience is not bound by any positive moral constraints. Long concludes that:

> spiritual development must mean enabling one to better make the connection between particular types of experience and particular interpretations within a distinct metaphysical framework rather than indulging in some type of unmediated experience . . . What seems important in an educational context is to expose what meaning or significance is being attached to any experience of transcendence.
>
> (Long 2000: 155)

This seems to reinforce the rather simpler way of putting it in the Stapleford Centre's guidance that spiritual understanding is needed alongside capacity and experience, and spiritual response needs to take understanding into account.

35. I therefore contend that a religious and philosophical education is an essential component and a necessary companion of spiritual (and moral) development. Such education operates with a similar dynamism as spirituality and religion. There are, of course, other areas of the curriculum that also help to promote such spiritual understanding, such as literature, humanities, and the arts.

36. Secondly, citizenship and personal, social and health education (PSHE) are now very much on the educational agenda. They raise many issues involving values and beliefs about identity, community, society, the world, life, purpose, etc. In other words, these new areas of the curriculum are also vehicles for carrying on the debate about spiritual, moral, social and cultural development. The preamble to the statutory order for citizenship states that citizenship should promote pupils' spiritual development. A series of wide-ranging learning objectives is set out, including religious diversity. The use of imagination and reflection is required, as is the study of topical spiritual and other issues (though these are not specified). It is clear that, for the government, citizenship (with PSHE, although less often mentioned) is regarded as a significant agent for personal and social development. Where the spiritual actually comes in in this new

area is not obvious at first glance, but closer reading of what is covered in the citizenship curriculum soon reveals many areas in which the spiritual is closely involved. Examples include the study of rights and respons-ibilities, justice and morality, diversity of identities, conflict resolution and global issues of different kinds. In my view, an effective religious and philosophical education is needed alongside citizenship to help pupils deal with these aspects of citizenship. RE should promote the development of pupils' ability to critique citizenship, including its spiritual implications, in the same way as a good religious and philosophical education should help pupils to interpret the meaning of their spiritual capacities and experi-ences and help them to shape their response.

CONCLUSION

37. What has perhaps become most obvious in this broad history of the QCA's involvement with spiritual development, and brief consideration of some of the issues raised, is the variety of language employed in trying to articulate spiritual development in a school context. The spiritual is associated with religion, beliefs, the transcendent; with values and how they are practised; with citizenship and PSHE. It is almost as if the spiritual represents the hidden, elusive, secret ingredient in these important but difficult areas. In the recently published White Paper *Schools: Achieving Success* and the Green Paper *14–19 Extending Opportunities, Raising Stan-dards*, a phrase 'education with character' appears. This seems to be a code for essential aspects of students' personal and social development that does not take place in the qualifications or other courses which they may choose to take. The phrase itself is interesting, reflecting perhaps rich traditions of character-building in English education, 'character formation' in other systems, e.g. the USA, and Gandhi. The recognition of the importance of character is welcome, though what exactly is signified is not clear. The papers themselves indicate that included in this general category are citizenship, RE, careers, health, sport, arts and culture. Citizenship is regarded in these documents as a necessary component for all students through to age 19, though in precisely what way is not so obvious. RE is also stated in these papers as being necessary for personal development, at least as far as age 16. Nothing is said beyond that.

38. Whatever may be intended by the phrase 'education with character', many would want to establish a connection with the spiritual. At one level the notion of spirit and character are almost synonymous – think of a sports team. At a deeper level, perhaps, there is the question of what drives character formation and determines the type of character people develop. Here issues of meaning and purpose, assumptions, values such as integrity, trust and reliability, may play a crucial role. It seems as if no

matter what the ways in which the school and college curriculum is formulated, the underlying concern of education with values is inescapable. The debate about spiritual development continues in yet another language.

REFERENCES

Department for Education and Employment/Qualifications and Curriculum Authority (DfEE/QCA) (1999) *National Curriculum Handbooks for Primary and Secondary Teachers*, London: HMSO.

Department of Education and Science (DES) (1977) *The Curriculum 11–16*, London: HMSO.

Department of Education and Science (DES) (1985) *The Curriculum from 5–16*, London: HMSO.

Long, J. (2000) 'Spirituality and the idea of transcendence', *International Journal of Children's Spirituality* 5, 2: 147–61.

OFSTED (1993) *Handbook for Inspection*, London: Office of Standards in Education.

OFSTED (1994) *Handbook for Inspection*, London: Office of Standards in Education.

OFSTED (1995) *Handbook for Inspection*, London: Office of Standards in Education.

Qualifications and Curriculum Authority (QCA) (2000) *RE: Non Statutory Guidance*, London: QCA.

School Curriculum and Assessment Authority (SCAA) (1995) *Spiritual and Moral Development, Discussion Paper 3*, London: SCAA (originally published by National Curriculum Council in 1993).

School Curriculum and Assessment Authority (SCAA) (1996) *Education for Adult Life, Discussion Paper 6*, London: SCAA.

Smith, D. (1999) *Making Sense of Spiritual Development*, Nottingham: Stapleford Centre.

Watson, J. (2000) 'Whose model of spirituality?', *International Journal of Children's Spirituality* 5, 1: 101.

Yates, P. (1999) 'The bureaucratization of spirituality', *International Journal of Children's Spirituality* 4, 2: 179–93.

Chapter 12

Longing to connect

Spirituality and public schools[1]

Daniel Vokey

> We all know that what will transform education is not another theory, another book, or another formula, but educators who are willing to seek a transformed way of being in the world.
>
> (Parker Palmer 1999: 15)

A growing number of authors are proposing one or another form of spirituality for inclusion within the curricula of public schools.[2] Many see spirituality as a 'safe' alternative to religion – safe in the sense of being free of ties to any particular religious tradition and therefore acceptable for public schools in pluralistic liberal democracies. These authors typically take spirituality to be universal where religion is particular, and so believe that implementing proposals to re/introduce it into public education would not compromise liberal principles protecting individual autonomy and cultural diversity.[3] In this paper I discuss in very general terms the prospects for success of such proposals. In the first section I briefly review the anticipated benefits – for students, teachers, and our communities – of some of the different conceptions of spirituality-in-schools. In the second section I argue that, in the short term at least, efforts to integrate spirituality within our public school curricula would be unlikely to meet with success, even granted considerable variation among the initiatives proposed. In the third section I endorse three long-term projects that I hope would help to create the conditions under which spirituality could be promoted within public education in a comprehensive and meaningful way. Although I write with Canadian educational systems in mind, my paper is addressed to all those who believe that we should be doing more to encourage and support both our own spiritual development and that of the students in our public schools.[4]

ANTICIPATED BENEFITS OF SPIRITUALITY IN SCHOOLS

Renewed life, energy, and enthusiasm for learning

Many of its advocates believe that re/introducing spirituality into public schooling would enliven classes that too often are deadly dull – for teachers no less than students. One concern of these authors is that secularised schooling has squelched students' sense of wonder and with it their motivation to learn: 'The modern age and its forms of education and mass media can readily kill awe . . . Education that ignores awe kills the soul' (Fox 1998: 50, cf. Palmer 1999: 17–19). These writers recommend that teachers bring spirituality into their classrooms in the form of inspirational, liminal, or other experiences that arouse student inquisitiveness and so restore their enthusiasm for education. In one case, teachers are enjoined simply to encourage students to slow down and 'smell the roses' (Scheindlin 1999). Other authors observe that there may be no need to instil a sense of mystery in younger children, as most will bring their innate thirst for learning with them to school. From this latter point of view, the task facing teachers – particularly in the early grades – is not so much to create *ex nihilo* a sense of wonder and awe in students as to keep schooling from killing their natural energy and curiosity.[5]

Some of the authors concerned about dis-spirited classrooms attribute the perceived lack of student enthusiasm to a perceived absence of higher purposes for school learning. These authors protest that contemporary curricula stifle curiosity in students by requiring them to absorb fragments of unconnected information that students (and even teachers) experience as meaningless (Iannone and Obenauf 1999: 738). They worry that students are not encouraged to ask the 'big questions' about what life and learning are all about, and that teachers (not without good reason) tend to avoid such questions, and the controversies that go with them, like the proverbial plague (Kessler 1998: 51). The belief is that students and teachers are 'turned off' schooling when they perceive no intrinsic meaning in what they are required to do.

> When we fail to honour the deepest questions of our lives, education remains mired in technical triviality, cultural banality, and worse: it continues to be dragged down by a great sadness. I mean the sadness one feels in too many schools where teachers and students alike spend their days on things unworthy of the human heart – a grief that may mask itself as boredom, sullenness, or anger, but that is, at bottom, a cry for meaning.[6]

Neil Postman (1995: 4) expresses a similar concern about the loss he sees in American society of a shared narrative about the intrinsic value or higher purposes of education: 'Without a narrative, life has no meaning. Without meaning, learning has no purpose. Without a purpose, schools are houses of detention, not attention.'

Some proponents of spirituality in schools argue that when students find their lessons boring and meaningless they are compelled to seek excitement in danger or an outlet for their frustration in aggressive behaviour. Kessler (1998: 49), for example, claims that 'Drugs, sex, gang violence, and even suicide may be both a search for connection and meaning and an escape from the pain of not having a genuine source of spiritual fulfilment.' On the flip side, Kazanjian (1998) reports that, when students are able to make connections between schooling and 'real life', they experience learning as meaningful, inspiring, and even joyful. In particular, lessons or discussions that encourage students to grapple with the 'big questions' at the centre of their lives are recommended as a way to bring 'soul' back to the classroom (Kessler 1998). For those of us who might worry that restoring a higher purpose to learning would involve imposing some master narrative on students in the name of spirituality, Palmer (1998: 8) reassures us that 'spiritual mentoring is not about dictating answers to the deep questions of life. It is about helping young people find questions that are worth asking because they are worth living, questions worth wrapping one's life around.'

Acceptance of self and compassion for others

On some accounts, re/introducing spirituality into public schools would not only help students to find meaning in and enthusiasm for their studies but also help them to learn to accept themselves and feel compassion for others. Here, teachers are enjoined to invite students to encounter their 'inner selves' and the interior lives of others in a more open, caring, and profound way than is usually possible in schools:

> When soul enters the classroom, masks drop away. Students dare to share the joy and the talents they feared would provoke jealousy. They risk exposing the pain or shame that might be judged as weakness. Seeing deeply into the perspective of others, accepting what they thought unworthy in themselves, students discover compassion and begin to learn about forgiveness.
>
> (Kessler 1998: 50)

Some authors propose that students would discover through spirituality a core of common humanity within their differences (Foxworth 1998), and that such experiences would lead students to active concern for the well-being of others outside as well as inside schools. For example, Iannone and Obenauf (1999) contend that 'once we recognize the spirituality in us, we then will recognize in others, especially the enslaved and oppressed, that need to be set free and enter into the world of justice.' Other authors go further, maintaining that we can learn to extend compassion to all beings through an appreciation of our interdependence. 'All education worthy of the name is education in compassion', says Fox (1998: 49), and 'We teach compassion by teaching interdependence.' For these authors, re/introducing spirituality into public schools would mean bringing students to an experience of the sacredness of all life and to an apprehension of the intrinsic worthiness of all beings.

The call for schools to cultivate in students acceptance of self and compassion for others closely parallels the demand for education of the whole person (Watson 2000a: 49, cf. Foxworth 1998: 51). Holistic educators insist that schools are responsible for promoting all dimensions of human development by attending to the physical, emotional, aesthetic, social, moral, and spiritual potential of students as well as to their intellectual abilities. They maintain that incorporating spirituality within public education would alleviate its chronic crises by addressing the needs that students have for acceptance, community, and moral guidance that too often are neglected in modern secular schools.

THE TRANSFORMATION OF CONSCIOUSNESS NEEDED TO SAVE THE WORLD

Many of spirituality's advocates believe that the problems experienced by students and teachers in public schools are symptoms of a broader social crisis that is rooted in human alienation. Such things as the warfare of nations, the deterioration of the environment, the persecution of minorities, the oppression of women, the growing gap between the rich and the poor, and many other sources of human suffering are all seen as evidence of our current condition of estrangement from '——', where the blank might be filled in with God, Gaia, our Inner/Higher Selves, our True Nature, or our Shared Humanity. (This is not, of course, an exhaustive list.) Here, re/introducing spirituality into public schools would mean setting students (and perhaps even teachers) on a path to the transformed state of consciousness that our very survival as a species requires. Holistic Education again represents a case in point, as many of its programmes include both personal and social transformation among their developmental goals: 'Seeing the interconnectedness of all things, with nature as the foundation, is the basis of the new mind that the world needs for survival and . . . the creation of this mind is the first responsibility of education' (Forbes 1996, cf. Miller 1998: 47). The paths to transformed consciousness that have been proposed for the salvation of schools and society are as varied as the interpretations of what it is that we are currently alienated from.

In sum: if there is one overarching theme in the literature on spirituality in education, it is that of connection. Spirituality is typically presented either as consisting of, or as leading to, experiences of connectedness with (a) our deepest selves, with all our secret hopes and fears; (b) other human and non-human souls, in all their similarities and differences; (c) the natural world and the cosmos beyond, in all its awe-inspiring complexity, beauty and mystery; and/or (d) the larger purposes, potentials, and powers that transcend ego's limited concerns. Precisely in virtue of their potential to foster these and other connections, various conceptions of spirituality-in-schools have been presented as antidotes to a wide variety of student problems and social ills. Experiencing one or another form of connectedness has been seen as the cure for such things as indifference towards a fragmented curriculum, rampant materialism and random vandalism, callous indifference to social injustice, and appalling apathy in the face of impending environmental catastrophe.

> Students who feel deeply connected don't need danger to feel fully alive. They don't need guns to feel powerful. They don't want to hurt others or themselves. Out of connection grows compassion and passion – passion for people, for students' goals and dreams, for life itself.
>
> (Kessler 1998: 52)

PROSPECTS FOR SPIRITUALITY IN PUBLIC SCHOOLS

I am sympathetic to concerns that public schooling is neglecting, and even perhaps obstructing, the spiritual development of its students and teachers. I believe that many of the educational initiatives proposed by spirituality's advocates are worthy of further exploration. At the same time, I believe that the following three general features of our current social, cultural, political, and economic context make it unlikely that attempts to re/introduce spirituality into public school curricula would succeed.

The absence of a widely shared understanding of spiritual education

Even the brief survey above illustrates that its contemporary advocates have quite different understandings of what 'spirituality' is and of what it would mean to re/introduce it into schools. This presents a problem when it comes time to establish what is and is not genuine, wholesome, or fruitful within spirituality. This question arises however spirituality is under-

stood; that is, whether as beliefs to be transmitted, feelings and dispositions to be fostered, insights and perceptions to be cultivated, higher
levels of consciousness to be attained, codes to be followed, rites to be
celebrated, disciplines to be practised, or some combination of these.
To leave to individual students judgements about what is and is not desirable within spirituality – for surely it also has its 'dark side' – would be to
abdicate our responsibility as educators. In this regard I think criticisms
of Values Clarification's 'laissez-faire' approach to moral education are
instructive.[7]

Where are the criteria of genuine spirituality to be found? I would argue
that, although the potential for spiritual experience or development might
be the same among all of us – and even this is not universally agreed –
our potential is only actualised through our initiation into the normative
practices of one or more socially and historically conditioned traditions.
(The same could be said, I suspect, about the development of the human
capacity for speech, aesthetic appreciation, artistic performance, and much
else.) Spirituality is not safe, then, in the sense of being as tradition-
independent as is sometimes supposed. The challenges to public education
presented by cultural pluralism cannot be avoided simply by declaring
spirituality independent of religious or institutional affiliations.[8] The fate
of Lawrence Kohlberg's claim to have discovered a culturally neutral
schema of moral development should makes us suspicious of any similar
claims for a universal or tradition-free programme of spiritual education.[9]

The political organisation of public schooling

Let us imagine that, on some happy day in the future, a combination of
psychological research, philosophical enquiry, contemplative practice, religious study, critical social theory, and cross-cultural dialogue produces a
characterisation of human spirituality that enjoys the unqualified approval
of humanistic psychologists, philosophers of education, scholars of religion, spiritual seekers, deep ecologists, critical pedagogues, and religious
authorities of all stripes. Let us further imagine that this account of
spirituality is integrated within a coherent, comprehensive, and compelling
account of human experience such that no 'rational' person (however
her qualifications are conceived) could, after due consideration, doubt its
validity. Even such a remarkable accomplishment would not in itself
guarantee the successful integration of spirituality into public schools – at
least, not in Canada. One problem is gaining access to 'the system', for
there is no clear set of procedures for (a) reaching agreement on what the
broad aims of public schooling should be; (b) evaluating the extent to
which – and for what reasons – public schools are or are not achieving
their full range of objectives; and (c) holding those in public office accountable for supporting systems of public education adequately to achieve

those objectives. A case in point is the Atlantic Provinces Education Foundation (APEF) documents, which define the knowledge, skills, and attitudes that all graduates of Atlantic Canada's public school systems should possess. In these documents, many laudable educational goals are set forth under such headings as 'Citizenship', 'Problem-Solving' and 'Personal Development'.[10] However, the documents say very little about who was consulted to arrive at the list of desired outcomes, who will revisit that list in the light of feedback from the curriculum implementation process, and – perhaps most importantly – who will make the changes to existing systems of public education that will be required for those outcomes to be achieved.[11]

My general point here is that public school curriculum policy decisions are not (at least, in any obvious way) the outcome of reasoned public debate.[12] This is in part because *there is no general social agreement on what public schools should be for* – a consensus that would provide a large part of the common ground required for productive argument on curriculum issues. If I am correct on this point, the lack of an empirically supported, philosophically sound, and cross-culturally accepted conception of spiritual education is less an obstacle to bringing spirituality into public schools than the lack of effective procedures to address competing educational priorities based upon conflicting political and economic agendas. For example, even if we could demonstrate that spiritual education is in the best interests of public school students, that would accomplish little if, as some have argued, serving the needs of its students are not what public schools are really for (Miller 1999: 190–91; also Fox 1998: 49; Gatto 1999: 158).

A related concern is the centralised, outcome-oriented structure of most publicly funded school systems. Even if advocates of spirituality in schools could effect changes in the standard curriculum, they would still be confronted with the question of whether spirituality is something that ever could or should be fostered through state-run bureaucracies. Parker Palmer (1999: 30) suggests a negative answer: 'I don't think that institutions are well suited to carry the sacred. Indeed, I think distortion is a great risk when the sacred gets vested in an institutional context or framework.' Iris Yob (1995) suggests why when she notes that spiritual quests are typically all-consuming affairs, observing that

> if a school program is to become involved in meaningful spiritual education, an occasional unit on spirituality in some social studies classes will be ineffectual at worst, merely supplemental at best, for pilgrimage is a way of life, the vehicle in which all other activities are carried along.
>
> (Yob 1995: 109)

Taken together, the political and economic priorities of our liberal institutions, and the corresponding centralised, bureaucratic, control-oriented structure of government systems of education, make it unlikely that spirituality will be taught or practised in public schools in any meaningful way.

The scarcity of reliable spiritual guides

In response to concerns such as I have raised, advocates of spirituality in schools could propose that it be re/introduced by teachers into their curricula in an *ad hoc* way using whatever opportunities exist in their particular educational contexts. I raise this possibility because, if the literature is correct, almost any aspect of schooling can become a vehicle for spiritual development under the direction of the right teacher.[13] Indeed, some authors have maintained that teachers cannot help but bring spirituality into their classrooms in the form of their own heart and soul: 'Whoever our students may be, whatever subject we teach, ultimately we teach who we are' (Palmer 1998: 10; cf. Mehlman 1991: 306).

But there's the rub. In whatever scenario we envision, the success of initiatives to bring spirituality (back) into schools will depend upon the abilities of the teachers involved, and particularly their degree of spiritual maturity. The problem facing advocates of spirituality in education is similar to that faced by proponents of Kohlberg's programme of moral education, which requires teachers at the appropriate stages of human development to serve as role models and guides: Who shall teach the teachers? Some authors do provide some suggestions for how to encourage the spiritual development of pre-service and in-service teachers, but they say very little about who will conduct these programmes. If current post-secondary educational institutions are the product of the same secularised society that has shaped elementary and secondary schools, and if current teacher educators are, like myself, the products and present occupants of those institutions – not to mention the former students of public schools – the prospects for a spiritual revolution seem very dim indeed.[14] It is not clear that there are enough people in teacher education qualified to hire, much less educate, the trustworthy spiritual mentors and guides that even *ad hoc* educational initiatives would require.

CREATING THE CONDITIONS FOR SPIRITUALITY IN SCHOOLS

For the reasons outlined above, I think the chances for success of efforts to re/introduce spirituality into classrooms are rather dim, at least in the short term. I am more optimistic about the prospects of long-term projects to create the proper conditions for spiritual education in public schools. I see many people engaged in a variety of such projects; I would like particularly to endorse these three.

Articulate a new world-view

Re/introducing spirituality into public schools in a responsible way would require greater consensus on the nature and conditions of genuine spiritual development and on the forms of education that foster it. Creating such a shared understanding of spiritual development would not necessarily require that we all come to belong either to the same historical tradition or to some new synthesis concocted in a spiritual melting pot.[15] What it would require, in part, is reaching general agreement on at least the basics of a post-positivistic metaphysics and epistemology in which the claims of science and of spirituality could be reconciled.[16] To this point, the conflict between science and religion has not been resolved so much as postponed by a policy of détente in which each is granted a separate sphere of influence. Co-existence based on mutual distrust is not enough because, as long as science and religion remain unreconciled, either spirituality will be denied a legitimate place in public schools or it will be admitted in an educationally inadequate form.[17]

The articulation of a new world-view is, of course, a large task.[18] I endorse efforts in that direction because the materialism, determinism, and reductionism associated with the mechanistic world-view leave no room for a spiritual dimension to reality. Also, the mechanistic world-view can support scientism, the assumption that what objectively exists can be known through scientific method, positivistically conceived; and that what cannot be so known lies within the realm of imagination, opinion, emotion, or (perhaps more charitably) 'the arts'. Once science conceived positivistically is accepted as the paradigm of knowledge, spirituality – along with morality and aesthetics – is typically seen to fall on the wrong side of the objective/subjective divide. Scientifically speaking, the mechanistic world-view is long out of date. Unfortunately, however, this does not mean that it no longer influences what we do and do not accept as real.[19] My concern here is that, as long as corresponding biases for 'hard' over 'soft' subjects continue to shape curriculum priorities, spirituality will be denied the status of a genuine form of knowledge and will have a very difficult time justifying its presence in schools.[20] Conversely, I believe that legitimising the inclusion of spirituality within public school curricula will require reference to a view of the world and of human potential that goes far beyond what is conceivable within a mechanistic universe.

Creating a shared understanding of spiritual development to inform educational initiatives in public schools would require, along with a new world-view, agreement on a set of elemental moral principles or virtues for schools to promote. This agreement would establish the basic moral framework within which cultural pluralism could flourish. If Alasdair MacIntyre (1988) is correct, it is neither necessary nor possible to meet the challenge of pluralism by attempting to discover or construct tradition-independent standards of moral and spiritual progress. To the extent that consensus on such standards is possible, it will be achieved through on-going critical dialogue between competing points of view that can both discover and create common ground. According to my understanding of what is involved in critical dialogue, reaching agreement on a new world-view and on a framework of basic moral principles or virtues are two aspects of the same multi-faceted process.[21]

Demonstrate that spiritual education 'works'

As I have argued above, arriving at consensus on the nature and conditions of spiritual development would not guarantee that corresponding proposals for curriculum change would be implemented. Where public education is understood to reflect the economic and political priorities of the powers that be, it seems unrealistic to expect that even well-conceived proposals will suffice to bring about significant changes in schools. The least one could say is that those who wish to resolve one or another perceived shortcoming in public education by re/introducing spirituality into public schools must address the social and political dynamics that are keeping it out of the curriculum in the first place. In short, they must direct their attempts to effect change to the cultural chicken as well as to the educational egg.[22]

I profess no expertise in engineering large-scale social change. Even so, I would suggest that one factor contributing to successful institutional reforms, educational and otherwise, is the tension created when the gap between the goals and values professed by an organisation and those embodied in its practices exceeds some undeterminable limit. To help mobilise and direct the energy for change created by that tension, proposals for new initiatives should be accompanied by evidence that they are workable. All this is to suggest that efforts to re/introduce spirituality into public schools could only increase their chances of success by pointing to successful precedents, prototypes, and pilot programmes. Establishing and maintaining viable alternative schools is one way in which the efforts of those working for change outside the public educational system can complement the efforts of those working for change inside.[23]

Attend to our own spiritual development in the academy

If I am correct that qualified spiritual guides are in short supply, those of us who believe in the importance of spiritual development, whether inside or outside of schools, are advised to attend to our own disciplines of spiritual study and practice. There is nothing, of course, more powerful than leading by example; or more suspect than failing to practise what is preached. I hasten to add that the necessity of taking time for one's own spiritual 'work' need not and should not serve to rationalise narcissistic self-preoccupation: taking responsibility for oneself does not excuse failure to attend to one's responsibilities for others. Yet, we should not forget that the reverse also holds true. While many traditions would assert that our progress in spiritual development is arrested if we do not share its fruits with others, they would also caution that our efforts to benefit others will go astray if we have not ourselves experienced some relaxation of ego's fixations.[24]

A related point is that, if schools are to become hospitable environments for the spiritual development of teachers and students, universities and colleges with teacher education programmes must become hospitable environments for the spiritual development both of their faculty and of pre-service teachers. For if 'higher' education cannot be persuaded to take holistic education seriously, I see little hope that it will be championed by the government ministries responsible for public schools. What modern, secular universities could become if they began to take spirituality seriously is beyond my ability to imagine. However, I do think Eli Bay (1999: 55) is on the right track in saying: 'we need to get beyond judging ourselves and others solely by the standards of doing and open up to the importance of being.'

CONCLUSION

In this paper, I have presented a brief survey of what proponents of spirituality in education believe their initiatives would offer students and teachers. I have identified three features of our cultural, social, political, and economic context that bode poorly for the success of such initiatives, and have endorsed three projects in response. I must acknowledge, however, that even if those projects were undertaken with enthusiasm, their success would by no means be assured; and even their success would by no means guarantee spirituality a place in schools.

By speaking in general terms about their common themes, I have passed over many significant differences among the varied proposals to re/intro-duce spirituality into public school curricula. This is in part because a nuanced treatment of individual programmes is beyond the scope of a single article. It is also because, if my claim is correct, all such initiatives face the obstacles I have identified. Therefore, although generalisation in this context is hazardous, I believe that those who wish to promote personal and social development through proper attention to spirituality in schools should take a long term-view of their enterprise. Yet, it should also be said that bringing ever greater energy, purpose, and compassion to education is worthy of our best efforts inside and outside public schools.

NOTES

1 An earlier version of this paper appeared in *Paideusis* 13, 2: 23–41.
2 A review of the titles in the References below will indicate the authors to whom I refer. Some of those cited speak more of educating holistically or of inviting soul into classrooms than of spiritual education, but the recommendations repeat essentially the same themes. For a critical interpretation from an American perspective of the cultural and social factors contributing to this revival of interest in spirituality, see Elias (1991).
3 Foxworth (1998: 51; cf. Minney 1991) provides a summary statement of this position: 'Spirituality is not peculiar to "a people" or to a religion but is what makes us all "people." It is universal.'
4 When referring rather grandly to 'our' public schools, I have in mind the educational systems of modern, pluralistic liberal democracies such as Canada, the United States, and the United Kingdom, the important differences among the systems within the different countries – and within the different regions, provinces, and states within countries – notwithstanding.
5 On this point, Hayward (1999) is particularly emphatic.
6 Palmer (1998: 8). My own visits to schools suggest that this generalisation applies more to secondary than elementary grades; and even then by no means universally.
7 For critical analyses of Values Clarification, see Boyd and Bogdan (1984, 1985); Carter (1984: 49–53); and Lockwood (1975).
8 On this point, see Watson (2000b: 96–100); Noddings (in Halford 1998: 29); and Blake (1996). For a complementary critique of the 'scatter-shot' response to the variety of conceptions of spirituality, see Carr (1995).
9 For critical analyses of Kohlberg's cognitive-developmental approach to moral education, see Broughton (1985); Carter (1985: 19); Gilligan (1982); and Locke (1980, 1985).
10 The Atlantic Canada Framework for Essential Graduation Learnings in Schools can be viewed at http://www2.gov.pe.ca/educ/publications/apef.asp.
11 I doubt, not the intentions or the abilities of those who produced the APEF documents, but that their mandate was broad enough to ensure successful implementation of their educational objectives.
12 Pinar (1998: 14) claims: 'Schools are no longer under the jurisdiction . . . of curriculum theorists.'
13 See, for example, Orr's (1999) discussion of 'architecture as pedagogy'.
14 For a related caution, see Gawitrha (1999).

15 Watson (2000a: 48) is concerned that 'consensus models of spirituality do a disservice to the richness of lived spiritualities and are not based in any enduring reality.'

16 The works of Huston Smith (e.g. 1989, 1990, 1992) and Ken Wilbur (e.g. 1985, 1997) are examples of the kind of project I have in mind.

17 On this point, see Nord (1999); also Singham (2000); cf. Larson and Witham (1999).

18 I do not wish to suggest that no progress has been made in this area. See Kidder and Born (1998); Suhor (1998/99: 12); and Teasdale (1997).

19 Regarding the persistence of positivistic views of knowledge, see Mayer (2000: 38–9) on defining educational research. For a broader discussion of mechanism and positivism, see Vokey (2001: 86–92).

20 See Nixon (1999: 628–9) for a historical perspective on the aversion of curriculum theorists to such things as 'mystical illumination'. Labaree (1998) provides an analysis of how the distinction between hard and soft knowledge operates within programmes of teacher education.

21 For more on the nature and possibility of such critical dialogue, see Vokey (2001).

22 For a claim that it is unrealistic to expect significant social change to result only from initiatives in schools, see Miller (1999: 193).

23 For one example, the Shambhala School (www.shambhalaschool.org) shows how it is possible for teachers to attend to their own spirituality and to that of their students without compromising more conventional educational goals.

24 As Luke 17:2 reminds us, a blind or untrustworthy guide is worse than no guide at all.

REFERENCES

Bay, E. (1999) 'The relaxation response', *Orbit* 30, 2: 54–5.

Blake, N. (1996) 'Against spiritual education', *Oxford Review of Education* 22, 4: 443–56.

Boyd, D. and Bogdan, D. (1984) '"Something" clarified, nothing of "value": a rhetorical critique of values clarification', *Educational Theory* 34: 287–300.

Boyd, D. and Bogdan, D. (1985) 'Rhetorical realities: a response to McAnich's interpretation of values and teaching', *Educational Theory* 35: 327–30.

Broughton, J.M. (1985) 'The genesis of moral domination', in S. Modgil and C. Modgil (eds), *Lawrence Kohlberg: Consensus and Controversy*, London: Falmer Press, pp. 363–85.

Carr, D. (1995) 'Towards a distinctive conception of spiritual education', *Oxford Review of Education* 21, 1: 83–98.

Carter, R.E. (1984) *Dimensions of Moral Education*, Toronto: University of Toronto Press.

Carter, R.E. (1985) 'Does Kohlberg avoid relativism?', in S. Modgil and C. Modgil (eds), *Lawrence Kohlberg: Consensus and Controversy*, London: Falmer Press, pp. 9–20.

Elias, J.L. (1991) 'The return of spirituality: contrasting interpretations', *Religious Education* 86, 3: 455–67.

Forbes, S. (1996) 'Values in holistic education', http://www.putnampit.com/holistic.html.

Fox, M. (1998) 'A spiritual renewal of education', *Tikkun* 13, 6: 49–50.

Foxworth, M. (1998) 'Putting spirituality in public schools', *Tikkun* 13, 6: 51–4.

Gatto, J.T. (1999) 'Education and the Western spiritual tradition', in Steven Glazer (ed.), *The Heart of Learning: Spirituality and Education*, New York: Jeremy P. Tarcher/Putnam, pp. 115–71.

Gawitrha (1999) 'Toward a 'new world' order: a native perspective', in A. Walter Dorn (ed.), *World Order for a New Millennium: Political, Cultural and Spiritual Approaches to Building Peace*, New York: St Martin's Press, pp. 213–18.

Gilligan, C. (1982) *In a Different Voice*, Cambridge, MA: Harvard University Press.

Halford, J.M. (1998) 'Longing for the sacred in schools: a conversation with Nel Noddings', *Educational Leadership*, 56, 4: 28–32.

Hayward, J. (1999) 'Unlearning to see the sacred', in Steven Glazer (ed.), *The Heart of Learning: Spirituality in Education*, New York: Jeremy P. Tarcher/Putnam, pp. 61–75.

Iannone, R.V. and Obenauf, P.A. (1999) 'Toward spirituality in curriculum and teaching', *Education* 119, 4: 737–41.

Kazanjian Jr., V. (1998) 'Moments of meaning', *Connection* 13, 3: 37–40.

Kessler, R. (1998) 'Nourishing students in secular schools', *Educational Leadership* 56, 4: 49–52.

Kidder, R.M. and Born, P.L. (1998) 'Resolving ethical dilemmas in the classroom', *Educational Leadership* 56, 4: 38–41.

Labaree, D.F. (1998) 'Educational researchers: living with a lesser form of knowledge', *Educational Researcher* 27, 8: 4–12.

Larson, E.J. and Witham, L. (1999) 'Scientists and religion in America', *Scientific American* September: 88–93.

Locke, D. (1980) 'The illusion of Stage Six', *Journal of Moral Education* 9, 2: 103–9.

Locke, D. (1985) 'A psychologist among the philosophers: philosophical aspects of Kohlberg's theories', in S. Modgil and C. Modgil (eds), *Lawrence Kohlberg: Consensus and Controversy*, London: Falmer Press, pp. 21–38.

Lockwood, A.L. (1975) 'A critical view of values clarification', *Teachers College Record* 76: 35–50.

MacIntyre, A. (1988) *Whose Justice? Which Rationality?*, Notre Dame: University of Notre Dame Press.

Mayer, R.E. (2000) 'What is the place of science in educational research?', *Educational Researcher* 29, 6: 38–9.

Mehlman, C. (1991) 'Walden within', in Ron Miller (ed.), *New Directions in Education*, Brandon, VT: Holistic Education Press, pp. 306–18.

Miller, J.P. (1998) 'Making connections through holistic learning', *Educational Leadership* 56, 4: 46–8.

Miller, R. (1999) 'Holistic education for an emerging culture', in Steven Glazer (ed.), *The Heart of Learning: Spirituality in Education*, New York: Jeremy P. Tarcher/Putnam, pp. 189–201.

Minney, R. (1991) 'What is spirituality in an educational context?', *British Journal of Educational Studies* 39, 4: 386–97.

Nixon, G.M. (1999) 'Whatever happened to "heightened consciousness"?', *Journal of Curriculum Studies* 31, 6: 625–33.

Nord, W.A. (1999) 'Science, religion, and education', *Phi Delta Kappan* 81, 1: 28–33.

Orr, D.W. (1999) 'Reassembling the pieces: architecture as pedagogy', in Steven Glazer (ed.), *The Heart of Learning: Spirituality in Education*, New York: Jeremy P. Tarcher/Putnam, pp. 139–49.

Palmer, P.J. (1998) 'Evoking the spirit in public education', *Educational Leadership* 56, 4: 6–11.

Palmer, P.J. (1999) 'The grace of great things: reclaiming the sacred in knowing, teaching, and learning', in Steven Glazer (ed.), *The Heart of Learning: Spirituality in Education*, New York: Jeremy P. Tarcher/Putnam, pp. 15–32.

Pinar, W.F. (1998) 'Gracious submission', *Educational Researcher* 28, 1: 14–15.

Postman, N. (1995) 'What does the future hold for public education?', Paper prepared for the Canadian Teachers' Federation National Conference, 'Public Education: Meeting the Challenges', May.

Scheindlin, L. (1999) 'Preparing children for spirituality', *Religious Education* 94, 2: 190–201.

Singham, M. (2000) 'The science and religion wars', *Phi Delta Kappan* 81, 6: 424–32.

Smith, H. (1989) *Beyond the Post-modern Mind*, revised edition, Wheaton, IL: The Theosophical Publishing House.

Smith, H. (1990) 'The central curricular issue of our age', in Mary E. Clark and Sandra A. Wawrytko (eds), *Rethinking the Curriculum: Toward an Integrated, Interdisciplinary College Education*, New York: Greenwood Press, pp. 123–34.

Smith, H. (1992) 'Is there a perennial philosophy?', in J. Ogilvy (ed.), *Revisioning Philosophy*, Albany: State University of New York Press, pp. 247–62.

Suhor, C. (1998/99) 'Spirituality – letting it grow in the classroom', *Educational Leadership* 56, 4: 12–16.

Teasdale, W. (1997) 'The interspiritual age: practical mysticism for the third millennium', *Journal of Ecumenical Studies* 34, 1: 74–90.

Vokey, D. (2001) *Moral Discourse in a Pluralistic World*, Notre Dame: University of Notre Dame Press.

Watson, J. (2000a) 'From transcendence to ethics: shaping spirituality to schools', *Journal of Beliefs and Values* 21, 1: 39–50.

Watson, J. (2000b) 'Whose model of spirituality should be used in the spiritual development of school children?', *International Journal of Children's Spirituality* 5, 1: 91–101.

Wilbur, K. (1985) *No Boundary: Eastern and Western Approaches to Personal Growth*, Boston: Shambhala Publications.

Wilbur, K. (1997) *The Eye of Spirit: An Integral Vision for a World Gone Slightly Mad*, Boston: Shambhala Publications.

Yob, I.M. (1995) 'Spiritual education: a public school dialogue with religious interpretations', *Religious Education* 90, 1: 104–18.

Chapter 13

Education, spirituality and the common school

Terence H. McLaughlin

The claim that education (and more specifically schooling) should be concerned with 'spirituality' and with 'spiritual development' invites immediate attention to two related questions which are fundamental, pressing and inescapable. These questions are: (i) How are 'spirituality' and 'spiritual development' to be properly understood? and (ii) What constitutes justifiable educational influence in relation to the spiritual domain? Progress in relation to both (i) and (ii) involves, amongst other things, the making of important distinctions. In relation to (i) I have argued elsewhere in work with Hanan Alexander that a useful distinction for educational purposes can be drawn between 'religiously tethered' and 'religiously untethered' conceptions of spirituality (Alexander and McLaughlin 2003: 359–60). In relation to (ii) I have argued in that work that distinctions between education in spirituality 'from the inside' and 'from the outside' respectively and between differing schooling contexts and mandates for the exercise of educational influence (separate religious schools and common schools) are also of significance (Alexander and McLaughlin 2003: 361–73).

This chapter seeks to explore central aspects of these two fundamental questions and the distinctions proposed in relation to them from a broadly philosophical perspective and in relation to a specific question: What form might 'education in spirituality' justifiably take in the common school? Three preliminary points can be usefully made at the outset of the discussion. First, the discussion is concerned with education and schooling in societies of a broadly liberal democratic kind, and although England is taken as a particular point of reference, the points which are made have broader application to other liberal democratic societies. Second, the various distinctions drawn in the discussion are rather stipulative and imprecise and are intended merely to provide a set of analytical tools based on discriminations which are seen as both intuitively plausible (at least in general terms) and useful in bringing into focus key issues in the educational debate. Third, it is acknowledged that the questions which arise in this discussion cannot be fully illuminated, let alone resolved, by philosophical considerations alone. Any merely philosophical approach to these questions is but necessarily incomplete.

The chapter has three sections. The first section offers a brief outline of the notion of the common school and the specific mandate it enjoys for the exercise of educational influence. The second section explores two concerns which arise in relation to 'education in spirituality' in the context of the common school, which I shall describe as a concern for clarity and coherence and a concern for 'admissability for common educational influence' respectively. The third section addresses the forms which 'education in spirituality' might justifiably take in the common school.

THE COMMON SCHOOL AND ITS EDUCATIONAL MANDATE

The term 'common school' is not widely or unproblematically used in England (or, for that matter, in the United States). I use the term to refer to schools which are open to, and intended for, all students within a liberal democratic society regardless of specific differentiating characteristics of the students and their families such as spiritual belief and practice. Common schools can therefore be identified in broad terms with 'non-voluntary' or 'community' schools in England in the 'maintained', or publicly funded, sector, and with 'public' schools in the USA. Such schools are contrasted with separate schools of one kind and another in these contexts, such as religious schools, whether or not (as in England) such schools receive some measure of support from public funds. In confining itself to some of the central principles relating to common schools, this section is not unaware of the dangers of undue idealisation and abstraction inherent in appearing to ignore the fact that common schools take particular forms in particular societal contexts. The implications of the contextualised nature of common schools will be alluded to in due course. At this stage, attention to matters of general principle will help to bring important central points into focus for the purposes of our discussion.

The common school forms the major part, and in some cases the sole part, of the publicly funded schooling system in liberal democratic societies. The mandate for educative influence possessed by common schools emphasises the importance of influence which is broadly acceptable to society as a whole. The concept of 'broad acceptability to society as a whole' is, of course, in need of more precise definition. One familiar resource for providing such a definition is the political theory of liberalism in which the theory of common schooling in liberal democratic societies is frequently articulated. From this perspective, the ideal of the common school specifies not only a particular institutional arrangement for schooling but also a 'conception of common education' based on liberal democratic philosophical and educational ideals with which it is presumptively associated.[1] From the point of view of this ideal, common schools lack a mandate to assume the truth of, or promote, any particular, overall, 'thick' or 'comprehensive' vision of the good life as a whole, in virtue of the 'significantly controversial' character of these visions in contemporary liberal democratic societies. Such schools cannot, for example, assume the truth of any particular religious faith and seek to shape its students into religious believers, and nor can they shape the beliefs, values and practices of students in the light of any substantive conception of 'spirituality'. In this context, religious and spiritual beliefs, values and practices are seen as 'significantly controversial' and therefore as matters for the reflective evaluation, decision and response of individuals and families. On such controversial matters, the common school is required either to remain silent, or to open up the issues at stake for critical reflective discussion and consideration by students. In contrast, in relation to the 'common' or 'public' values which articulate a liberal democratic society, such as respect for the autonomy and dignity of individuals, and a concern for the demands of education for democratic citizenship and civic virtue (including the development of appropriate forms of empathy and tolerance), the common school seeks to achieve a substantial influence on the beliefs of students and on their wider development as persons. At the heart of the educational influence of the common school is therefore the need to achieve a balance between unifying and diversifying imperatives and forces which are characteristic of pluralist liberal societies themselves. The fact that the common school must exercise a form of forbearance from undue substantive influence on controversial matters means that the claim that we should 'educate the whole child' in the common school is problematic (McLaughlin 1996).[2]

An acceptance of these general principles outlining the educational mandate of the common school does not depend solely upon an acceptance of the theory of liberalism in which they have been articulated, but corresponds to widely held intuitions among educational professionals and the public at large in liberal democratic societies. In England, for example, there is little widespread general enthusiasm for developing (say) an explicitly Christian form of spiritual belief and practice in students in the common school, despite the non-neutrality towards religious faith in common schools in England which is reflected in the history of the development of these schools and the continuing requirement that they hold a daily act of collective religious worship.[3]

In contrast to the common school, 'separate' schools (such as 'religious' or 'faith' schools) enjoy a mandate to educate students in the context of a fuller view of life as a whole such as a religious faith and to include a formation in particular religious and spiritual belief and practice as part of their overall educational influence. (On such schools and their related conceptions of education, see, for example, McLaughlin 1992.)

The concept of the common school and its educational mandate which has emerged from this brief outline is not, of course, unproblematic. Challenges to this broad account of the concept and mandate arise from articulations of the common school which do not invoke the philosophical theory of liberalism and which point to the acceptability of such schools transmitting 'default norms' based on the dominant norms (including religious norms) prevalent in a society.[4] Even within the theory of philosophical liberalism there is dispute about precisely how the concept and mandate of the common school should be precisely characterised. In the light of this theory, for example, I have argued elsewhere that common schools face a series of complex and neglected burdens and dilemmas relating to the public domain, the non-public domain and the interface between the two (McLaughlin 2003).

Leaving aside these complexities, however, it seems clear that two general concerns arise in relation to the claim that the common school should engage in 'education in spirituality', and that these concerns are experienced in general terms as much by educational practitioners and teachers on widely accessible grounds as by educational theorists. These concerns can be described respectively as a concern for clarity and coherence and a concern for 'admissibility for common educational influence'. The concern for clarity and coherence expresses an aversion to imprecision and vagueness in relation to central notions such as 'spirituality' and 'spiritual development'. The concern for 'admissibility for common educational influence' expresses a desire to ensure that the forms of 'education in spirituality' envisaged are genuinely acceptable as part of the 'conception of common education' being offered by the common school.

TWO CONCERNS AND THEIR IMPLICATIONS

A concern for both clarity and coherence and for 'admissibility for common educational influence' have been a marked characteristic of the debate concerning 'education in spirituality' in common schools in England. With regard to clarity and coherence, it has long been acknowledged in this debate that the concepts of 'spirituality' and 'spiritual development' are resistant to easy clarification and definition and that educational policy and practice in relation to these notions have been underinformed by necessary forms of transparency and comprehensibility. The concern with 'spirituality' and 'spiritual development' in common schools in England and its discussion and implementation at the policy level have struggled, not always successfully, with these issues[5] and more general discussions of education in spirituality by educational theorists and philosophers of education have also been preoccupied with these questions.[6] Terence Copley describes the area as 'a beguiling mist' (Copley 2000: 11) and John Haldane observes that when educational theorists talk about 'spiritual development' 'they are usually either struggling to take a last dip in the shallows of the ebbing tide of faith, or engaged in the practice of aggrandising the ordinary, or else doing both at once' (Haldane 2000: 54). David Carr expresses a widely felt view in observing that notions of spirituality in an educational context often amount to little more than 'a hotchpotch of only vaguely connected items of cognition, intuition and feeling between which it is well nigh impossible to discern any coherent conceptual connections' (Carr 1995: 84).

This lack of clarity and coherence gives rise to several kinds of reaction. At one level, the lack of clarity and coherence is seen simply as undermining the prospect of intelligible educational practice. Terence Copley, for example, complains that schools 'neither know clearly what they are trying to do, how they are trying to do it, nor how they are going to evaluate their efforts' (Copley 2000: 136). The difficulty of being able to specify clear criteria for 'spiritual development' is one aspect of this phenomenon (on this, see, for example, J. White 1994). A different kind of reaction, however, expresses a concern with a range of actual or potential dangers which a lack of clarity and coherence is seen as leaving room for. A prominent concern is that 'spirituality' and 'spiritual development' in the common school may act as a Trojan horse for more specific religious influence seen as objectionable on various grounds (Beck 1998: ch. 3; J. White 1994, 1995) as well as for influence, seen as equally objectionable, of a more general, metaphysical, kind (Blake 1997; Flew 1997).

A further concern is that an emphasis on 'spirituality' and 'spiritual development' may act in various ways as a distortive influence on other areas of the work of the school, such as education for citizenship and social and moral development (P. White 1994). A different reaction to a lack of clarity and coherence can be seen in Copley's description of a 'tendency to sanitise and secularise spiritual development within the UK educational system, to render it a benign, consensus-driven, self-exploratory process, at pains to offend no one' (Copley 2000: 128; cf. Blake 1997). John Hull, for example, argues that 'spirituality' and 'spiritual development', properly conceived, have an important but neglected critical role to play in relation to contemporary materialism (Hull 1996). Another reaction to lack of clarity and coherence is a claim that defensible educational activities which may be conducted under the labels of 'spirituality' and 'spiritual development' would be better approached under labels which are more transparent and acceptable. John White, for example, writes: 'I would advocate an absolute embargo on the use of the terms "spirituality" or "spiritual development" in all official documents on education, all conferences on education, all in-service courses for teachers . . . The words simply get in the way of thinking' (J. White 1995: 16).[7]

It should be stressed that a concern with a lack of clarity and coherence in relation to 'spirituality' and 'spiritual development' does not depend upon an unreasonable demand that educational policy-making and practice should or could wait upon fully articulated and philosophically approved conceptualisations of these matters. (On the complex relationship between philosophy and educational policy, see McLaughlin 2000.) Nor does it depend on a claim that educational policy-makers and teachers in this area have been wholly insensitive to the demands of clarity and coherence.

The concern for clarity and coherence leads on to the second concern which has been identified: 'admissibility for common educational influence'. Here the concern is to specify forms of educational influence in relation to 'spirituality' and 'spiritual development' which can satisfy the kinds of criteria for common educational influence identified earlier. This task requires attention to the spiritual domain and to the possibility of making useful distinctions both within this domain and in relation to educative processes concerning it.

EDUCATION IN SPIRITUALITY IN THE COMMON SCHOOL

In the light of the foregoing discussion, what forms might education in spirituality justifiably take in the common school?[8] This question is brought into clearer focus by two sets of distinctions: between 'religiously tethered' and 'religiously untethered' forms of spirituality and between 'education in spirituality from the inside' and 'education in spirituality from the outside' respectively.

Before turning to these distinctions, however, it is necessary to explore why the area of the 'spiritual' broadly conceived should feature in the work of the common school at all. Perhaps the strongest line of argument in relation to this matter[9] concerns the need for any education worthy of the name to address fundamental questions about the nature and context of human life which are open to responses of a 'spiritual' kind. Peters insists that education should include attention to attempts to 'make sense of and give sense to the human condition' (1981: 41), requiring students to be made aware of various perspectives on this matter which are acceptable within, if not demanded by, a democratic way of life – 'in the hope that many will develop insights and sensitivities that may become of increasing significance to them' (Peters 1981: 41). Also included in this process is attention to the 'predicaments' of life for which, in contrast to 'problems', there are, in principle, no solutions (Peters 1981: 45).

This last emphasis of Peters resonates with John Haldane's account of the 'quiet desperation and other non-eccentric conditions of the soul or psyche' (Haldane 2000: 66) which he sees as a starting point for reflections about the meaning of life associated with forms of spirituality not confined to the religious. John White argues that all students need to be introduced to a secular 'cosmic framework' within which their well-being can be conceived and pursued and which relates to 'the widest horizons of our being' (J. White 1995: 19).Whilst White imposes a strictly secular conception of these 'horizons' and resists talk of 'spirituality' in relation to them, Martha Nussbaum insists on a recognition of the difficulty, mysteriousness and continuing openness of ultimate questions relating to life and death, and our need to recognise the shortcomings of our current explanations (Nussbaum 2003). Charles Taylor explores the neglected dangers of an 'exclusive humanism' which excludes a transcendental vision altogether and which involves, in his view, a kind of 'spiritual lobotomy' (Taylor 1999). Nussbaum and Taylor can be read as calling for an openness in relation to the interpretation of questions of a fundamental or 'cosmic' kind to which the common school can be invited to respond.[10]

If a general justification along these lines for the involvement of the common school with 'spiritual' questions can be provided, how should 'spirituality' be understood? The spiritual domain involves a wide range of kinds of human sensitivity, experience, belief, judgement, response, disposition, motivation, commitment, virtue and achievement.[11] The domain is in many cases related, by implicit presupposition and implication if not by explicit avowal, to a range of perspectives and beliefs concerning underlying fundamental questions such as the nature of reality, of persons and of the good. The resistance of the spiritual domain to easy clarification and definition consists in part in the inherently opaque nature of some of its elements, the wide variety of phenomena included under its name, and its close affinity with related areas such as the aesthetic. A central issue claiming attention is what can be said to be *distinctive* of the spiritual (see, for example, Carr 1995, 1996; Haldane 2000).

In previous work with Hanan Alexander, I have drawn a rough distinction between 'religiously tethered' and 'religiously untethered' forms of spirituality (Alexander and McLaughlin 2003: 359–60). In part, the aim of this distinction is to try to pin down 'spirituality' more clearly by marking out at least one general aspect of spirituality which it is relatively easy to bring into focus.

Religiously 'tethered' spirituality takes its shape and structure from various aspects of the religion with which it is associated and which makes it possible to identify the nature and shape of 'spirituality' within that context, including criteria for spiritual development. As John Haldane observes, within religious domains 'spirituality' has definite meanings (Haldane 2000: 54). In the Christian tradition, for example, 'developmental criteria' for spiritual development can be discerned in the life and work of figures such as Ignatius of Loyola, St John of the Cross, and St Francis de Sales, whose experiences and reflections are located within an extended and elaborated tradition of belief, practice and value and infused with its central tenets and commitments.[12] The theological, epistemological, ethical and collective aspects of religion all have their spiritual correlates. The theological aspects of religion provide an intentionality to spirituality by delineating the nature of a divine reality or favoured state of contemplation or consciousness seen as the object or goal of the spiritual quest. The epistemological aspects of religion underpin and give direction to the search for meaning which is such a marked feature of the spiritual domain and which is reflected in many religious traditions in the search to know God through prayer. The ethical aspects of religion infuse forms of spirituality which are part of, and support, a life configured to the acquisition, cultivation and maintenance of the virtues as part of a religiously inspired conception of the good and flourishing life. The collective aspects of religion are expressed in part in forms of spirituality developed and exercised in the different communal contexts of a faith community, especially in different forms of liturgy. 'Religiously tethered' spirituality therefore is typically both substantive and elaborated.

As is widely argued, spirituality extends beyond the religious domain, and much attention has been given to the question of how a non-religious form of spirituality can be characterised (on this, see, for example, Haldane 2000). Religiously 'untethered' spirituality involves beliefs and practices that are disconnected from, and may even be discomforting to, religions. Religiously untethered spirituality takes many forms. Some forms are substantive and elaborated in much the same way as some 'religiously tethered' forms of spirituality are. Other forms may lack a definite shape and structure and may be unconnected to any wider tradition of belief, practice and value, thereby making it difficult to specify criteria for spiritual development in relation to them.

The contrast between religiously 'tethered' and 'untethered' conceptions of spirituality can be illustrated by reference to five interrelated strands which often characterise the spiritual domain (a search for meaning, the cultivation of 'inner space', the manifestations of spirituality in life, distinctive responses to the natural and human world, and collective or communal aspects) (Alexander and McLaughlin 2003: 359–60).

The distinction between 'religiously tethered' and 'religiously untethered' conceptions of spirituality needs, of course, to be handled with considerable caution. The domain of religion is not itself one with clear features and boundaries. It is not always easy, therefore, to distinguish with any degree of rigour a religious from non-religious perspective, and the phenomenology of spirituality does not correspond to any rigid distinction of the sort that has been drawn. Nevertheless, despite its imprecision, the distinction may serve a useful purpose for the present discussion.

The second set of distinctions pertinent to the present discussion involves a distinction between 'education in spirituality from the inside' and 'education in spirituality from the outside',[13] which can also be brought to bear on education in religion (Alexander and McLaughlin 2003: 361–73). 'Education in spirituality from the inside' refers to forms of education in spirituality which are seen as appropriate for those *within* a particular spiritual tradition, or those who are being initiated into such a tradition. Central to these forms of education in spirituality is the attempt to *form* and *nourish* a commitment to the particular beliefs, values and practices of a specific spiritual tradition. The aim of such forms of education in spirituality is therefore not merely to bring about understanding of the spiritual domain but a particular form of spiritual belief and practice. This kind of education in spirituality, which need not necessarily involve indoctrination, is most appropriately located in separate religious schools, where it will be linked with 'religiously tethered' forms of spirituality. (For an example of education in spirituality of this kind, see Haldane 1999).[14]

'Education in spirituality from the outside' refers to forms of education in this domain in which no assumptions are made about the belief and involvement or otherwise of students in relation either to the spiritual domain as a whole or to particular spiritual traditions within it. Initiation into this domain and into these traditions does not constitute an aim of the enterprise. Spiritual belief, commitment and practice on the part of individuals are therefore neither presuppositions of, nor aims of, the process. The aim rather is to engage in exploration, discussion and critical assessment of the spiritual domain and issues of meaning, truth and value relating to it. For these reasons, education of this kind can be described as 'from the outside' of particular spiritual traditions. It is important to insist, however, that education of this form cannot remain 'on the outside' in the sense that no attempt is made to understand the spiritual domain from the insider's point of view. Such attempts are necessary if spiritual traditions and ideas are to be properly illuminated for the purposes of understanding and assessment.

In the light of these distinctions, what can be said about the nature of 'education in spirituality' in the common school? In relation to 'religiously tethered' spirituality, any form of 'education in spirituality from the inside' would amount to formation in a particular religious faith, and would thereby be incompatible with principles relating to 'admissibility for common educative influence' of the sort discussed earlier. 'Education in spirituality from the outside' in the case of 'religiously tethered' spirituality would seem to be justified on very much the same grounds as similar forms of Education in Religion in common schools and be subject to the same kinds of problems and dilemmas, particularly those relating to the achievement of an internal perspective on the domain for students.[15] Any exploration of the domain of spirituality in the common school cannot ignore 'religiously tethered' spirituality, and an examination of this form of spirituality 'from the outside' is therefore appropriate and necessary.

In the case of 'religiously untethered' spirituality, 'education from the outside' is in principle compatible with the requirements of 'admissibility for common educative influence'. A general difficulty encountered by 'education from the outside' in relation to spirituality of whatever kind is captured in David Carr's querying of the extent to which students can achieve a genuine understanding of spirituality short of 'a substantial examination of (even initiation into) the reflection, practices and achievements of some actual spiritual tradition or other' (Carr 1996: 173). The diffuse nature of 'religiously untethered' spirituality and a temptation to approach the area in an eclectic way might be thought to exacerbate the difficulty to which this remark draws attention. One dimension of this difficulty is that students may come to see the spiritual domain exclusively under the aspect of the kind of distorted 'consumerist' mentality associated with the culture of 'authenticity' or expressivist self-awareness in relation to spiritual things to which Charles Taylor has pointed (Taylor 2002).

'Education in spirituality from the inside' seems to be incompatible with the requirements in the case of 'religiously untethered' spirituality for much the same general reasons as in the case of its 'religiously tethered' counterpart. Whilst the form of influence here may not amount to formation in a religious faith, it may involve initiation into practices and perspectives which embody to a greater or lesser extent controversial assumptions and beliefs.

This aversion to 'education in spirituality from the inside' in the case of 'religiously untethered' spirituality is challenged by Clive Erricker, who argues that 'spiritual development involves – . . . self-transformation through practice' (Erricker and Erricker 2001: 58). For Erricker, 'knowledge', 'the conceptual', 'rationality' and the like cannot achieve the necessary forms of understanding, and he insists that 'You actually have to carry out the practices, techniques or strategies that relate to spirituality and reflect upon the effects' (Erricker and Erricker 2001: 58). Erricker and others argue that students should be encouraged to engage in the practice of meditation in common schools. Included among the benefits claimed in relation to this activity are the alleviation of stress and other physical ailments, the enhancement of awareness and clarity, the facilitation of experiential learning, the promotion of calm, a sense of inner strength, self-reliance, well-being and the like (Erricker and Erricker 2001: especially chs 7–9). Whilst being alert to potential objections arising from a perception that engagement of students in this kind of activity may involve the imposition of controversial imbedded beliefs,[16] it has been claimed that

'Meditation does not presume a particular faith or non-faith stance but is a means to calming the mind and acquiring insight into the nature of experience and how the mind works' (Erricker and Erricker 2001: 21). Things may not, however, be this simple.[17] An alertness to the assumptions and beliefs which are imbedded in all spiritual practices is part of the responsibility of the common school.[18] 'Education in spirituality from the inside' of whatever kind in the common school is inherently problematic.

Education in spirituality in the common school faces a range of difficulties and dilemmas, many of which have been indicated. It is important to note that many of these can be resolved only via a form of practical judgement by educational leaders and teachers at school level. Teachers who can realise the complex mandate of the common school must be *certain sorts of people* who possess not merely an abstract understanding of matters of principle relating to this mandate, but can also bring to bear the kind of pedagogic *phronesis* needed for its interpretation and application in practical contexts. Whilst this is a point of general application (McLaughlin 2003: 145–47) its significance in the case of 'education in spirituality' is manifest.

NOTES

1 On the general conception of education associated with liberal democratic societies, see, for example, Callan 1997; Gutmann 1987; Levinson 1999; Macedo 2000; Reich 2002; Tomasi 2001: ch. 5; J. White 1990; P. White 1996.
2 On the concept of the common school see, for example, Callan 1997: especially ch. 7; Feinberg 1998; McLaughlin 1995a, 2003; Salomone 2000.
3 On the relationship between Church and State in education in England, see, for example, Chadwick 1997.
4 On this notion, see, for example, McLaughlin 1995a: 245–8. On the 'neutrality' or otherwise of the common school, see Sandsmark 2000.
5 On the development of educational policy with respect to 'spirituality' and 'spiritual development' in England, see, for example, Copley 2000: Introduction and ch. 2; Erricker 2000; Wright 2000: ch. 6. On policy and discussion documents dealing with these matters, see, for example, Department of Education and Science 1977a, 1977b; National Curriculum Council 1993; Office for Standards in Education 1994; Schools Curriculum and Assessment Authority 1996.
6 For such discussions, see, for example, Best 1996; Blake 1996, 1997; Carr 1995, 1996; Copley 2000; Erricker 2000; Hull 1996; Thatcher 1999; Wright 1998, 2000.
7 See also Beck 1998: especially 63–5; Lambourn 1996.
8 For an extended discussion of this matter, see Mott-Thornton 1998.
9 Included among these perspectives by Peters are '[a] . . . sense of the beauty of the world . . . of man's strivings to give concrete embodiment to intimations about the human condition that he cannot explicitly articulate . . . the place of man in the natural and historical orders . . . the contingency, creation and continuance of the world, which are beyond the power of man to comprehend . . . [giving rise to] . . . awe and wonder . . . [T]he human condition . . . viewed in

a wider perspective, under "a certain aspect of eternity" . . . [generating] . . . ways of life . . . that transcend and transform what is demanded by morality and truth' (Peters 1981: 41; cf. Peters 1972: especially Lecture 4; Elliott 1986).

10 On the relationship between the cosmic imagination and specific beliefs and values, see Hepburn 2000.

11 For general treatments of the spiritual domain, see, for example, Alexander 2001; Hadot 1995; Haldane 2000; Hick 1999; McGhee 2000; Wright 1998, 2000. On the notion of the spirituality of childhood, see, for example, Coles 1992; Hay with Nye 1998.

12 On the Christian tradition in spirituality, see, for example, Jones *et al.* 1992; McGrath 1999. For an accessible appropriation of aspects of this tradition, see, for example, Norris 1993, 1996, 1998.

13 For complexities in the meaning of the terms 'from the inside' and 'from the outside' in this context, see Alexander and McLaughlin 2003: 372, fn. 1.

14 On the contribution which a Catholic philosophy of education might make to education in general in relation to spiritual matters, see Groome 1998.

15 For philosophical aspects of these problems and dilemmas, see, for example, Alexander and McLaughlin 2003: 363–9; McLaughlin 1995b; Hobson and Edwards 1999.

16 One writer observes that such processes 'may be viewed only as something associated with new age thinking or religious belief which if imposed upon students could be harmful' (Erricker and Erricker 2001: 4).

17 See the following passages in Erricker and Erricker (2001) which are selected from a range which give rise to questions about presupposed assumptions or beliefs: 'opportunities to balance the external and inner world' (p. 6); 'To learn how to simply be' (p. 7); 'the abstract needs of their inner being' (p. 7); 'the laws of polarity, positive and negative, impermanence and change' (p. 10); 'to allow things to be as they are' (p. 22); 'beyond thought and concept, a place of direct awareness' (p. 33); 'the investigation of experience without ultimately relying on conceptual thinking . . . challenges conceptual maps of reality. It challenges and undermines doctrines, whether religious or secular, that say that this is how the world is, this is what we must do, and this is how we should behave. This challenge to authority comes from determining that there is higher authority, whether within one's own consciousness and conscience or beyond oneself, that cannot be denied. Meditative experience is a basis of that authority: a being true to oneself' (p. 53); 'a path beyond thought and imagination into the indwelling presence within our hearts' (p. 129).

18 For a range of 'spiritual exercises' giving rise to the need for this kind of care, see, for example, Hadot 1995; cf. Haldane 2000.

REFERENCES

Alexander, H.A. (2001) *Reclaiming Goodness: Education and the Spiritual Quest*, Notre Dame: University of Notre Dame Press.

Alexander, H.A. and McLaughlin, T.H. (2003) 'Education in religion and spirituality', in N. Blake, P. Smeyers, R. Smith and P. Standish (eds), *The Blackwell Guide to the Philosophy of Education*, Oxford: Blackwell.

Beck, J. (1998) *Morality and Citizenship in Education*, London: Cassell.

Best, R. (ed.) (1996) *Education, Spirituality and the Whole Child*, London: Cassell.

Blake, N. (1996) 'Against spiritual education', *Oxford Review of Education* 22, 4: 443–56.

Blake, N. (1997) 'Spirituality, anti-intellectualism, and the end of civilisation as we know it', in R. Smith and P. Standish (eds), *Teaching Right and Wrong. Moral Education in the Balance*, Stoke-on-Trent: Trentham Books.

Callan, E. (1997) *Creating Citizens. Political Education and Liberal Democracy*, Oxford: Clarendon Press.

Carr, D. (1995) 'Towards a distinctive conception of spiritual education', *Oxford Review of Education* 21, 1: 83–98.

Carr, D. (1996) 'Rival conceptions of spiritual education', *Journal of Philosophy of Education* 30, 2: 159–78.

Chadwick, P. (1997) *Shifting Alliances. Church and State in English Education*, London: Cassell.

Coles, R. (1992) *The Spiritual Life of Children*, London: HarperCollins.

Copley, T. (2000) *Spiritual Development in the State School. A Perspective on Worship and Spirituality in the Education System of England and Wales*, Exeter: University of Exeter Press.

Department of Education and Science (1977a) *The Curriculum 11–16*, London: HMSO.

Department of Education and Science (1977b) *Supplement to The Curriculum 11–16*, London: HMSO.

Elliott, R.K. (1986) 'Richard Peters: a philosopher in the older style', in D.E. Cooper (ed.), *Education, Values and Mind. Essays for R.S. Peters*, London: Routledge and Kegan Paul.

Erricker, C. (2000) 'A critical review of spiritual education', in C. Erricker and J. Erricker (eds), *Reconstructing Religious, Spiritual and Moral Education*, London: RoutledgeFalmer.

Erricker, C. and Erricker, J. (eds) (2001) *Meditation in Schools. A Practical Guide to Calmer Classrooms*, London: Continuum.

Feinberg, W. (1998) *Common Schools/Uncommon Identities. National Unity and Cultural Difference*, New Haven and London: Yale University Press.

Flew, A. (1997) 'What is "spirituality"?', in L. Brown, B.C. Farr and R.J. Hoffman (eds), *Modern Spiritualities. An Inquiry*, Oxford: Prometheus Books.

Groome, T.H. (1998) *Educating for Life. A Spiritual Vision for Every Teacher and Parent*, Allen, Texas: Thomas More.

Gutmann, A. (1987) *Democratic Education*, Princeton: Princeton University Press.

Hadot, P. (1995) *Philosophy as a Way of Life. Spiritual Exercises from Socrates to Foucault*, Oxford: Blackwell.

Haldane, J. (1999) 'The need of spirituality in Catholic education', in J.C. Conroy (ed.), *Catholic Education: Inside-Out/Outside-In*, Dublin: Veritas.

Haldane J. (2000) 'On the very idea of spiritual values', in A. O'Hear (ed.), *Philosophy, the Good and the Beautiful*, Cambridge: Cambridge University Press.

Hay, D. with Nye, R. (1998) *The Spirit of the Child*, London: Fount.

Hepburn, R. (2000) 'Values and cosmic imagination', in A. O'Hear (ed.), *Philosophy, the Good and the Beautiful*, Cambridge: Cambridge University Press.

Hick, J. (1999) *The Fifth Dimension. An Exploration of the Spiritual Realm*, Oxford: Oneworld Publications.

Hobson, P.R. and Edwards, J.S. (1999) *Religious Education in a Pluralist Society. The Key Philosophical Issues*, London: Woburn Press.

Hull, J. (1996) 'The ambiguity of spiritual values', in J.M. Halstead and M.J. Taylor (eds), *Values in Education and Education in Values*, London: Falmer Press.

Jones, C., Wainwright, G. and Yarnold, E. (eds) (1992) *The Study of Spirituality*, London: SPCK.

Lambourn, D. (1996) '"Spiritual" minus "personal-social" = ?: a critical note on an "empty" category', in R. Best (ed.), *Education, Spirituality and the Whole Child*, London: Cassell.

Levinson, M. (1999) *The Demands of Liberal Education*, Oxford: Oxford University Press.

Macedo, S. (2000) *Diversity and Distrust. Civic Education in a Multicultural Democracy*, Cambridge, MA and London: Harvard University Press.

McGhee, M. (2000) *Transformations of Mind. Philosophy as Spiritual Practice*, Cambridge: Cambridge University Press.

McGrath, A.E. (1999) *Christian Spirituality. An Introduction*, Oxford: Blackwell.

McLaughlin, T.H. (1992) 'The ethics of separate schools', in M. Leicester and M.J. Taylor (eds), *Ethics, Ethnicity and Education*, London: Kogan Page.

McLaughlin, T.H. (1995a) 'Liberalism, education and the common school', *Journal of Philosophy of Education* 29, 2: 239–55.

McLaughlin, T.H. (1995b) 'Wittgenstein, education and religion', in P. Smeyers and J. Marshall (eds), *Philosophy and Education: Accepting Wittgenstein's Challenge*, Dordrecht: Kluwer Academic Publishers.

McLaughlin, T.H. (1996) 'Education of the whole child?', in R. Best (ed.), *Education, Spirituality and the Whole Child*, London: Cassell.

McLaughlin, T.H. (2000) 'Philosophy and educational policy: possibilities, tensions and tasks', *Journal of Educational Policy* 15, 4: 441–57.

McLaughlin, T.H. (2003) 'The burdens and dilemmas of common schooling', in K. McDonough and W. Feinberg (eds), *Citizenship and Education in Liberal Democratic Societies: Teaching for Cosmopolitan Values and Collective Identities*, Oxford: Oxford University Press.

Mott-Thornton, K. (1998) *Common Faith. Education, Spirituality and the State*, Aldershot: Ashgate.

National Curriculum Council (1993) *Spiritual and Moral Development: A Discussion Paper*, London: National Curriculum Council.

Norris, K. (1993) *Dakota. A Spiritual Geography*, New York: Houghton Mifflin.

Norris, K. (1996) *The Cloister Walk*, New York: Riverhead Books.

Norris, K. (1998) *Amazing Grace. A Vocabulary of Faith*, New York: Riverhead Books.

Nussbaum, M.C. (2003) 'Judaism and the love of reason', in M. Bower and R. Groenhout (eds), *Philosophy, Feminism and Faith*, Bloomington: Indiana University Press.

Office for Standards in Education (1994) *Spiritual, Moral, Social and Cultural Development. An OFSTED Discussion Paper*, London: OFSTED.

Peters, R.S. (1972) *Reason, Morality and Religion*, Swarthmore Lecture 1972, London: Friends Home Service Committee.

Peters, R.S. (1981) 'Democratic values and educational aims', in R.S. Peters (ed.), *Essays on Educators*, London: George Allen & Unwin.

Reich, R. (2002) *Bridging Liberalism and Multiculturalism in American Education*, Chicago: Chicago University Press.

Salomone, R.C. (2000) *Visions of Schooling. Conscience, Community and Common Education*, New Haven and London: Yale University Press.

Sandsmark, S. (2000) *Is World View Neutral Education Possible and Desirable? A Christian Response to Liberal Arguments*, Carlisle: Paternoster Press.

School Curriculum and Assessment Authority (1996) *Education for Adult Life: The Spiritual and Moral Development of Young People*, SCAA Discussion Papers No. 6, London: SCAA.

Taylor, C. (1999) 'A Catholic modernity?', in J. Heft (ed.), *A Catholic Modernity? Charles Taylor's Marianist Award Lecture*, New York and Oxford: Oxford University Press.

Taylor, C. (2002) *Varieties of Religion Today. William James Revisited*, Cambridge, MA and London: Harvard University Press.

Thatcher, A. (ed.) (1999) *Spirituality and the Curriculum*, London: Cassell.

Tomasi, J. (2001) *Liberalism Beyond Justice. Citizens, Society, and the Boundaries of Political Theory*, Princeton and Oxford: Princeton University Press.

White, J. (1990) *Education and the Good Life. Beyond the National Curriculum*, London: Kogan Page.

White, J. (1994) 'Instead of OFSTED: a critical discussion of OFSTED on "spiritual, moral, social and cultural development"', *Cambridge Journal of Education* 24, 3: 369–77.

White, J. (1995) *Education and Well Being in a Secular Universe*, London: Institute of Education, University of London.

White, P. (1994) 'Citizenship and spiritual and moral development', *Citizenship. The Journal of the Citizenship Foundation* 3, 2: 7–8.

White, P. (1996) *Civic Virtues and Public Schooling. Educating Citizens for a Democratic Society*, New York and London: Teachers College Press.

Wright, A. (1998) *Spiritual Pedagogy. A Survey, Critique and Reconstruction of Contemporary Spiritual Education in England and Wales*, Abingdon: Culham College Institute.

Wright, A. (2000) *Spirituality and Education*, London: RoutledgeFalmer.

Chapter 14

Spirituality, pluralism and the limits of common schooling

Kevin Mott-Thornton

WHOSE TRADITIONS? WHICH SPIRITUALITY?

How should we think in a liberal-democratic and culturally pluralist society about the place of spirituality and spiritual education in state-funded schooling? On the face of it, a common conception of spiritual education for any such context would seem to presuppose some cultural or political consensus on spiritual and moral values. Indeed, the kind of liberal philosophical reflection that has played a large role in the development of British and other western political and public institutions since the Enlightenment suggests that any such proposal would have to avoid particular cultural or religious bias. However, the basic trouble with this idea, as contemporary debates in social theory between liberals and communitarians well demonstrate, is that it is doubtful whether any philosophical reflection is culturally or normatively non-partisan.

At all events, the present chapter will question the assumption that more particular religious or theological approaches to spiritual development have no place in state-funded schools, and that – as much secular liberal thinking on spiritual education seems to have maintained – a common approach can only be constructed upon some philosophically neutral or value-free rational foundations. In this respect, the views set out here should chime well with those other contributions to this volume which have argued that philosophy and spiritual traditions are inevitably intertwined: on such perspectives, a spiritually neutral philosophy is as unrealistic as that of a philosophically neutral spirituality.

However, if all philosophy draws upon or is to some extent tied to particular cultural traditions, we need to be clear which philosophical tradition or traditions have predominant influence upon current educational policy-making in such western liberal democracies as Great Britain. Again, if education in Britain is largely though not exclusively carried out in publicly funded state schools, the *political* context of educational provision may also need to be taken into account when devising or assessing policies for moral and spiritual development. Although all this takes us into complexities of cultural and political analysis that cannot be adequately pursued here, it may be appropriate to clarify some of the political and cultural assumptions within which the present author takes himself to be working. First, British society is a plural society – perhaps one of the most plural in the world – drawing together people of diverse and often incompatible beliefs and lifestyles. Secondly, it seems central to the mainstream of contemporary British social and political culture to regard this diversity as itself valuable, and as something to be nurtured rather than discouraged. The freedom of individuals and communities to direct their own lives, according to their own authentic understanding of what is good and right, is of course deeply grounded in the liberal-democratic mainstream of British political thought.

All the same, I shall try to show that these very general cultural values have interesting and at times problematic implications for the construction of policies in moral and spiritual education for common schools. In particular, they seem to require the formulation of a universal and therefore tradition-free pattern of spiritual education, which at the same time does not neglect the plurality and cultural diversity of conceptions of spiritual *development*.

COMMON SPIRITUALITY AND SPIRITUAL DEVELOPMENT

Liberal thinkers who wish to adapt policy-making to conditions of pluralism will incline to a neutralist approach to policy. Liberal educational theorists and policy-makers may feel obliged to show that a centrally prescribed programme of moral or spiritual education does not constitute illegitimate state imposition of a particular mode of normative development on the children of all citizens. From this perspective, it may appear to be a precondition of the legitimacy of any national approach to spiritual education that the human development it aims to foster is not unduly skewed towards this or that 'comprehensive theory of the good'. Clearly, an expressly Christian concept of the 'spiritual' would fall short of meeting this requirement insofar as it embodies ideals quite unacceptable to other groups or individuals with an equally legitimate stake in the common school.

So, in order to be generally acceptable to all cultural constituencies of a given society, any approach to spiritual education for the purposes of state-funded schooling would need to be couched in more formal or general developmental terms. It goes without saying, of course, that some such more formal concept of spirituality must be presupposed to any formulation of policy for spiritual education in conditions of cultural diversity. In view of recent communitarian and other social-theoretical critiques of liberal approaches to education, and the internal connections between personal formation and cultural, religious, spiritual and moral values to which they have drawn attention (raising the possibility, not least in countries where education is both compulsory and mostly publicly funded, of serious conflicts between state education and such other important institutions as the family), some such general account of spirituality would appear presupposed to the political and moral evaluation of any and all candidate conceptions of spiritual education.

However, any such concept also presupposes the identification of some common feature or features underlying the bewildering range of apparently diverse conceptions of human spiritual development. In my recent book *Common Faith* (Mott-Thornton 1998), I have attempted to spell out some such view of common spirituality uncoupled from any particular system of values, and to that extent free from any trace of particular developmental bias – and I here offer a brief outline of those ideas.

The meaningfulness of human experience seems dependent on its connections with personal and social values, goals and ideals which give direction and purpose to the lives of individuals and communities. These goals and ideals may be regarded as constitutive of a spiritual dimension, which some may also conceive as an unobservable and non-material source of *inspiration*. As David Carr has pointed out (Carr 1995), the etymology of the word 'spirit' is suggestive: it is derived from the Latin term for 'breath' (spiritus) – that very breath which is both the *source* of life and *constitutive* of it. In this regard, it is possible to link the idea of spirit to notions of inspiration and aspiration. Although this spiritual aspect of experience is not necessarily linked to any religious perspective, it is in principle open to construal – as in certain religious views – by reference to some 'supernatural' transcendent and enduring reality beyond the empirically experienced world. At all events, thus broadly conceived, common spirituality is apt for particular interpretation in a virtually limitless number of ways, and remains open to development by particular individuals or communities according to particular needs, tastes and interests. For present purposes I will refer to this common form of human spirituality as a '*de facto* spirituality'.

It is only to the extent that this *de facto* spirituality is conceived at a more abstract or meta-developmental level that it can hope to command any adequate degree of social consensus, and avoid bias towards any particular spiritual developmental goal. If it does not work at this level, allowing for a range of more particular possibilities of spiritual expression, it must fail to secure the wide consensus needed to justify any form of common schooling in a plural society. An analogy might help to clarify the role of such a formal or *de facto* conception of spiritual development in educational policy-making.

It is clearly of some importance to the general civil enterprise of providing habitable human accommodation that the design and development of new buildings is subject to appropriate regulation. From this viewpoint, it is reasonable to require that – for official building permission – the plans of architects should respect commonly agreed standards of design and construction in the interests of public health, safety and security: building approval will be precisely dependent upon the conformity of plans to an acceptable basic standard of private and/or public accommodation. For example, any plan may be expected to conform to key requirements for living space, proper ventilation, appropriate sanitation, adequate lighting, sufficient storage space and so on.

That said, official regulations will also need to offer some scope for personal and local architectural taste and preference, and to avoid introducing unnecessary restrictions on individual freedom of creative design. In short, insofar as building regulations will seek not to prevent individual architects or designers from expressing their aesthetic preferences, they may be said to observe neutrality with regard to this or that particular style of architecture. Any requirement for plans to conform to certain basic standards of adequate living space or sanitation will be in this sense architecturally neutral and non-evaluative regarding particular architectural styles or preferences. On the other hand, any attempt to specify (say) how the walls of a flat should be decorated, or the materials the door handles should be made of, would not be in this sense architecturally neutral.

Mindful of the limits of this analogy, we might regard educational theorists and policy-makers and/or religious communities as spiritual architects and developers concerned with the educational design and building of particular types of persons. In this respect, my own previously proposed conception of common spirituality and its basic dimensions aims to provide educational legislators, as well as those on the receiving end of legislation, with a view of spiritual education which seeks to balance freedom and restriction in a not dissimilar way to that in which building regulations allow for architectural freedom. Such a conception aims to provide a generally plausible overall conception of spirituality which similarly avoids commitment to particular socio-culturally defined spiritual values. All the same, a number of definitive features of spirituality – to which any more particular conception of spiritual development might be expected to conform – are built into this general account of common spirituality. It is these spiritual equivalents of building regulations which underpin the *de facto* spiritual framework of particular individuals and/or local social spiritualities.

I have elsewhere (Mott-Thornton 1998: ch. 6) identified a group of eight formal dimensions of spirituality and suggested how they might be used by educational policy-makers. Generally, however, some such distinction between 'common spirituality' and spiritual development would seem presupposed to any and all useful discussion of most key issues of spirituality and spiritual education. Indeed, a failure to observe some such distinction may have made a number of fashionable policy approaches to spiritual development seem more attractive than they are – precisely insofar as they appear more accommodating to the prevailing secular climate of the common school classroom than to the basic features of *de facto* spiritualities.

At all events, we need to observe a distinction between the *de facto* or common spirituality and the *developmental* spiritual frameworks used by those operating within particular contexts of nurture and education. The openness aimed for in the *de facto* account of the 'spiritual' is not available when we are operating at specific levels of 'development'. At such levels, we are not committed, on grounds of either pluralism or neutrality, to non-judgemental openness to the full range of possible spiritualities. Any idea of spiritual development cannot but incorporate some particular view of human well-being, even if it is characterised – minimally or negatively – only in terms of avoidance of what is allegedly morally or otherwise harmful. Indeed, we have to recognise that a given expression of *de facto* spirituality might well be secular, materialist or even – from some other perspective – amoral or immoral.

However, we should also resist the assumption that because this or that concept of 'spiritual' development is in some sense expressive of *de facto* spirituality, it must qualify for accommodation in any reasonable policy for spiritual development. All the same, the developmental frameworks of school policies on spiritual development can hardly avoid commitment to some normative conception of spiritual development. Such normative commitments and preferences will also inevitably enshrine assumptions about the best interests of young people on the basis of some more specific conception of human flourishing. In turn, this may not be disassociated from a view of spiritual progress or regress that would take some possible expressions of the *de facto* spiritual conception to be positively harmful.[1]

LIBERAL EDUCATION, AUTONOMY AND SPIRITUAL DEVELOPMENT

Liberals who regard the development of personal autonomy as the key aim of education might still be drawn to basing a nationally common approach to spiritual development upon the idea of spirituality as an individual journey or quest for meaning. However, recent philosophical work on autonomy suggests that any such attempt to ground a common conception of spiritual development in liberal individualist spiritual preference is not unproblematic. Autonomy has two aspects, which seem also to engender tensions within any idea of autonomy as a key educational aim. On the one hand, autonomy suggests self-creation, self-government (autarchy) or self-direction. This aspect of autonomy seems to require individuals to make critical rational assessments at some distance from their current or inherited commitments. Raz, for example, emphasises this aspect of autonomy in the following way:

> The ruling idea behind the ideal of personal autonomy is that people should make their own lives. The autonomous person is a (part) author of his own life. The ideal of personal autonomy is the vision of people controlling, to some degree, their own destiny, fashioning it through successive decisions throughout their lives.
>
> (Raz 1986: 369)

On the other hand, accounts of autonomy offered by recent liberal political theorists and educationalists, in response to communitarian criticism of earlier liberal views, have inclined to emphasise a second feature of autonomy. On this view, autonomous agents operate not from a perspective of complete critical detachment from their social contexts and circumstances, but from one that is more personally, socially and culturally *situated*. Indeed, some liberal thinkers have gone still further by arguing that the self-creative aspects of autonomy actually *require* individual personal development from within some particular tradition of value (see, for example, Macedo 1995: 213ff; Thiessen 1993: 118f; and also Kekes 1989).

Autonomous choosing, to be sure, requires to be contrasted with *arbitrary* choosing. However, if meaningful decisions and choices can only be made from within established normative frameworks, it would appear hard to envisage any universal notion of autonomy that is not at the same time tied to some particular and/or substantive conception of the good.[2]

But now, commitment to a national common school conception of personal education is unlikely – to the extent that such schools may only promote nationally common values – to assist young people to development of the second aspect of autonomy which requires situatedness within some particular primary culture. Irrespective of the status of autonomy as a primary educational aim, of course, responsibility for initiation into any and all values that are not common is effectively given to parents. The trouble here, however, is that initiation into the more particular values of good primary socialisation and parenthood may fail to occur in the socially or culturally impoverished familial circumstances of a fair number of children. In that case, ironically, the degree to which the necessary conditions of situated autonomy can be satisfied would seem to depend upon the ability of *parents* to satisfy them, and – as I will shortly try to show – many children may therefore stand to be disadvantaged precisely in consequence of educational commitment to common schooling. At all events, any liberalism in which autonomy is held to be a key educational aim must also require school learning to be reinforced by the values of the home and to be committed to formation in these values as a primary educational entitlement for all children.

Some attempt might be made to avoid this conclusion by suggesting that the curriculum of the common school could be rooted in some national consensus on what constitutes adequate primary care and culture for all children. But any argument to this effect would appear to depend either upon denial of the genuine cultural pluralism of British society, or upon an implausibly 'thin' conception of consensual values. For the most part, however, liberal conceptions of values education in general and spiritual education in particular seem to have erred in assuming that a completely open-ended concept of spiritual or other development, as indicated above, could provide a satisfactory common school framework for spiritual and other development. I have elsewhere tried to show the folly of attempting to construct a *common* conception of spiritual development upon an 'individual quest for meaning' model. Insofar as such approaches refuse to acknowledge the deep normativity of all rational human decision and choice, they fail, in a dangerously individualistic way, to add up to any coherent concept of self-determination.[3]

THE LIMITS OF COMMON SCHOOLING: CONSENSUS, SPIRITUALITY AND JUSTICE

The ideal of the common school has two distinguishable aspects. First, it incorporates a commitment to some notion of common education for all: secondly, it subscribes to the idea that the membership of common schools should reflect the *diversity* of cultural and other differences to be found in the wider society (McLaughlin 1995: 239). Amy Gutmann offers, from a liberal perspective, the following principle as an important criterion of any common conception of education:

> Any conception of common education based on liberal principles must be alert to the dangers of basing educational influence on a form of communitarian solidarity which requires that children be educated to accept the singularly correct and comprehensive conception of the good life.
>
> (Gutmann 1993: 3)

This principle seems defensible with regard to the state educational provision as a whole: that is, to any conception of common education as centrally imposed upon *all* state schools. As applied to the work of this or that particular school, however, it might be held to represent a denial of the broader educational requirement for schools to acknowledge or reflect the basis of personal development in local community and/or family values. The 'thin' approach to school values which seems to follow from the application of Gutmann's principle also threatens to inhibit or preclude serious educational attention to a range of key normative issues (Strike 1993: 178). This may also create an educational vacuum, which parents may have neither the ability nor the means to fill, but which may nevertheless be filled for good or ill by media and other influences from beyond the school and the family.

Moreover, however much a school *aims* to confine its attention to a 'thin' set of procedural values, aspiring perhaps to the development of capacities for disinterested rational appraisal, it is hard to see how the values and principles of more comprehensive perspectives could be entirely purged from the curriculum – for, to be sure, such values are likely to be manifest in the very selection of issues for curricular inclusion or exclusion. Indeed, since it is hard to see how teachers in any school could avoid discussion of questions of human value in the course of teaching this or that subject or activity, it is impossible to see how a school committed to liberal neutrality could reasonably avoid the influence of this or that particular normative conception of positive human development. More particularly, insofar as teachers are moral exemplars themselves, the procedural neutrality of liberal teachers must *itself* provide a particular moral or spiritual model for pupils. Hence, an education based upon liberal neutral discussion of issues could itself encourage the view that good lives are best chosen or constructed exclusively on the basis of *individual* or individualistic rational deliberation. Above all, however, it is unlikely that any teachers would be able to observe such strict liberal neutrality to the point of complete success in concealing their own beliefs and values in any genuine discussion of controversial issues – not least on issues about which they have passionately held views.

In response to these difficulties concerning basic values formation and education, some have been tempted to reconsider the possibility of arriving at some national consensus on values. For example, some theorists and policy-makers have clearly hoped to build a degree of national consensus on some cross-culturally shared notion of what is unacceptably harmful to others. More positively, one might also seek some agreement about the general social value or utility of such personal dispositions as 'responsibilty', 'honesty' or 'tolerance'.

Again, the trouble is that in a plural and free society there will precisely be much room for disagreement even about the nature of personal and social harm. Whereas those who regard such sexual preferences as homosexuality as contrary to religious or family values may consider tolerance of homosexuality to be socially undermining, others with a more open attitude to sexuality are likely to view such attitudes as themselves socially harmful expressions of prejudice and intolerance. Indeed, even if universal agreement could be secured concerning the common value of some set of virtues and personal qualities, at least two considerations suggest that such consensus could not be used to ground an adequate policy on personal development. First, it is a feature of such general virtues and values as (say) 'responsibility', 'honesty' and 'fairness' that they are susceptible to wide interpretation and/or contextually specific instantiation. However, any general attempt to identify what 'being responsible' means in this or that concrete moral situation – which must also be a fundamental requirement of any public policy which stands a chance of working in practice – is precisely prone to wreck on the rocks of more particular disagreements about whether or not this or that actual behaviour is responsible or irresponsible. One has only to think of the controversies which rage over questions about how responsible it might be for nurses to strike in protest at alleged health service 'cuts', or about the fairness or justice of liberal abortion laws, to appreciate the problems surrounding any attempt to base a satisfactory common policy on personal development upon such abstractly conceived values.

Given the moral disunity of many culturally plural liberal-democratic polities, the chances of producing a national consensus on such issues *thin* enough to secure the agreement of all, and *thick* enough to support an adequate programme of personal development, are therefore likely to be remote (see also, on this question, Galston 1989). Although what we require from a national value consensus is a set of normative principles able to plug the formative gap left by the liberal neutral approach, it is difficult to see how any such set could – in violation of Gutmann's principle – be entirely innocent of some 'singularly correct and comprehensive conception of the good life' at the level of actual practical application.

Regardless of this, I have argued that it must be impossible for individual schools to avoid having some normative influence on the children in their care, whether they decide to promote only a thin set of common values or no values at all. Even where a school does not set out to promote a specific set of positive values, then it will no doubt – intentionally or not – hand over control of its pupils' moral and/or spiritual development to benign or other external influences. Insofar as the general ethos of the school cannot but affect the spiritual development of its pupils, schools will be either active promoters or passive accomplices in spiritual development.

At all events, if a consensually based central policy cannot adequately provide for the moral and spiritual needs and development of all the moral and cultural constituencies of plural societies, we might ask who should be responsible for deciding the appropriate value system for this or that local school. Liberal philosophers of education often seem to assume that either the state, professional educationalists or perhaps some independent committee of appropriate stake-holders are best placed to decide the direction of moral and spiritual development in state schools. This viewpoint probably rests on assumptions to the effect that school-based spiritual development is a matter for public or political endorsement, and that spiritual development needs – since it is delivered at public expense in most schools – to be rationally justifiable and democratically *accountable*. All the same, the idea that there is a legitimate public interest in common school spiritual development falls well short of the conclusion – built, by design or default, into much liberal thinking on this issue – that a child's primary formative culture should be a matter for public or political *determination*. Indeed, there is surely a *prima facie* case for holding that spiritual development belongs very much in the sphere of the family, and is the prime responsibility of parents or carers. On the other hand, as we have argued, the spiritual values adopted by the school may also have a direct impact upon the primary culture of the child. So, in that case, primary culture cannot be wholly provided without formal school support.[4]

In my own view, however, no one else is either *better placed* or entitled than the parents of a child to make policy decisions regarding formative personal development for that child's school. In short, while we can admit that there may be circumstances in which parents can be said to have forfeited their rights in this matter, there is a reasonable case for saying that parents should have a large say in what constitutes the best spiritual developmental direction for their own children.

If this is right, it follows that arrangements should be made to ensure that the views of the school are not inconsistent with parental views, and (ideally) that the values of parents – albeit reflecting some substantive conception of the good life – should be taken into account in determining the educational policies which will directly affect the schooling of their own children (see also Almond 1994; McLaughlin 1994). Moreover, ensuring that personal and spiritual development policies are formulated at the school and community level in relative freedom from central or other outside interference would also appear to be the best way to ensure this.

On this view, individual schools should involve and collaborate with parents and be encouraged, over time, to accommodate parental requirements where possible. As individual schools throughout the system develop their policies in accordance with the views of different parental constituencies, the resulting diversity of provision should naturally begin to reflect more accurately the diversity within society. It should also improve relationships between schools and parents, give grounds for a greater sense of community within society, and devolve real power to the ordinary tax-paying financiers of public schooling. Indeed, such a strategy might also be a means to the promotion of wider civic responsibility, as well as conducive to the general reinvigoration of civil society. Fundamental to the success of this strategy would be the framing of legislation which aims to remove any and all unreasonable limitations on parental choice of school.

This need not mean, of course, that either individual parents or some parental constituency would have absolute control over the policies of the school. In the first place, as members of the larger parental constituency of a school, the voices of individual parents will in general be subject to the parental consensus of the wider community. Secondly, however, the wider community of parents will itself be subject to further constraints as only one of three powerful influences on policy formation within particular schools. In this regard, any given policy will also need to take account of the professional educational expertise of teachers working in the school, as well as of central government initiatives and strategies for the maintenance of national educational standards.

The above considerations also provide a reason for rejecting the common school ideal to 'aspire to achieve a broad range of mix in its student body' (McLaughlin 1995: 239). I have shown that policies for the primary personal development of pupils ought to be worked out at the individual school level, on the grounds that this enables the key players (parents-in-community) to influence decision-making. School policies are likely to be regarded as most acceptable (to parents themselves, as well as to those wishing to maintain the diversity of society) if their developmental aims reflect, *as far as possible*, the values of the home and community. Indeed, it may well be that the closer schools come to meeting any goal of maximum cultural diversity within particular institutions, the smaller will be the chances of achieving the kind of value consensus apt for the development of school policies acceptable to all relevant stake-holders. The trouble is that if particular school communities aim to reflect the cultural pluralism of wider society, the problems which plagued the attempt to find an adequate national consensus on personal development are likely to be recapitulated at the local level. Indeed, in the pursuit of some chimera of policies *acceptable* to all, one would be likely to produce policies that *no one* would regard as adequate.

On the other hand, allowing school communities free rein over the construction of the primary personal development policies need not preclude recognition and observance of some common normative goals for all schools. There is no reason, for example, why a common state-prescribed conception of civic education might not be promoted in all schools irrespective of their particular allegiances to local community values (see Halstead 1994). However, this would require us to address, both theoretically and practically, the issue of how tensions between local school policy and central requirements for civic education might be resolved in the event of value conflict.

At all events, a system of schooling conceived to enable different cultural constituencies to provide the kind of personal development for their children which adequately reflects and reinforces their local family and community values would appear to be a reasonable goal. Some such arrangement seems particularly pertinent given current sequestering, via taxation, of financial resources for the provision of schools which *compel* parents to relinquish much control over the personal development of their children to professionals employed and guided by the state. Indeed, it is arguable that such compulsion can *only* really be justified if state-funded schools are free to develop policies that meet the criteria of adequacy and acceptability set out above.

The kinds of organisational arrangements suggested here are, at the time of writing, enjoyed within the state-funded system by only a minority of parents. Some religious practitioners of Christianity, Judaism and Islam can send their children to state-funded schools that provide for a particular religious version of personal development. In addition, parents whose preference is for their children to be developed along the lines of the very thin set of liberal and multiculturalist values – which, as we have argued, prevail by default in the vast majority of state schools – are also in this position. A further extension of recent school admissions reforms, giving parents more choice of school, would have the effect of *reducing* diversity amongst the clientele of state schools, in the interests of promoting more acceptable or adequate personal development policies for particular schools across the state sector (see Halstead 1995; also Carr 1996). In my view, this would be greatly preferable to the imposition of a centrally or profession-ally designed one size fits all conception of spiritual or other normative development, and better reflect the personal and communal sources of human spiritual values.[5]

NOTES

1 Interestingly, guidance issued on the implementation and inspection of spiri-tual education provided in the early 1990s by the National Curriculum Council (1993) and the Office for Standards in Education (1993), for state schools in England and Wales, suggests that policies should be developed at school rather than at national level, in line with what I have suggested here. However, as I tried to show in more detail elsewhere (Mott-Thornton 1998: 140–2), both of these documents fail to draw upon the crucial distinction outlined here between common spirituality and developmental spiritual frameworks. As a result, they may encourage school policy-makers to adopt a non-judgemental approach to the moral and spiritual development of their pupils, which will, nonetheless, have developmental implications.

2 For a more detailed discussion of this issue in relation particularly to the work of Joseph Raz, see Mott-Thornton 1998: 124–33.

3 Mott-Thornton 1998: 144f has further discussion of the kinds of problems associated with experientialist, non-realist and intrumentalist approaches to spiritual education.

4 For further discussion on the extent of the public domain in a variety of liberal theories, especially the political liberalism of John Rawls, see Mott-Thornton 1998: ch. 5 ('Varieties of liberalism, public values and education'). Against the widely held assumption that, in situations of cultural pluralism, the only way to avoid conflict between those holding rival value systems is for public policy to be based on an intellectual consensus, see Rescher (1993).

REFERENCES

Almond, B. (1994) 'In defence of choice in education', in J.M. Halstead (ed.), *Parental Choice and Education*, London: Kogan Page, pp. 68–82.

Carr, D. (1995) 'Towards a distinctive conception of spiritual education', *Oxford Review of Education* 20: 83–98.

Carr, D. (1996), 'Rival conceptions of spiritual education', *Journal of Philosophy of Education* 30, 2: 159–78.

Galston, W. (1989) 'Civic education and the liberal state', in N. Rosenblum (ed.), *Liberalism and the Moral Life*, Cambridge, MA: Harvard University Press.

Gutmann, A. (1993) 'Democracy and democratic education', *Philosophy and Education*, 12, 1: 3.

Halstead, J.M. (ed.) (1994) *Parental Choice and Education: Principles, Policy and Practice*, London: Kogan Page.

Halstead, J.M. (1995) 'Voluntary apartheid?: problems of schooling for religious and other minorities in democratic societies', in *Journal of Philosophy of Education* 29, 2: 257–72.

Kekes, J. (1989) *Moral Tradition and Individuality*, Princeton: Princeton University Press.

Macedo, S. (1995) 'Multiculturalism for the religious right? Defending liberal civic education', *Journal of Philosophy* 29, 2: 223–8.

McLaughlin, T.H. (1994) 'The scope of parents' educational rights', in J.M. Halstead (ed.), *Parental Choice and Education: Principles, Policy and Practice*, London: Kogan Page, pp. 94–107.

McLaughlin, T.H. (1995) 'Liberalism, education and the common school', in *Journal of Philosophy of Education* 29, 2: 239–55.

Mott-Thornton, K. (1998) *Common Faith: Education, Spirituality and the State*, Aldershot: Ashgate.

National Curriculum Council (1993) *Spiritual and Moral Development: A Discussion Paper*, York: NCC. Reissued by the School Curriculum and Assessment Authority (1995), London: SCAA.

Office for Standards in Education (1993) *Handbook for the Inspection of Schools*, London: HMSO.

Raz, J. (1986) *The Morality of Freedom*, Oxford: Oxford University Press.

Rescher, N. (1993) *Pluralism: Against the Demand for Consensus*, Oxford: Clarendon Press.

Strike, K. (1993) 'Ethical discourse and pluralism', in K.A. Strike and L.P. Ternasky (eds), *Ethics for Professionals in Education*, New York: Teachers College Press.

Thiessen, E.J. (1993) *Teaching For Commitment*, Leominster: Gracewing.

Chapter 15

Three conceptions of spirituality for spiritual education

David Carr

RECENT CONCERN WITH SPIRITUAL EDUCATION

The appearance in the UK alone of several major policy documents from such hallowed sources as the NCC (National Curriculum Council), OFSTED (Office for Standards in Education) and the SCAA (School Curriculum and Assessment Authority) – as well as the proliferation of professional conferences, academic books and journal articles on moral and spiritual education – attests to a recent explosion of official and professional educational interest in spirituality and spiritual education.[1] This interest seems to have been driven by at least three main concerns: first, a socio-political worry about the decline of social co-operation and common purpose in contemporary conditions of cultural pluralism and liberal individualism; second, anxiety about the breakdown of traditional values under the influence of secularism and materialism evident in the decline of youth discipline as well as in recent events (notably in Britain and the USA) of anomic murder and mayhem; third, a professional concern that recent political interest in improving educational standards has focused more on the economic than the moral benefits of education. Indeed, some would regard recent British and other educational reforms as in themselves symptomatic of that obsession with economic consumerism that has fuelled the spread of selfish materialism and hedonism in western society.

Notwithstanding my own sympathy with these overall concerns, not least with the complaint that issues of values and morality have too often taken a back seat in recent educational policy-making to more instrumental or economic interests, I share some of the doubts of those who have wondered precisely what useful role the idea of spiritual education might serve in addressing such matters (e.g. Blake 1996; Lambourn 1996; see also Carr 1996a for a reply to Blake). Indeed, one might first ask what light is likely to be shed on problems of contemporary social or *moral* decline by describing them as precisely 'spiritual', though this need not be to deny – in the manner of some sceptics – that the discourse of spirituality is entirely devoid of meaning. All the same, my aim in this chapter will be to try to see what possible sense (or senses) might be made of spiritual education in the light of latter-day reflections on the topic. I shall not try, of course, to arrive at any precise *definition* of the spiritual: the language of spirituality is clearly far too protean for that. Still, it is reasonable to suppose that in the absence of some fairly coherent or consistent account of the purpose of spiritual discourse – one which effectively distinguishes the language of spirit and spirituality from other sorts of usage – the very idea of spiritual education must also lack any determinate sense or direction. In light of this assumption, I shall now try to distinguish and evaluate *three* broad conceptions of or strategies for spiritual education from the abundance of recent literature on the topic.

SPIRITUALITY WITH AND WITHOUT RELIGION

Religion would seem to be the most obvious place to encounter discourse of spirit and/or spirituality: from this viewpoint, we might refer to any religious conception of spiritual usage as the *conventional* or *traditional* view. On this view, any initiation into a religious creed, system of beliefs or set of practices would be tantamount to induction into a mode of spiritual life. Moreover, in some religious systems the term 'spirit' may be taken to refer to a particular aspect of the human soul or psyche which it is the main task of religious initiation or education to nurture and cultivate. This object of religious attention has also sometimes been regarded – for example, by Platonic and Cartesian dualists – as distinct from or opposed to corporeal or bodily nature. On the other hand, as Aristotelian Thomism shows, it is possible to conceive the life of the soul or spririt in rather less dualist and more naturalistic terms. At all events, many religious traditions have promoted specific pedagogies or programmes of spiritual instruction – for example, the spiritual exercises of Christian mystics, Buddhist meditational techniques and so on – expressly designed to assist the soul's progress to salvation or enlightenment. From this viewpoint, indeed, it might be supposed that traditional religions already provide coherent basic frameworks for spiritual education.

Still, much of what educational policy-makers have recently written about the need for spirituality to counter contemporary materialism, hedonism and nihilism would seem mostly at odds with any such identification of spirituality with religion. Indeed, widespread suspicion that spirituality has declined, in tandem with the general demise (in Britain at any rate) of religious commitment, has not fuelled much optimism about the prospects of any great modern revival of traditional religious faith. Moreover, insofar as traditional religious belief could be held to reinforce the potentially divisive socio-cultural pluralism of modern liberal democracies, educational policy-makers may have regarded this as reason enough for attempting to decouple spirituality from particular historically formed religions. Additional points that might be made against the connection of spiritual education with religion are: first, that other areas of the school curriculum besides religious education such as *literature* and *music* would appear to have spiritual educational potential; secondly, that any close association of spiritual experience with religious experience seems to deny spiritual experience to the non-religious; thirdly, that traditional spiritual pedagogies of meditation and the like may appear far from suitable for inclusion in the common school curriculum.

In this light, much recent British policy documentation and academic literature on spirituality and spiritual education has sought to distinguish the spiritual from the religious in the name of what we may here call an *attitudinal* or *postmodern* account. Although this conception does appreciate links between the spiritual and the religious, it denies that religion has any monopoly on the development of spirituality, and it appears to focus attention mainly on the *experiential* or *phenomenological* dimensions of spiritual life, or upon those moments of intense or heightened awareness of reality to which spiritual terminology is often popularly applied. I have elsewhere argued (Carr 1996b) that this emphasis on the *epiphanic* aspect of spirituality seems to have at least two dimensions: first, there seems to be a stress upon the *wondrous* or *sublime* qualities of things – focused perhaps upon some capacity to appreciate the apparent 'miracle' of creation; secondly, there is concomitant emphasis upon the *mysterious* or *ineffable* character of things, and on the limits of any human attempts to explain them. Moreover, insofar as such natural and artificial items as sunsets and sonatas are prime objects of awe and wonder, there is some tendency here towards general assimilation of spiritual to *aesthetic* experience.

It could also be regarded as an advantage of this account, however, that it gives a potentially *cross-curricular* role to spiritual education. On the one hand, insofar as spiritual experience is held to be a matter of *self-transcendence* – of, as it were, curbing the self-interested desires of ego – moral, religious, and personal and social education may continue to play a role in cultivating empathy for or some sense of transpersonal unity or continuity with other living things. But *science* and *mathematics* might be regarded as significant vehicles of spiritual education insofar as these may also promote a sense of self-transcendence: biological science, indeed, might be held to provide opportunities for *both* awe and wonder at the sheer mystery of existence, *and* for aesthetic appreciation of the beauty of creation; and so on for other areas of the curriculum. In brief, some alleged advantages of the attitudinal account are: (i) that it provides

a potentially common non-religiously affiliated basis for spiritual education; (ii) that it is not thereby committed to any controversially dualist
doctrine of spirit as a distinct metaphysical entity; (iii) that it also seems
to make some reasonable sense of cross-curricular spiritual education.

All the same, the all-purpose model is not without problems. First,
the account is not especially strong on *coherence*. For one thing, there
seems no obvious connection between those features of experience
which engender attitudes of awe and wonder, and those which occasion
a sense of mystery: I may well find mysterious (or inexplicable) what I do
not regard as awe-inspiring, or experience wonder at what seems quite
unmysterious. Again, it seems less than clear how the episodes of awe
and wonder prompted by different curriculum experiences are related:
how, for example, the mystery of infinity in mathematics might be linked
to that of the origins of life in biology, or what the aesthetic celebration
of the beauty of a sunset might have to do with any general reverence for
life cultivated in zoology or botany. Moreover, despite its separation of
the spiritual from the religious, the cross-curricular approach to spiritual
education of the attitudinal account may nevertheless be in its own way
reductive of the spiritual to a range of quite other human concerns.

In this regard, insofar as cultivating appreciation of beauty is part of
what we mean by good art teaching, promoting respect for life appears
central to any effective learning in environmental studies, fostering self-
transcendent regard for others is integral to moral education, communi-
cating some sense of our epistemic limits is part and parcel of good science
teaching and so on, the attitudinal account of spiritual education seems
prone to division without remainder into the sum of conventional curriculum areas. In short, it is difficult on this view to discern anything
particularly *distinctive* about the spiritual dimension of human experience –
anything, that is, which might mark it off from the aesthetic, the moral, the
religious or whatever – and that might therefore secure a place for *spiritual*
education as such. Indeed, the 'phenomenological' focus upon the *experience* rather than the *content* of spiritual engagement makes it hard to
see *what* someone might actually have *learned* when they have learned
spiritually rather than aesthetically, morally or scientifically, and hence
provide the basis for a distinctive spiritual *pedagogy*. Above all, despite
their appeal to notions of spirituality and spiritual education to offset contemporary instrumentalism and consequentialism, recent policy proposals
have often been themselves unashamedly *instrumental* in their explicit
focus upon the social, economic and therapeutic benefits of sprituality.
Moreover, it is arguable that the attitudinal view offers a rather shallow
'rose-tinted' perspective on spiritual experience which fails to acknowledge that spiritual life and growth may concern struggles with setback,
grief, humiliation, guilt and despair no less (if not more) than the cosy
contemplation of sunsets.

IN SEARCH OF A THIRD WAY

The difficulties lately aired about the traditional and attitudinal or post-modern accounts may already suggest a need to steer some more reasonable middle course between the Scylla of controversial allegiance to specific religiously grounded spiritual traditions and the Charybdis of vague, evasive and perhaps ultimately vacuous talk of awe and wonder. It is also arguable that the most promising alternative to such views lies in some theoretical trimming of the loose ends of received spiritual usage in the interests of a more formal or systematic psychology of spiritual experience and/or development. Although this general approach to the problem of spiritual education is mostly programmatic in the context of educational theory, much latter-day work in the social sciences of anthropology and psychology provides clues as to the ways in which the theory and practice of spiritual education might go. From an anthropological perspective, for example, much modern structuralist work on the religious and moral narratives of humankind has suggested that the apparently diverse myths and legends of different cultures may nevertheless express and/or celebrate the fundamentally common spiritual experiences and developmental processes of a basically universal 'hero with a thousand faces' (Campbell 1993). Again, from a psychological viewpoint, recent theorists of religious education (Fowler 1981) have also drawn upon the highly influential moral developmentalism of such modern cognitivists as Piaget and Kohlberg in a bid to identify the stages of growth through which individuals might be held to progress on their journey to religious or spiritual maturity.

Although such approaches to the study of human norms and values and their relevance to questions of spiritual education remain controversial – for example, whereas at least one contributor to this volume is sceptical about applying stage analyses of faith to spiritual development, the reflections of another are clearly more in harmony with a kind of spiritual structuralism – what we might here call a 'modernist' or *constructivist* view of spiritual development and education does represent a possible alternative to traditionalist and postmodern perspectives. At heart, any such constructivist approach to spiritual education would turn precisely upon the structuralist insight that, behind the apparent variety and diversity of personal or socio-culturally conditioned perspectives on this or that aspect of human interest or concern, we may expect to find common principles or strategies of psychic organisation. Indeed, the claim that there are such features might appear presupposed to regarding different perspectives *as* focused on common concerns: for how might students of comparative religion set out to examine the differences and similarities between various world faiths if they could not be fairly confident that Christianity, Islam, Judaism, Hinduism, Animism and so on are all to be regarded as *religions* as opposed to (say) scientific theories, artistic creations or political ideologies? Thus, the idea that there is some common logical form to the course of religious and spiritual development fits well with the general structuralist thesis that this is also the case in the realms of scientific, mathematical, moral and other reflection and enquiry.

At all events, such a constructivist conception would appear to concentrate upon rather different aspects of spirituality and spriritual development from traditional and 'postmodern' conceptions. We have already seen that there are familiar features of usage which dwell upon the more *subjective*, emotional or attitudinal aspects of spiritual response – and it seems to be just such trends upon which the postmodern conception of spiritual experience focuses. This is also not at all a perverse conception of spirituality: there are, to be sure, traditions of eastern and western religious mysticism that have not only been inclined to reject conscious reflection or ratiocination as useful routes to salvation or enlightenment, but in which any use of intellect has sometimes been regarded as an active *impediment* to spiritual progress. That said, any extreme non-cognitive construal of spirituality must give rise to familiar Wittgensteinian problems about the precise identity of spiritual experiences – not least for any attempt to isolate spiritual awareness from any and all religious content. Indeed, such problems must spell particular disaster for the very idea of *spiritual education,* and we have already observed some of the difficulties to which they may be vulnerable in the 'postmodern' problem of distinguishing spiritual from aesthetic, religious, moral or even scientific engagement.

Mystical emphases on spiritual experience, of course, need present no particular difficulties for traditional conceptions insofar as such experiences are definable by reference to specific patterns of religious formation. From this viewpoint, this or that spiritual experience will have at least implicit aims and content: for example, whereas for Christians the main object of spiritual awareness is *God* and its key aim is love of God, for Buddhists the goal is (presumably) to achieve *enlightenment* via the extinction of desire. It may thus be of little consequence on traditional conceptions that some have, in the name of advanced spiritual development, rejected intellectual enquiry as a route to direct knowledge of God, since – in the light of more or less clearly defined religious beliefs and goals – mystical endeavours may yet conform to an otherwise rationally articulable salvific conception. Hence, the view of the traditional mystic, that in arriving at true knowledge of God it may be ultimately necessary to leave intellectual enquiry behind, need not be incompatible with regarding some theological conception as a nevertheless necessary point of departure for any spiritual traveller hoping to get somewhere or *anywhere*. In any case, it would appear that any viable conception of spirituality for spiritual *education* would have to eschew inherently subjective or 'private language' perspectives on spiritual experience – for whereof we cannot speak it is not obvious that we can *educate* either.

In this respect, a 'modernist' or constructivist conception might aspire to steer a safe course between traditionalism and postmodernism. First, unlike the all-purpose account, it may avoid the subjectivism that precludes clear distinction of spiritual from such other forms of experience as the aesthetic and the moral – though it is not thereby bound, any more than the traditional account, to deny that spiritual experience has a subjective or personal dimension. Secondly, although this may also incur the traditionalist 'cost' of defining spiritual goals in something like religious terms, it might yet aspire – via abstraction of a general form of spiritual development from the manifold of culturally conditioned religious perspectives – to evade *particular* religious bias. In short, the constructivist view seeks to identify a general pattern of spiritual development predicated on the idea of a universal human search for ego-transcendence and/or eternal truth. It remains an open question, however, whether this idea makes much coherent sense. Indeed, the constructivist account appears vulnerable to a range of familiar objections to related structuralist, modernist or cognitivist accounts of moral, scientific and other forms of enquiry, and the key difficulty is perhaps that of how one might separate the form of any human aspiration or enquiry from some specific or substantial content. It is to the possibility or otherwise of providing some such content to ideas of spiritual development and education that we now turn.

THE POSSIBILITY OF SPIRITUAL KNOWLEDGE AND TRUTH

What we have called traditional, postmodern and constructivist (or modernist) conceptions of spirituality and spiritual experience would certainly appear to have rather different implications for spiritual *education, teaching* and *learning* in the context of public schooling. In general, however, it may be hard to make sense of spiritual *education* in the absence of some distinctive *content* or subject matter by reference to which we can distinguish spiritual from aesthetic, moral or other activities or experiences. In turn, this might mean giving some sense to the idea of spiritual *knowledge* – construed either *theoretically* as a concern with the discovery of *truth*, or more *practically* as a concern with the cultivation of *virtues* or *skills*. In this respect, it would also seem that traditional and constructivist views offer more scope for the idea of spiritual knowledge than postmodern perspectives. The trouble with any postmodern 'attitudinal' notion of spirituality is that it makes it hard to see how spiritual education might be regarded as either *spiritual* or *educational*. But constructivism seems vulnerable to not dissimilar problems. Much 'ordinary language' philosophy, for example, has sought to resist modern positivist claims that insofar as moral and aesthetic statements are not *descriptive* of reality they can have little or no sense at all: thus, theorists of 'meaning-as-use' have argued that although moral, aesthetic, religious and other judgements are not concerned to state the truth about the nature of things, they may nevertheless have *prescriptive, commendatory* or *expressive* functions. But it is also more than likely that some such non-realist semantics underpins the moral educational constructivism of such cognitive developmentalists as Piaget and Kohlberg: on such views, the objectivity of moral claims rests not upon their truth to the facts, but upon their role as expressions of consistent personal commitment.

The difficulty with any such view of normative or evaluative discourse, however, is that it precisely secures *meaning* at the price of *truth*: more especially, insofar as such discourse collapses – like ethical prescriptivism – into a kind of non-cognitivist expressionism, it no longer provides much scope for genuine *enquiry*, and can only therefore be of limited or problematic *educational* utility. Indeed, it has long been argued that no such account of moral language could be coherent, for in general we do not call this or that good because we are inclined to commend it, but commend it because we regard it as good (Geach 1972: part 8). But why should we not suppose that broadly the same considerations also apply to non-cognitive or expressive views of the meaning of religious or spiritual discourse? If, in short, recognising that it is bad to neglect the state of our souls makes sense only insofar as we have some objective reason for believing that it is bad so to do – rather than because it seems a good idea to live as *if* it were so – any meaningful spiritual reflection might also seem to rest on the possibility of some non-subjective or mind-independent spiritual reality or truth.

But even granting some objective basis to our moral evaluations and prescriptions – for holding that there are at least some absolute standards of right or wrong to which human conduct ought to conform – it might be doubted whether this does much to advance the case for a distinctive form of spiritual knowledge or enquiry. To whatever extent one might reasonably make sense of moral or aesthetic truths – or at least of the idea of objective or naturalistic standards of moral and/or aesthetic judgement – any talk of spiritual truth or objectivity is bound to seem more problematic. That said, it is possible that the main obstacle to allowing any objective basis to moral, aesthetic and other non-scientific claims has been an ultimately implausible modern scientism which has sometimes aspired to indiscriminate physicalistic reduction of all knowledge, explanation and truth (Smart and Haldane 1996, 2003). However, just as it is not obvious how any claim that plants gain nourishment by photosynthesis might be translated without loss into the language of chemistry or physics, it is not clear how a psychological claim about the human rational need to resolve cognitive dissonance might be explained in purely biological terms, how a socio-economic claim that communities above a certain level of economic complexity are prone to class divisions is entirely explicable in terms of psychological generalities, or how a claim that slavery is unjust might be given an exclusively sociological explanation. All these claims, in their different ways, may be judged true or false on the basis of objective experience – but they also appeal to different orders or levels of that experience.

Elsewhere (Carr 1995, 2002) I have argued for an essentially non-reductive realist or naturalistic appreciation of spiritual truth, precisely in the interests of making sense of spiritual life, reflection and education. Drawing on the Christian Gospels, for example, such claims as 'man does not live by bread alone', 'no man can serve two masters', 'render unto Caesar the things that are Caesar's' and 'what shall it profit a man if he shall gain the whole world and lose his soul', might well be offered as examples of such truths: but similar claims – some of which are close analogues of such key Christian asseverations – can be found in most major world faiths. It should also be clear that such claims are not 'scientifically' reducible to psychology, biology or chemistry: just as 'man does not live by bread alone' cannot be considered a piece of dietary advice, so 'no man can serve two masters' is concerned more with matters of divided value and loyalty than with questions of empirical or practical impossibility. More interestingly, spiritual truths are often fairly distinguishable from ethical or moral claims. Thus, unlike the so-called 'Golden Rule', the recently noted spiritual claims are not primarily *prescriptions*: for though I can certainly be *unfair* in failing to do unto others as they would do unto me, I need not by so doing necessarily be guilty of *untruth,* as I precisely might by denying a spiritual claim. Arguably, then, the point of saying 'what shall profit a man that he shall gain the whole world and lose his soul' is to claim with respect to *actual* ruthless seekers of wealth or power that they *have* lost their souls in pursuit of the world: that, in short, it is a plain spiritual *fact* – ignored at our peril – that our souls will precisely fail to flourish if we neglect the *truth* in question. Furthermore, very many spiritual lessons – for example, that at the heart of Christ's parable of the workers in the vineyard – may be quite deliberately *subversive* of conventional moral intuitions concerning justice as fairness.

Is this not just to reduce spiritual truths to religious truths? Although something here may depend on how broadly or narrowly one conceives religious truths, it seems that spiritual truths are certainly distinguishable from many religious truths or claims. These, to be sure, come in rather different forms: some, such as 'Christ's teaching was for the Gentiles as well as the Jews', may be an historical claim testable by biblical textual analysis; others, however, such as 'By the power of the Holy Spirit, Jesus Christ became incarnate of the Virgin Mary and was made man', are

doctrinal, and aspects of these – or, at any rate, questions of their interpretation – continue to be matters of heated theological debate within
and across different Christian confessions. However, spiritual claims are
not in this sense religious claims: on the one hand, such claims of religion
have rather different evidential grounds from spiritual claims: on the other,
it seems that the latter, unlike the former, often have near equivalents in
other religions.

However, insofar as spiritual life would seem to be no less concerned
with the cultivation of a range of *practical* dispositions and capacities
than with truth-focused reflection, we might also seek to identify a range
of distinctive spiritual *virtues* – likewise not reducible to familiar moral
virtues. In this respect, mainstream Christianity does appear to have recognised a class of such essentially spiritual virtues in its distinction between
the *cardinal* virtues (courage, temperance, justice and wisdom) of ordinary
moral engagement and the *theological* virtues (of faith, hope and charity),
and it is arguable that the latter are not reducible to the former. Moreover,
it seems reasonable to regard a range of other practical dispositions – such
as forgiveness, and even chastity – as irreducible (Christian) spiritual
imperatives or virtues.

TRUTH AND ERROR IN THE THREE PERSPECTIVES

We may conclude with a summary of the three approaches to spirituality
and spiritual education distinguished in this paper. First, on what we
have called the traditional conception, spiritual life and experience acquire
their identity from particular faith perspectives: to that extent, the rival
'postmodern' and 'constructivist' approaches would probably agree in
regarding traditional views as both sectarian and potentially *indoctrinative*.
Secondly, the postmodern conception loosens the connection between
spirituality and religion and claims to make sense of spiritual education
as a cross-curricular concern: but from the other viewpoints any such
'attitudinal' construal of spiritual experience may appear too *subjective* and
open-ended, as well as liable to general assimilation to other curriculum
concerns. Thirdly, however, although the constructivist perspective aims
to identify a universal pattern of spiritual experience and reflection, its
rivals would probably reject (albeit for different reasons) the rather *abstract*
and contentless conception of spiritual experience presupposed to this
approach. That said, it may also be that each of these perspectives
enshrines a partial truth about spiritual life and its educational implications
which we may now proceed to consider.

Approaching the three views in reverse order, the appeal of the constructivist view of spiritual growth is likely to be much the same as that

of the constructivist view of moral education. As already noted, it draws some support from the idea that different evaluative conceptions must have something in common if they are precisely to be regarded *as* diverse conceptions of *morality, spirituality* or whatever. Moreover, in seeking to identify a universal course of human moral or spiritual development, the constructivist perspective promises to free us from this or that partisan normative allegiance. The trouble is, however, that any such conception of spiritual life and education seems prey to recent communitarian as well as naturalistic objections to constructivist views of moral formation: thus, it is not just that we commend the good because it is good, but that any attempt to derive the essence of morality or whatever by abstracting *form* from *content* in this way must – since 'thoughts without content are empty'[2] – sail close to the *meaningless*.

Moreover, although they have sometimes been supposed to yield *universal* conceptions of morality or spirituality, constructivist accounts (such as prescriptivism) focused upon the rational contours of enquiry often tend to forms of subjective or conceptual idealism which may be indifferent to contradictions *between* perspectives, as long as they are individually consistent. On the other hand, communitarian or 'rival tradition' conceptions of moral and spiritual value[3] – though often linked to moral relativism – are not inherently at odds with a moral or religious *realism* which allows for serious consideration of the actual *truth* or falsehood of rival views. Thus, notwithstanding the possible objection that initiation into a rival conception of belief or practice cannot but be other than *indoctrination* into some controversial perspective, it seems that although this *can* be so, it *need* not be: just as learning a first language can be more of a positive *aid* than an impediment to learning a second one, so initiation into a given spiritual perspective may offer a valuable basis for the appreciation of its rivals (see Carr 1996b).

A traditional approach to spirituality and spiritual education may therefore be able to accommodate the constructivist point about the human universality of spiritual experience without necessarily falling prey to charges of indoctrination. Indeed, I think that only a traditional conception of spiritual life and experience can explain what is almost unintelligible on a constructivist view – namely, the need that individuals reared in one spiritual tradition may feel to *convert* to another quite different one. If the spiritual perspectives enshrined in particular faith traditions are genuinely controversial – in a way that, say, my taste for jazz is not – then they can be *wrong* or mistaken, and the urge to abandon or embrace a spiritual perspective may follow recognition that it no longer adequately expresses what one has come to regard as true to one's spiritual experience. To that extent, spiritual perspectives seem answerable to much the same rational constraints as other (moral, scientific or whatever) perspectives: just as someone might abandon Christianity because Christian views of divine justice are contrary to otherwise deeply held moral convictions about justice as fair distribution – so conversion to Christianity might also follow recognition in the light of some personal stocktaking of one's spiritual life to date that gaining the whole world is not worth the price of one's soul.

On the other hand, what certainly seems to be missing from any 'post-modern' conception of spirituality and spiritual education is just this possibility of coherence among spiritual experiences – the idea that there might be a domain of typically spiritual concerns which it could be the task of spiritual understanding to bring into some meaningful order. The main advantages to be claimed for the postmodern view, of course, are that it seems to make cross-curricular sense of spiritual education, and that its very reductionism avoids any 'occult' reference to metaphysically or ontologically queer realms of soul or spirit. But while endorsing the time-honoured relationship between spiritual and religious experience, the traditional view readily acknowledges the contribution that other areas of human enquiry can make to spiritual education, and – with respect to the point that a traditional spiritual conception must license subscription to some dubious Platonic or Cartesian ontology – we have already observed that Christian or other talk of spiritual concerns as focused on the welfare of the *soul* is quite compatible with a non-dualist anthropology drawing on Aristotelian and Thomist resources. This, in turn, sits well with the central tenet of this essay that the best prospects for spiritual education rest on the possibility of reflection on truths and/or the cultivation of virtues that also admit of an essentially naturalist construal. From this viewpoint, if the idea of spiritual education is to have any contemporary currency, I would argue that this would have to be in terms of some reworking of a *traditional* as opposed to a postmodern or a constructivist conception of spiritual life and experience.

NOTES

1 In the way of recent UK official documentation, see NCC 1993; OFSTED 1994; SCAA 1995, 1996. For a sample of recent work on values education, see Best 1996; Halstead and Taylor 1996; Haydon 1997; Jarrett 1991.
2 This is, of course, the first half of Immanuel Kant's much quoted observation: 'Thoughts without content are empty, intuitions without concepts are blind' (Kant 1968: 93).
3 The expression 'rival tradition' is mainly associated with the work of Alasdair MacIntyre (1981, 1987, 1992).

REFERENCES

Best, R. (ed.) (1996) *Education, Spirituality and the Whole Child*, London: Cassell.

Blake, N. (1996) 'Against spiritual education', *Oxford Review of Education* 22, 4: 443–56.

Campbell, J. (1993) *The Hero with a Thousand Faces*, London, HarperCollins, Fontana Press.

Carr, D. (1995) 'Towards a distinctive conception of spiritual education', *Oxford Review of Education* 20: 83–98.

Carr, D. (1996a) 'Songs of immanence and transcendence: a rejoinder to Blake', *Oxford Review of Education* 22: 457–63.

Carr, D. (1996b) 'Rival conceptions of spiritual education', *Journal of Philosophy of Education* 30: 169–78.

Carr, D. (2002) 'Metaphysics, reductivism and spiritual discourse', *Zygon* 37, 2: 491–509.

Fowler, J. (1981) *Stages of Faith: The Psychology of Human Development and the Quest for Meaning*, San Francisco: Harper & Row.

Geach, P. (1972) *Logic Matters*, Oxford: Blackwell.

Halstead, M. and Taylor, M.J. (eds) (1996) *Values in Education and Education in Values*, London and Washington, DC: Falmer Press.

Haydon, G. (1997) *Teaching about Values: A New Approach*, London: Cassell.

Jarrett, J. (1991) *The Teaching of Values: Caring and Appreciation*, London and New York: Routledge.

Kant, I. (1968) *The Critique of Pure Reason*, trans. Norman Kemp Smith, London: Macmillan.

Lambourn, D. (1996) '"Spiritual" minus "personal-social = ?: a critical note on an "empty" category', in R. Best (ed.), *Education, Spirituality and the Whole Child*, London: Cassell, pp. 150–58.

MacIntyre, A.C. (1981) *After Virtue*, Notre Dame: University of Notre Dame Press.

MacIntyre, A.C. (1988) *Whose Justice, Which Rationality?*, Notre Dame: University of Notre Dame Press.

MacIntyre, A.C. (1992) *Three Rival Versions of Moral Enquiry*, Notre Dame: University of Notre Dame Press.

National Curriculum Council (1993) *Spiritual and Moral Education: A Discussion Paper*, York: NCC.

OFSTED (1994) *Spiritual, Moral, Social and Cultural Development: An OFSTED Discussion Paper*, London: Office for Standards in Education.

School Curriculum and Assessment Authority (1995) *Spiritual and Moral Development*, Discussion Paper No. 3, London: SCAA.

School Curriculum and Assessment Authority (1996) *Education for Adult and Moral Life*, Discussion Paper No. 6, London: SCAA.

Smart, J.J.C. and Haldane, J.J. (1996) *Atheism and Theism*, Great Debates in Philosophy, Oxford: Blackwell.

Index